MW00559991

Aesthetic Apprehensions

Transforming Literary Studies

Series Editors: Ranjan Ghosh, University of North Bengal, and Daniel T. O'Hara, Temple University

Transforming Literary Studies is dedicated to exploring how our reading and understanding of literature and culture within modernity is continually about "going beyond." It focuses on the modern and contemporary experiences of literature and the critique of literary studies arising from them at the crossroads of disciplines, traditions, and cultures where the politics and aesthetics of historical embeddedness emerge across such determinants. Works in the series encourage us to rethink the strictures and limitations of modelling literature and literary studies upon one static paradigm because literature cannot have a life without "crossing boundaries"—being ever mobile, transitive, and transmuting. The series acknowledges that literary studies today is a transformative site. It is committed to deciphering, discovering, and conceptualizing anew a variety of embeddings in such sites through a deep and fresh reading of texts from across world literature (both in English and translation), theory, and cultural events.

Advisory Board

Muhsin Jassim Al-Musawi, Columbia University; Bill Ashcroft, University of New South Wales; Diana Brydon, University of Manitoba; Timothy Campbell, Cornell University; T J O Clark, Durham University; Bruno Clement, University of Paris; Thomas Docherty, Warwick University; Susan Stanford Friedman, University of Wisconsin-Madison; Keya Ganguli, Minnesota University; Paul Giles, University of Sydney; Vesna Goldsworthy, University of East Anglia; Priya Joshi, Temple University; Donald E. Pease, Dartmouth College; Jean Michel Rabate, Pennsylvania University; and Karen Thornber, Harvard University

Titles in the Series

Aesthetic Apprehensions: Silences and Absences in False Familiarities, edited by Jena Habegger-Conti and Lene M. Johannessen

Repetition, Recurrence, Returns: How Cultural Renewal Works, edited by Joan Ramon Resina and Christoph Wulf

Emerging Aesthetic Imaginaries, edited by Lene Johannessen and Mark Ledbetter

The Postcolonial Subject in Transit: Migration, Borders and Subjectivity in Contemporary African Diaspora Literature, edited by Delphine Fongang

Playing Offstage: The Theatre as Presence for the Real World, edited by Sidney Homan

Community Boundaries and Border Crossings: Critical Essays on Ethnic Women Writers, edited by Kristen Lillvis, Robert Miltner, and Molly Fuller

Aesthetic Apprehensions

Silences and Absences in
False Familiarities

Edited by
Jena Habegger-Conti and Lene M. Johannessen

LEXINGTON BOOKS
Lanham • Boulder • New York • London

Published by Lexington Books
An imprint of The Rowman & Littlefield Publishing Group, Inc.
4501 Forbes Boulevard, Suite 200, Lanham, Maryland 20706
www.rowman.com

6 Tinworth Street, London SE11 5AL, United Kingdom

British Library Cataloguing in Publication Information Available

Library of Congress Control Number: 2020946691

ISBN 978-1-7936-3366-8 (cloth : alk. paper)
ISBN 978-1-7936-3367-5 (electronic)

♾™ The paper used in this publication meets the minimum requirements of American National Standard for Information Sciences—Permanence of Paper for Printed Library Materials, ANSI/NISO Z39.48-1992.

Contents

Figures   vii

Acknowledgments   ix

Introduction: Apprehending Aesthetic Apprehensions   xi
Jena Habegger-Conti and Lene M. Johannessen

1   Drawing *Closer*: Liminal Medievalism in the Post-Punk Gothic   1
Aidan Conti

2   A Chair Is Not a House: Sepulchral Intimacies in *Sharp Objects*   17
Janne Stigen Drangsholt

3   "The Immortal Conception, the Perennial Theme": Reading the
Modern Body in Willa Cather's "Coming, Aphrodite!"   31
Ingrid Galtung

4   Not Reading the Signs in Nick Drnaso's *Sabrina*   47
Jena Habegger-Conti

5   Apprehensive Figurations: Monuments in "Site-Specific
Performances"   63
Lene M. Johannessen

6   Apprehending the Past in the National Parks: False Familiarities,
Aesthetic Imaginaries, and Indigenous Erasures   77
Jennifer Ladino

7   The Garrulous Eye: Allegorizing Rape in Djuna Barnes's *Ryder*   97
Helle H. Lapeniene

8 Metonymy and the "Art of Reading the World Slowly" 113
Genevieve Liveley

9 Aesthetic Apprehension, Hauntology, and Just Literature 127
Ruben Moi

10 Close Reading and Critical Immersion 143
Timothy Saunders

11 Indians, Aliens, and Superheroes: Countering Silence
and the Invisual in David Mack's *Echo: Vision Quest* 161
Sara L. Spurgeon

12 Listening to Ourselves: The Musician as Listener in
Rafi Zabor's *The Bear Comes Home* 177
Zoltan Varga

13 Harlem to World and World to Harlem: Revisiting the
Transnational Negotiations of Harlem Renaissance Narratives 189
Nahum Welang

Index 205

About the Editors 211

About the Contributors 213

Figures

Figure 1.1   *Closer*, Joy Division, Factory Album 1980   6

Figure 1.2   The Appiani Family Tomb at the Cimitero monumentale di Staglieno, Genoa, Italy   9

Figure 1.3   Giotto di Bondone, *The Lamentation of Christ*, Scrovegni Chapel, Padua, Italy (c. 1305)   11

Figure 4.1   Many of the Images in *Sabrina* Position the Readers at a Distance (Drnaso 2018, 3)   49

Figure 4.2   Teddy Screams in the Middle of the Night, Waking Calvin (Drnaso 2018, 46)   56

Figure 4.3   Sabrina's Bedroom (Drnaso 2018, 11)   57

Figure 4.4   A Gray Cat, a Gray Mobile Phone, and a Gray Gun (Drnaso 2018, 49)   58

Figure 5.1   Equal Justice Initiative, Crawford Memorial Plaque, Abbeville, SC   68

Figure 5.2   Equal Justice Initiative, Crawford Memorial Plaque, Abbeville, SC   73

Figure 6.1   NPS Display Sign Overlooking English Camp, San Juan Island   81

Figure 6.2   Two NPS Signs Overlooking South Beach in American Camp, San Juan Island   83

Figure 6.3   Tourists Visit the USS *Arizona* Memorial, Pearl Harbor   85

Figure 6.4   Military Technology Onshore with USS *Arizona* Memorial in the Distance, Pearl Harbor   87

Figure 6.5   Ranger Next to Display Sign, Sand Creek Massacre NHS   89

Figure 6.6   NPS Display Featuring Close-Up Image of Cheyenne Chief, Sand Creek Massacre NHS   91

Figure 7.1   The Beast, Ryder, c. 1928, by Djuna Barnes   100
Figure 11.1 David Mack, *Echo: Vision Quest*   166
Figure 11.2 David Mack, *Echo: Vision Quest*   169
Figure 11.3 David Mack, *Echo: Vision Quest*   173

Acknowledgments

We would like to thank the UH-nett Vest (the University and College Network for Western Norway) for funding the two workshops of sustained critical conversations. With their help we were able to gather scholars from different places inside and outside Norway to produce the present volume.

Introduction

Apprehending Aesthetic Apprehensions

Jena Habegger-Conti and Lene M. Johannessen

We approach figures we are not familiar with, with some hesitancy, waiting for them to make sense to us so that we can pass a judgment appropriate to our encounter, or the encounter we believe we are having. A sense of discomfort arises when we perceive the figure withholding something, when it avoids telling, when it hides, and prevents our apprehension of what it is. Too often, as Jena Habegger-Conti observes in her essay in the present volume, the question that then arises is "whether we read a text to listen to what it says, or whether we read to hear/comprehend the message that we already know" (47). The urge to capture what is other and accommodate it/ they into our zone of the familiar is a natural instinct; we seek what is shared and consequently safe. In his essay "Close Reading and Critical Immersion," Tim Saunders thus notes that "[l]acking an orientation towards a specific endpoint in time or space, to apprehend a work of literature is also to grasp it perceptually, but without an expectation of ever coming to perceive its scope or outer boundary in their totality, or to grasp and own them fully" (144). Apprehension in the sense of comprehension vies with all the other senses of apprehension, leaving the space of interpretation that could lead us further in our desire to understand a place of insecurity, defensiveness, perplexity.

A preliminary starting point for this introduction to *Aesthetic Apprehensions: Silences and Absences in False Familiarities* is consequently the reckoning with how reading the word governs our ways of seeing the world. Herein is presented the first obstacle: Our seeing is already directed by the world we have seen and our experiences of it. Hence, reading practices cannot be extricated from historical, cultural, economic, and sociological systems, but crucially and paradoxically, our ways of seeing are jeopardized by the always potential threat of ossification by those very systems, their words and their worlds, in turn restricting what Rancière calls the "topography of the thinkable" (Rancière 2010, 24). Thus, our reading and seeing, indeed, our sensing, can dangerously encourage and strengthen what we can think of as false familiarities with the world. Here the familiar is false, not because it is untrue, but because of the false comfort it provides with the knowable. Precisely because comprehension requires recognition—literally a knowing again of something, the "message precedes (the text) and dominates it" (Nancy 2010, 95). In so doing, the thinkable is reduced to circle in one, predetermined orbit (sense, in order to make sense, craves this "gathering" or "sheltering" (ibid., 117). As a consequence, the nonrecognizable, that which beckons to be listened to or seen, but which does not fit into known and therefore comfortable schemas, is refused entrance. It is in this context that we need to address the challenges of seeing and knowing *again* across aesthetic, cultural, and epistemic borders of traditions and received habits.

The phrase false familiarities as we use it in this book moreover names not that which is not true, but rather what is mistaken through comfort, or deceiving because apprehended too easily, and thus wrongful. There are any numbers of reasons why perceived difference and insecurity translate into mistaken conceptions of the figured and figuring world, but more often than not they are somehow related to what we cannot see or do not have access to. We tend either to ignore these spaces or fill them with something rather than to simply sit with their presence and listen to how they beckon us to listen and see, to sense further than what we are accustomed to. We should therefore heed Glissant's admonition when he writes about opacities that they "can coexist and converge, weaving fabrics. To understand these truly one must focus on the texture of the weave and not on the nature of its components" (1990, 190). The essays gathered here engage in conversations with "textures of the weave," not to arrive at essences to bring what is opaque into the totality of the fold, because as Glissant goes on to say, "[f]or the time being, perhaps, give up this old obsession with discovering what lies at the bottom of natures" (ibid.). In this sense, in order not to "obsess," the present collection of essays in many ways continues a conversation begun in the volume *Emerging Aesthetic Imaginaries* (2018, eds. Lene Johannessen and Mark Ledbetter), also in Lexington's "Transforming Literary Studies" series. If that volume focused on problematizing, theorizing, and testing the promises of the concept of the aesthetic imaginary, as inspired by Ranjan Ghosh's formulation (2015, 2017), the present volume picks up some of the challenges that surfaced during the work with *Emerging Aesthetic Imaginaries*. They arise from the gaps that open up between ideas and formations of "shared realities" and "entangled figurations," on which the aesthetic and social imaginaries that embed us rest. In a series of scholarly discussions, the contributors to the *Aesthetic Apprehensions* circle a set of auxiliary tropes that crystallize to more accurately pay attention to these gaps. Their more finely tuned theoretical explorations help bring the conversation about the role of aesthetics in the imaginary further. More specifically, the questions the essays engage attend to the anticipations, frustrations, and deep apprehensiveness trailing entangled figurations; more often than not, their closer scrutiny reveals realities not easily disentangled, familiar but not apprehended.

It is perhaps strange to qualify aesthetics, usually associated with the pleasurable and beautiful, with what comes trailing with the hesitant and the concerned, and yet the conversation of this volume began from a belief that aesthetics focused too narrowly on what is present, visible. The work of aesthetics is the striving to capture in forms and figures ways to test and try the way we see the world, circling the tropes of Silences, Absences, and False Familiarities. The three may seem straightforward enough, but a closer examination of their function in relation to social, cultural, and political assumptions and gestalts in aesthetic imaginaries reveals troubling oversights. The essays can be categorized according to where their primary interest lies, on the tropology of silence or on what is simply not there, or according to the genre or medium on which their gaze is focused, but because they are themselves interwoven methodologically and thematically we choose not to group them. Instead the volume as a whole comes to name troubling oversights, attempting to capture the outlier meanings residing in habituated receptions as well as the uneasy relations that result from aesthetic practices already in place.

That particular exercise also accounts for the main title of this book, *Aesthetic Apprehensions*, describing the various ways our aesthetic comprehensions and immersions are obfuscated by deep-seated epistemological and ideological apprehensiveness and unease. The seizing of relations in their tangled formations is the work of aesthetic analysis, a learning and teaching exercise that also comes with hesitation. It would of course make little sense to say that imaginative and epistemic contractions into bounded thinkability leave absences and silences in their wakes. For, how can what is not, be anything at all? And yet, on the topographic edges of the centripetal forces that perpetuate our perceptions of the familiar and the comfortable, fragments and traces of sense and sensing hover—apprehensively. In their hushed beckoning to us for a response, we as readers of words and worlds have choices, and it is what we do with those choices, that is, at the core of *Aesthetic Apprehensions: Silences and Absences in False Familiarities*. It signals the shift of conversations about aesthetics into a field that comes fraught with doubt, unknowables, and trepidations.

The dialogues that surface aim toward *praxis* rather than *poeisis*, at apprehending the silences and absences in the world, not for a better or more comprehensive understanding of it, but to transform the practice of sensing itself. As Nancy writes:

It is no longer a matter of interpreting the world, but of transforming it. It is no longer a matter of lending or giving the world one more sense, but of entering into this sense . . . "to transform" should mean, "to change the sense of sense," that is . . . to pass from having to being. Which means also that transformation is a *praxis*, not a *poiesis*, and action that effects the agents, not the work. (1997, 8–9)

In a series of interrelated essays, we seek to detect affects that surge from barely perceptible thresholds of senses and sensing, to locate vague traces of epistemological geographies, to listen to spectral possibilities residing in shadows and rifts, and to discover disruptions that lodge in lulls and silences. *Aesthetic Apprehensions* thus comes to name powerfully the kind of thresholds of sense that uphold the meaning of limen in psychology as "the minimum amount of stimulus or nerve-excitation required to produce a sensation." Herein, and in all senses of sense and sensation, resides the potential for rupture and creativity; such, after all, is the promise of the threshold, of the liminal: to encourage our leap into otherness, for then to find ourselves and our sensing again, and anew.

From the above considerations of ossifications and ruptures, it follows that this book's conversations are also bids for a kind of further dissection of the overarching structure of aesthetic imaginaries, themselves generator as well as receptacle for oscillations between thinkability and contraction. This moment of the threshold waits for recognition, maintaining the suspense of the unknown and unknowable moment after. And hence, rather than aiming for a new shared reality, or new shelterings of the familiar, it marks an absence, a silence that deserves attention, that demands to be listened to in its own right, in order to sense sense. This, now, is the concern that runs through the chapters in this book—listening and looking for aesthetic ripplings and disruptions.

While the essays in this volume have been arranged in alphabetical order, the first piece in this conversation, Aidan Conti's "Drawing *Closer*: Liminal Medievalism in the Post-punk Gothic" is an apt place to begin. In a consideration of periodization as a schema laden with aesthetic criteria and considerations, Conti uses the artwork on Joy Division's album *Closer* (1980)—Bernard Wolfe's photograph of the Appiani family tomb in the Cimitero di Staglieno outside Genoa—to suggest that it is not the correctness or priority of one or another way of seeing that demands our sensing, but rather the possibility of these varied apprehensions that position us to appreciate the multiple possibilities inherent in the moment of disaggregation and subsequent reformation. The album cover, habitually and reflexively pronounced a work of postmodern neoclassicism by its designer Peter Saville, can also be productively read in terms of medieval referents, which, Conti asserts, serve as a seductive, if hushed, beckoning to its audience. To sense this medieval presence, Conti proposes that we fruitfully disentangle, but not disconnect, the medieval from a temporally and geographically determined Middle Ages so as to understand the medieval as a sensed and sense-making space, the contours of which are formed by our perceptions of its contingent and localizing temporalities, namely, the classical and modern.

Janne Stigen Drangsholt's "A Chair Is Not a House: Sepulchral Intimacies in *Sharp Objects*" is focused on a more specific problem of representation and familiarity, namely, the idea of home, particularly in regard to motherhood and the female experience. The falsity of the familiar is acutely felt in conceptions of *oikos*, there were one dwells, in *Sharp Objects*, which was published as a novel in 2006, and adapted for television by HBO in 2018. Drangsholt undertakes an investigation into the representation of family and *oikos* in Flynn's text, unpacking the various mechanics of the sphere of intimacy which both make us belong to the earth and preclude us from bringing ourselves into dwelling, or "being in the world." The chapter examines silences, ghostly secrets, and the untellable narratives produced through a patriarchal structure that results in flawed perceptions.

A similar figuration of the unsettled familiar can be said about our relation to our bodies, historically aestheticized into self-contradictory relations of truth and lies, and always, as Ingrid Galtung's new reading of Willa Cather's "Coming, Aphrodite!" makes clear, in the service of larger imaginaries' directions. The essay considers how modernists were drawn to the contemporary body's expressivity, endeavoring to encompass and creatively utilize bodily events and experiences in their writing. In particular, the essay explores how Cather's story evokes and is shaped by the context-specific corporeal ideal of the New Venus. Here the close reading of the main protagonist brings to renewed attention how "she performs to satisfy the expectations of a given script, which aids her visibility at the cost of her vitality" (Galtung 41).

In its very distinct aesthetic form, Nick Drnaso's extraordinary graphic novel *Sabrina*, on the other hand, offers no script, or at least not one we detect as such. Jena Habegger-Conti argues that our accustomed reading for context distracts us from the absences of human connection that permeate the text, and which go unacknowledged lest we give to absence itself its due. This is a meditation on the problem of "what is not there," and suggesting that "[t]extual absences, indeterminacies, visual silences present opportunities, openings between the reader and the text, and between the reader and the world" (Habegger-Conti 61).

The problem of absence and familiarity is also central in Lene M. Johannessen's reading of an actual site where relationality carried in monuments and memorials reclaims its troubled place. As a confederate monument's monologue on the town square in a small town in the US South is disrupted by an Equal Justice Initiative plaque memorializing the lynching of an African American community member in 1916, the site and its discourse can be "read" along the lines of a chorographic, site-specific installation. The significance of its "work" is in this sense closely related to what Rancière describes as "issues of the configuration of a common world" (2010, 24), its potential promise residing in the aesthetic rupture the audience is invited to pause before and respond to.

Jennifer Ladino's "Apprehending the Past in the National Parks: False Familiarities, Aesthetic Imaginaries, and Indigenous Erasures" is also concerned with memorialization, and traces the role that the US National Park Service (NPS) plays in shaping a collectively imagined national identity. Approaching tourism as a kind of "slow reading" influenced by the environmental and textual features unique to each site, Ladino suggests that there is a consistent aesthetic imaginary associated with the NPS. The nostalgic tone of its rustic architecture, trail maps, and signage, and the quaint, militaristic uniforms with the iconic "Smokey Bear Hat," risk elegizing as much as they commemorate. Drawing out the affective dimensions of this aesthetic imaginary, she emphasizes apprehension as an affective as well as a cognitive, ideological process, suggesting that the aesthetic imaginary reinforces a false familiarity with the NPS which hides the fact that it is constrained by an ossified aesthetic that tends to historicize culture, silence present-day political concerns, and render the most unsettling aspects of the American past "unthinkable."

In a reading that shares some similarities with Galtung's analysis of Willa Cather's modernist short story, in "The Garrulous Eye: Allegorization of Rape in Djuna Barnes's *Ryder*" Helle Håkonsen Lapeniene examines aesthetic apprehension through Djuna Barnes's paradoxical image of the garrulous eye that merges pretext and visual sense as *sense*. She argues here that the chapter in Barnes's novel *Ryder*, "The Beast Thingumbob," is an allusion to the Rape of Proserpina, and not only addresses conditions for re-presenting the popular myth, but also artistic renderings of idealization and aestheticization of female suffering—seen through the peepholes of beauty and sacrifice. Focusing her discussion on Barnes's originally censored drawing in the chapter, Lapeniene suggests a reading of the image as emblematic of the garrulous eye where looking away and explaining away converge. While invisibility can be a form of silencing, silence in *Ryder* is also the familiar noise of the allegorizing eye.

Genevieve Liveley's "Metonymy and the 'Art of Reading the World Slowly'" explores the suspenseful sense-making that drives the art of slow reading—characterized here as the art of narrative metonymy. Its aim is to glean new insights into the narrative dynamics that shape aesthetic imaginaries in our encounters with stories of various forms. Narrative and narrative sense-making, Liveley demonstrates, are both predicated on silence and invisibility—what is left unsaid, untold, unrepresented, underrepresented. Taking as her case study a micro-narrative titled "Expenses for the Month," the essay sets out to look afresh at the pitfalls and possibilities opened up by the operations of narrative metonymy and to recognize its pivotal role in directing the ways that we think about silenced and absenced words (and worlds).

With a special focus on Northern Ireland and Guantánamo Bay, Ruben Moi's "Aesthetic Apprehensions, Hauntology and Just Literature" attends to how, where, and why literature justifies itself as an imaginative heterological possibility, but also as an unappeasable spirit to haunt the past, the living, and the generations to come. Derrida's concept of "hauntology" describes a type of just literature that unsettles, intervenes, and apprehends our ways of seeing the world, our reading practices, and our understanding of justice. Hauntology also tends to trace the absences and silences of the ideas, acts, and texts that do not manifest themselves as ruptures and heterotopia. To some extent, Derrida's hauntology could also be regarded as a tangential intellectual motion to Rancière's "topography of the thinkable": as restless wanderings into the unthinkable of heterotopia, and into the silenced and absented discourses to which such wanderings might lead.

The false familiarity Timothy Saunders specifically addresses in his "Close Reading and Critical Immersion" is the practice of close reading itself: the form of literary analysis most commonly advocated and employed in undergraduate textbooks and classrooms to teach students to appreciate and interpret the literariness of a work of literature. Despite its long-standing dominance within English Studies, close reading requires of its practitioners an attitude toward literature as an aesthetic phenomenon, including basic assumptions about the aesthetic structure and nature of a literary work. Saunders thoughtfully considers the ramifications of two principal modes of understanding a work of literature through close reading—comprehending and apprehending—to explain why the concept of literature to which close reading adheres no longer make sense to many of today's students. He then outlines an alternative reading practice ("critical immersion") that is every bit as analytical in its approach to literature as its forebear, but that embraces rather than rejects the forms of aesthetic apprehension with which modern students are already familiar. Saunders concludes that the sensorial experience of immersive reading may allow for different modes of understanding, particularly through senses other than sight, and in turn may produce different types of multimodal and multifaceted responses to literature.

Sensorial experience is also central to Sara L. Spurgeon's "Indians, Aliens, and Superheroes: Countering Silence and the Invisual in David Mack's *Echo: Vision Quest*" in which she examines an absence of sight and sound in a text by Cherokee comics artist and author David Mack that dismantles and rebuilds an aesthetic imaginary that has attempted to disappear nations, cultures, societies, and traditions. Mack's text is a native-centric memoir about an Indigenous artist's attempts to decolonize the silences and absences settler colonialism has imposed by subversively imagining the Indigenous refusal to disappear as a kind of superhero origin story on the level of the personal and the historical. In this comic featuring a deaf, Native American woman as a superhero, meaning is constructed layer by layer, the written word providing only one layer of meaning among many as it builds a narrative defined by its first-person narrator's negotiations of the experience of silence and absence. One accomplishment of this unusual blurring of text and image is to guide readers in how to read between, around, and within mainstream white hearing culture's false familiarities with indigeneity and deafness as things supposedly defined by lack, loss, or absence.

Zoltan Varga continues the conversation on sound, false familiarities, and the practice of listening to silences in "Listening to Ourselves: The Musician as Listener in Rafi Zabor's *The Bear Comes Home*." The tradition of listening to Western classical music, Varga argues, is deeply rooted in the anthropomorphization of musical sound, that is, linking the sound of the lead instrument to vocality, providing it with a voice. While assigning a voice, or imaginary consciousness, to music may originally stem from a view of the human body as the source and the measure of music, even today, music is essentially contingent on the structure of human body in its production, physical properties, and reception. Varga traces the possibilities that jazz brings to musicalized narrative fiction, seeking to complicate central terms in narratology and intermedial studies, namely, voice, embodiment, and temporality. Zabor's protagonist, a saxophone player who is a talking bear, tests the human limits of music and narrative. The Bear's *bearness* rearticulates human concepts such as self, cognition, pleasure, and beauty, in a way that is not dissimilar to how music, providing the closest analogy to language, may serve as a mirror to its (mal)functioning.

In the final essay to this volume, Nahum Welang's "Harlem to World and World to Harlem: Revisiting the Transnational Negotiations of Harlem Renaissance Narratives" further considers the silencing role that familiar conceptualizations may play in our interpretive lenses. Welang brings to light how a regional "reading" of the Harlem Renaissance limits its transcontinental reach and creates barriers to thinkable. In an analysis of Claude McKay's *Home to Harlem* (1928), Welang demonstrates that although this novel is set in Harlem, systemic oppression and the existential tensions between individual and collective identities are thematized in negotiation with transnational migration patterns and new imperialism. Pointing to creative reinterpretations that map and reorient the parameters of black expression by actors Josephine

Baker and Paul Robeson across the Atlantic, Welang shows that these artists were engaged with a literary and cultural topography that existed and thrived beyond national borders.

WORKS CITED

Ghosh, Ranjan. 2015. "The Figure that Robert Frost's Poetics Make: Singularity and Sanskrit Poetic Theory." In *Singularity and Transnational Poetics*, edited by Birgit Mara Kaiser, 134–154. New York/London: Routledge.

———. 2017. "Aesthetic Imaginary: Rethinking the 'Comparative.'" *Canadian Review of Comparative Literature* 44(3): 449–467.

Glissant, Édouard. 1997. *Poetics of Relation*. Translated by Betsy Wing. Ann Arbor: The University of Michigan Press.

Habegger-Conti, Jena. "Not Reading the Signs in Nick Drnaso's *Sabrina*." In *Aesthetic Apprehensions: Silences and Absences in False Familiarities*, edited by Jena Habegger-Conti and Lene M. Johannessen, 42–61. Lanham, MD: Lexington Books.

Nancy, Jean-Luc. 1997. *The Sense of the World*. Minneapolis: University of Minnesota Press.

———. 2010. "Art Today." *Journal of Visual Culture* 9(1): 91–99. https://doi.org/10.1177/1470412909354265.

Rancière, Jacques. 2010. "The Aesthetic Heterotopia." *Philosophy Today* 54: 15–25.

Saunders, Timothy. "Close Reading and Critical Immersion." In *Aesthetic Apprehensions: Silences and Absences in False Familiarities*, edited by Jena Habegger-Conti and Lene M. Johannessen, 143–160. Lanham, MD: Lexington Books.

Chapter 1

Drawing *Closer*

Liminal Medievalism in the Post-Punk Gothic

Aidan Conti

The medieval, as an often silent presence in our aesthetic apprehensions, tellingly speaks to us about how contemporary sovereign, perceptive, and participatory subjects see themselves in the here and now.[1] Readily visible in cultural productions that knowingly and expressly engage medieval sources as points of departure or comparison, a sense of the medieval is also reflected and refracted in less visible, less explicit manners, yielding complex, non-teleological temporalities. If the notion that the medieval constitutes the other against which the modern defines itself is tired, the idea nonetheless can serve as a point of departure for investigating the complicated temporalities at play in making such a distinction and indeed sets the stage for engaging the multiple temporalities, both residual and emergent, that the medieval occupies not only in aesthetic thought (Nolan 2004), but also in cultural production. The relationship, for example, between the medieval and the Gothic, often knotty and frequently problematized, is nevertheless widely recognized and discussed as a *relation* (Clery 2002). When less clear and explicit temporal frameworks and understandings are at play, relations become more difficult to see. In this chapter, I explore the multiple temporalities employed in aesthetic apprehensions as seen in the case of a living subculture that has been widely labeled and self-presented as gothic and its relation to a trace of the medieval, tantalizingly touchable, but generally silenced in public appreciation.

In order to grasp a sense of the medieval and, indeed, to comprehend the medieval as a sense, I suggest that we fruitfully disentangle, but not completely extricate, the medieval from the false familiarity of the Middle Ages. In this understanding, the medieval is not construed as a delineated period and demarcated place as it is situated in traditional forms of medievalism, but rather represents a sense or feeling for ways of being that do not conform to a normative present. In working through this sense of the medieval, contingent and localizing temporalities, that is the classical and the modern, provide points of orientation. These points allow us to apprehend the medieval as a form of inbetweenness that sits uneasily within (even as it is essential to) notions of modernity and its practices. As such, even when unnamed and so seemingly absent, a sense of the medieval can and does exert a seductive pull within and on the imaginary of the modern ordinary. To illustrate such an assertion, this chapter examines the art of Joy Division's *Closer* (1980) and critical apprehensions of the work. By critically reading the absent medieval in the art of the album sleeve, we see past the habituated rhetoric of a "postmodern neoclassical" tableau, which becomes a site of false familiarity, and better apprehend the coming into being of the post-punk gothic aesthetic. As a barely perceptible trace, a sense for the medieval represents an important, but not determinant, element within the disruptive desires characterized by the post-punk gothic.

The perception of the Middle Ages as negligible, and more importantly for our discussion, as outside of modern time is largely the result of a series of cultural operations that aimed to make the period appear irrelevant. As an epistemological entity and historical area of inquiry, the Middle Ages developed as an object of study within the professionalizing university of the nineteenth century. Frequently described as a period (ca. 500–1500 CE) with a specific geography (Western Europe), this academic elaboration of the idea of a middle age and the development of the period as an object of study created silences and absences in the name of recovery. Through "isolating methodologies," as Kathleen Biddick summarizes, "in order to separate and elevate themselves from popular studies of medieval culture, the new academic medievalists of the nineteenth century designated their practices, influenced by positivism, as scientific . . . isolated medieval artifacts from complex historical sediments and studied them as if they were fossils" (1988, 1–2). In particular, philology and archaeology, situating themselves as technologies of recovery (Dinshaw 2012, 99), removed texts and objects from their material contexts—namely, manuscripts and sites—and placed them in the curatorial spaces of the edition and the exhibition. These spaces facilitated an orientation of disinterested study, which, in turn, promoted the notion of irrelevance in the name of disinterestedness, an orientation distinct from the amatory attachment practiced by the amateur (ibid. 26–27). In the process of defining the Middle Ages, there emerged an overarching view of the period as one "of small quaint things and people, of miniatures, humble, little, overshadowed by its big neighbours—antiquity in its past and the Renaissance in its future" (Jaeger 2010, 5). This view enabled and continues to enable a persistent false familiarity with the period that "sets and limits what can be thought and claimed about medieval culture" (ibid.).

However, much as the disinterested study of the Middle Ages and the diminutive view of the period have rendered the period negligible and at times irrelevant, nonetheless as a descriptive term, the medieval has developed and continues to develop important connotations that tellingly reflect how we in the present position ourselves in relation to the past. Often, this use of "medieval" takes on dark significations. For example, "medieval" is frequently invoked to describe allegedly "premodern" practices such as torture, as in the case of the pear of anguish (Bishop 2014), or enforced abstemiousness, as in the use of chastity belts (Classen 2007). And yet, frequently, the practices invoked are first documented and become widespread in the postmedieval period. In these and such cases, the absence of evidence from the Middle Ages is subsequently filled in the spirit of recovery and based on preconceived ideas of the period. In a circular process, the false familiarity of what we believe we know engenders new knowledge about the period and reinforces the inscribed familiarity. Absorbed within these processes, "medieval" commonly stands for severity, cruelty, and barbarism, associations that facilitate a dark medievalism and strip the period of scientific exploration, philosophical thought and, perhaps most extreme, the very notion of individuality.

Perhaps nowhere is this use of the medieval more evident than in the phrase, "getting medieval," popularized in Tarentino's *Pulp Fiction* (1994). In a once oft-quoted scene that gave rise to an enduring phrase (Dinshaw 1999, 183–206), Marsellus Wallace (Ving Rhames) informs his captive, Zed (Peter Greene), that his associates will torture the victim with pliers and a blowtorch. In other words, Marsellus says, "Ima git medieval on your ass." Marsellus's threat is underpinned by a clever use of anachronism that incongruously suggests that blowtorches can somehow be medieval. Indeed, it is through the use of anachronism—that is by pairing "medieval" with diverse modern objects like synthesizers or automobiles—that the phrase "getting medieval" draws a particular resonance. For example, in a meandering column from 1999 the columnist Tony Kornheiser asks and answers himself: "I have no idea why we're talking about sending ground troops to Kosovo when we can send a fleet of Ford Expeditions and Lincoln Navigators over there. What's Milosevic going to throw at them—Yugos? These things will get medieval with Yugos" (Kornheiser 1999). Kornheiser's attempted humor seems to lie in the temporal disjunction presented. Contemporary machines, here American SUVs, will, through disparities in levels of technological accomplishment, enact a type of violence that belongs to another era. By incorporating un-modern ways of being within modern time, the phrase permits the audience to laugh alongside the teller, recognizing the temporal impossibility of "getting medieval," but also seeing the very possible barbarism that can be acted out in the present. In this manner, Kornheiser's example and other uses of the phrase exhibit a temporal sleight of hand, suggesting rather disingenu-ously that behavior that does not conform to modern ideals is somehow char-acteristic of a past outside of modern time, even when the behavior is enacted in the present. Baldly stated, the Balkan wars of the 1990s were very much a modern phenomenon; there was nothing medieval about their methods or ideologies. Naming events in the now as medieval or potentially medieval not only produces a temporal disjunction, which facilitates the humor of irony, but also politicizes temporality by situating others outside the scope of an achievable, liberal, and democratic now (Altschul 2020).

The politics of temporalizing modern violence as medieval stands in stark and telling contrast to our use of and relation to antiquity. Whereas "medi-eval," as a descriptive term derived from the Middle Ages, has generally (but not in certain, specific cultural contexts) become a term of abasement, the period of antiquity not only has a derived adjective, *ancient*, that has taken on status as "venerable," the field as an academic specialty has imported an outside descriptive term that intimates the elevated status of the period and its study. As classical studies, or even more regularly simply classics, antiquity and the ancient suggest not only timelessness, enduring interest and value, but also the exemplary character of its canon. In our most popular forms of periodization, antiquity is where we turn when we want to renew ourselves and so we often situate modern democratic and aesthetic ideals in a posited rediscovery of antiquity. For example, one can situate the emergence of the now dominant aesthetic regime in Johan Winckelmann's study of art in antiquity (Rancière 2013, 2–3), a body of work that continues to inform our present aesthetic periodizations.

In turn and by contrast, the medieval retains its sense as a time between. As such, the medieval is a term of relation that posits both a connection between us and the non-modern, as well as a break between now and then. In this ambiguous space, extraordinary phenomena may occur—such as the enactment of horrible forms of violence—but safely outside the well-known contours of everyday life. The way that we use and name the medieval as a point of reference in the present is not simply a form of medievalism, tra-ditionally understood as "the reception, interpretation or recreation of the European Middle Ages in post-medieval culture" (D'Arcens 2016, 1), but rather as an attachment to or experience of a non-modern feeling or way of being. As an attachment and relation, the medieval, or a sense of the medieval, can be found in certain modern works that exhibit little explicit knowledge of Middle Ages. Such modern works can be fruitfully read next to specific medieval acts and works, even if specific references to the Middle Ages were not envisaged during the process of creation. Here, in arguing for a silent medievalism, the album artwork for Joy Division's *Closer* (1980) serves as an illustration.

During the post-punk period of the late 1970s, the British music press began referring to a number of disparate, yet similar post-punk acts as "gothic" (Carpenter 2012, 29–33). Early reviews of Joy Division, Siouxsie and the Banshees and Bauhaus, employed "gothic" paired with descriptions like "sinister," "dark," and "gloom" to evoke a mood rather than a fixed historical, literary, or musical antecedent. Tony Wilson, cofounder of Factory Records, the label that produced and distributed Joy Division's albums, proclaimed that the band's music, "Because it is unsettling, it is like sinister and gothic, it won't be played" (Wilson 1979, 3:54). Similarly, in a review of a live performance of the band, *Melody Maker* situated Joy Division within a broader mood, declaring them "masters of this gothic gloom" (Bohn 1980). Indeed, in at least one case, critics endeavored to draw genealogical lines for the sound. The *NME* review of an early show of Siouxsie and the Banshees found that "parallels and comparisons can now be drawn with gothic rock architects like the Doors and, certainly, early Velvet Underground" (Kent 1978). Moreover, as much as acts could exemplify a gothic ideal, they could also fail to live up to a notion of the gothic. For example, Bauhaus's debut effort, *In the Flat Field* (1980), could at once be characterized as "Gothick-Romantick pseudo-decadence" (Gill 1980), but also as "Too priggish and conceited. Sluggish indulgence instead of hoped for goth-ness. Coldly catatonic" (McCullough 1980). More recently, scholarship has pulled out particular elements of the music and its attendant subculture to work through definitions of the post-punk gothic and indeed its relation to the Gothic (Bibby 2007; Langhorst 2018; Rovira 2018). Likewise, retrospectives often play with historically elastic reverberations found in "gothic," calling the period both "a new dark age" and as evoking "a hint of the 'Victorian'" (Harriman and Bontje 2014, 22), an elasticity that indicates the problematics in defining a fluid and changing set of practices and aesthetics. These retrospectively looking efforts, together with contemporary reviews, suggest that, while "gothic" was in the air as a descriptive term, the community was not a consolidated subculture (and arguably never will be (Van Elferen 2012, 128)), but rather a set of loosely affiliated bands and audiences that shared a common sound and disposition, frequently characterized by participants and critics as dark.

Consequently, in the years around 1980, "goth," which will later become further elaborated into a more or less recognizable aesthetic grammar, can be perhaps best described as "a structure of feeling" in the sense elaborated by Raymond Williams (1977), that is, a new formation of thought, not yet fully articulated, and yet clearly visible. In this cultural formation, the medieval plays a markedly ambiguous and often implicit role, but nevertheless perceptible in shaping the idea of the post-punk gothic. At first apprehension, in relation to the acts listed above, who are decidedly "modern" in juxtaposition to the "classic" rock that defined a previous generation, the medieval seems a rather distant, and arguably absent, concern. For example, one of the most iconic images from the time depicts radio waves from a pulsar. Featured on Joy Division's first album, *Unknown Pleasures* (1979), the image has since been elaborated in a remarkable array of commercial and noncommercial designs, such as a t-shirt retrofitted with the band's name in Cyrillic text available from Urban Outfitters and a gif-generator available on GitHub which allows the public to inscribe their own patterns on and within the radio waves (described in Spice 2016). In this manner, both the composition, designed by Peter Saville from an image found in the *The Cambridge Encyclopaedia of Astronomy*, and the cultural dynamics of its reappropriation are decidedly contemporary.

By contrast, and more relevant to the use of the medieval, the artwork for the band's subsequent and final album, *Closer* (1980), offers not only an interesting constellation of historical relations and attachments, but also a telling demonstration of the aesthetic apprehensions involved in its interpretation. Created again by Peter Saville, this time assisted by Martyn Atkins, the album cover sources an image from the photography magazine *Zoom* taken by French photographer Bernard Pierre Wolff in 1978 (figure 1.1). The

Figure 1.1 *Closer,* **Joy Division, Factory Album 1980.** Art direction: Peter Saville. Photography: Bernard Pierre Wolff. Design: Peter Saville.

photograph shows three figures—one kneeling and looking forward; the second kneeling with a bowed, hooded head; the third prostrate—before another figure in repose, seemingly resting on a clothed coffin. The arm of a fifth figure reaches down from the left of the frame; from this angle light seems to pour in, resting and spotlighting the prostrate figure. All of the figures are clothed, one might say draped, in loose, flowing garments. We see flowers at the head and feet of the prostrate figure, and also perhaps in the hands of the corpse. Above the image, centered on a white field we read the title of the album, *Closer*, in between two raised points. Title and photograph are framed within a thin black border that leaves generous off-white margins to all sides.

In a number of discussions of the image, and the attendant mythologization surrounding it, the picture is described and seen as "classical." In a retrospective exhibition of the visual works attached to Manchester music of the time, Fiona Corridan's text for the catalog, *True Faith*, asserts what has become common popular knowledge: "Saville believed the image to be fabricated and that Wolff had staged the sitting to create a postmodern neoclassical tableaux [*sic*]" (2017, 58). This description, which reflects Saville's own, similar words from interviews on the album artwork (as in Grundy 2011) as well as those of others (such as Poynor 2003, 36–37), offers a number of telling points. First, the image was believed to have been fabricated, or staged, and as such this belief permitted Saville to see the photograph as an aesthetic object removed from a local, physical site or historical situatedness. In turn and following thereafter, in light of the aestheticization of the image, the description offers a temporal framework for understanding the seemingly staged scene—it is both postmodern and neoclassical—but a temporal framework that does not adhere to a specific historically defined period. In describing the photo as "postmodern," we see the contemporaneity of the image asserted; a similar gesture is accomplished by asserting the "neo" nature of its classicism. Given the emphasis on the nowness of the image, the evocation of the classical suggests a desire to assert a notion of timelessness to the artwork. Indeed, the description does not adhere to strict historical understanding of the classical or the neoclassical as periods. The posture and stasis of the figures share little in common with the motion, idealized forms, and fluid lines of sculpture from ancient Greece and Rome or from the neoclassical period that imitated these forms. Moreover, the figures in the photograph look inward and downward—the figure on the bier, whose gaze we cannot see, tellingly faces upward—a dramatic contrast to the outward-looking gazes of, for example, the Belvedere Apollo and the Aphrodite Braschi. In this light, by using a term that has an historical referent, but also a broader ahistorical meaning, the designer and subsequent critics urge and reinforce an interpretation of this image as outside of historical time. Classical in these popularized descriptions is not a period, but a byword for ideals of timelessness and duration.

The assertion of a sense of timelessness is further augmented by the attention to the typography of the album cover. As an account of Factory records suggests, again repeating some of Saville's own characterization: "This Neo-Classicist imagery was complemented with typography based on a 2nd-century Roman alphabet" (Robertson 2006, 29). While the font is based on the square capitals of Roman epigraphy, the practical steps taken in the development of the lettering employed contemporary methods and models rather than ancient. The typeface does not borrow letter forms directly from the distant Pantheon or Trajan's column, but was found as an alphabet in a more accessible book, *The Development of Writing* (1958), by Hans Eduard Meier, in which important modifications, such as the letter 'J', were made to a 1st-century model. From images therein, photomechanical transfers for the album were made (Shaw 2010). In short, Saville employed modern practices to recreate the *feeling* of timelessness evoked by the seeming antiquity of the letter forms. For Saville, the "classical" artwork and lettering for the album contrasted with the modern music: "This cover for the band's second album was like a work of antiquity, but inside is a vinyl album, so it's a postmodern juxtaposition of a contemporary work housed in the antique" (Grundy 2011).

If Saville was intent on creating a relation between the contemporary and antiquity through an aestheticized image that he believed was staged, Wolff's framing of the sculptural group arguably allows for this apprehension. Wolff's image visibly crops the standing figure to the left, leaving only a shoulder and arm. The lighting also renders the posture of the pictured middle figure (between the kneeling and prostrate figures) uncertain. Perhaps most importantly, the aura of light surrounding the figure lying in repose obscures what one might be able to make out once the shape is made known, namely, the nimbus behind the head of the figure. In this sense, Wolff's photograph is indeed staged, not in that the figures therein are embodied actors, but in the editing of a scene into a cropped black and white image with a fixed perspective. The absences and obscurities in the photograph facilitate a reading of the image as both contemporary and timeless, an object outside of place and time, but always able to be viewed here and now.

Nevertheless, despite critical assertions and Wolff's staging, other complementary and juxtaposing readings of the image are not only possible but can be seen as fruitfully accretive by enabling a mode of understanding that situates the image not only in time but also within a time even as notions of timelessness continue to be asserted. Such readings have been undertaken through acts of participatory and amatory desires by fans who have identified the sculptural group in Wolff's photo as the Appiani family tomb, sculpted by Demetrio Paernio in ca. 1910, in the Cimitero monumentale di Staglieno, a vast cemetery in Genoa known for monumental sculpture. This identification facilitates differing perspectives on the album's artwork and indeed the artwork's importance within the idea of a post-punk gothic aesthetic. Additionally, reading with the identification in mind, our understanding can disrupt the ahistorical, but now familiar, secularizing characterization of the

Figure 1.2   The Appiani Family Tomb at the Cimitero monumentale di Staglieno, Genoa, Italy. *Source*: Photo: Aidan Conti 2017.

image. Once we consider the sculptural group in time, that is within historical understanding, we can also apprehend the album artwork within a time, that is in relation to other album artwork from comparable groups.

A visit to the cemetery reveals more distinctly the four figures next to the bier and their position vis-à-vis one another (see figure 1.2). The halos carved in the background behind the corpse and the standing woman come clearly into view. At the feet of the standing figure are evinced the words *Stabat mater eius*. The scene becomes intensely religious, proclaiming a faith notably absent from critics' characterization of the image. Moreover, the group, seen as a tomb, that is a marker for a specific grave in a particular cemetery, becomes situated in space and time rather than an image removed from both. An historical understanding begins to suggest itself, which, neither correct nor exclusive, intimates the silent presence of the medieval in the sculpture, a telling trace within the postpunk gothic.

The words at the feet of the figures echo the beginning of a thirteenth-century hymn to Mary, *Stabat mater*, a poem that affectively depicts Mary's suffering at the crucifixion. The first strophe of the hymn, suggestive of the rhyme and disposition, runs: *Stabat mater dolorosa/juxta Crucem lacrimosa,/ dum pendebat Filius* (The mother stood grieving, tearful by the Cross, while her son hanged). As the sentence *Stabat mater eius* (His mother stood by) at the foot of the Appiani tomb convincingly alludes to the medieval hymn, the words, in turn, together with the halo, identify the standing figure as Mary, who is notably obscured in Wolff's photograph, where only her arm, reaching down to the kneeling figure before her, can be ascertained. Once Mary is identified, the figure on the bier, above whom flies the holy spirit in the form of a dove bearing an olive-branch, is recognized as Jesus, who was only distantly discernible as such in Wolff's image and whose identity is omitted in most critical descriptions. One imagines that in the eyes of many critics and fans the figure in repose was simply a staple of classical or neoclassical imagery; a viewer steeped in Catholic iconography might more readily see the faint nimbus and apprehend the figure as Jesus.

This religious scene, conveniently secularized as classical and ancient in popular accounts, can then be reconfigured in relation to religious visual art, and specifically that of medieval and early modern Catholicism. In particular, the sculptural scene calls to mind scenes for the narrative cycle, the Life of Christ, found in medieval book illustrations as well as church paintings. Of particular relevance is the Lamentation of Christ in which figures, most often including the three Marys and Joseph of Arimathea and/or Nicodemus, mourn the body of Christ. The figures present varied, as did the gospel accounts of who was present at the crucifixion and the entombment, which renders specific identification of figures in Paernio's work difficult. Such scenes, appearing as early as the eleventh century, feature in works, for example, by Giotto (ca. 1267–1337) (see figure 1.3) and later Rubens (1577–1640). Additionally, the funerary sculpture can be related to the Entombment of Christ, which followed the Lamentation in narrative cycles. Appearing as early as the tenth century, Entombments are similarly popular, and found in the work of Michelangelo (1475–1564), Raphael (1483–1520), and Caravaggio (1571–1610) among others. Moreover, in addition to the words at Mary's feet, Paernio's work offers further textual references to Christological symbols. The word ICTHYS, both the Koine Greek word for "fish" and an acrostic for "Jesus Christ, son of God, [our] savior," appears in Greek letters in the upper right-hand side of the tomb. In short, the sculptural group presents a range of religious references that suggests a living medieval tradition in early twentieth-century Italy, a tradition, which, through the lens of the photography and the critical apprehensions of others, becomes portrayed as ancient, classical, and secular rather than religious, spiritual, and medieval.

Admittedly, it is unlikely that those purchasing *Closer* in 1980 saw allusive references to Giotto or Raphael in the artwork on the cover. Indeed, as we have seen, Wolff's photograph obscures a range of graphic codes that identify the figure as Jesus. Yet, as the album was to be released in the wake of the suicide of the band's lead singer, Ian Curtis, Saville privately acknowledged what would likely be grasped by the public: that a tomb appeared on the cover (Grundy 2011). As a result, even as popular appraisals of the

Figure 1.3   Giotto di Bondone, *The Lamentation of Christ,* **Scrovegni Chapel, Padua, Italy (c. 1305).** Fresco, 200 × 185 cm. Image in the public domain from Web Gallery of Art.

cover disconnect the photographed art from the medieval referentiality in the sculpture, the sense that there was something more to the image has exerted a seductive pull on fans of the album as evidenced by the efforts to track down the cemetery and websites that continue to document the origins for the artwork. In other words, a historical reading of the album sleeve represents not a singular, exclusive, or even predominant hermeneutic for the work. But the pregnant possibility of further referentiality, a possibility explored by a public intent on finding further ways of reading the image, tantalizes and entices.

Fan engagement with the pregnant referentiality of the artwork for *Closer* fits well with a description of gothic subculture as "more dialectically engaged with the past than is typical of most youth cultures" (Goodland and Bibby 2007, 4). However, in the years around 1980, this aspect of the subculture was very much taking form. Examples of this engagement can be seen, for example, in the lyrics of Joy Division's "Atrocity Exhibitions" which allude to both Roman coliseums and death camps "to portray a world in which torture and murder are spectacles for entertainment" (Bibby 2007,

237). Likewise, in certain examples from the album artwork of acts that have subsequently been grouped together with Joy Division as foundational for the postpunk gothic, we see hints of veiled historical referentiality. Notable in this regard is Siouxsie and the Banshees's *Join Hands* (1979), which features four soldiers from the Guards Memorial in London. Similar to the reuse of photography exhibited on *Closer*, Bauhaus's *In the Flat Field* (1980) features a repurposed photograph. Reportedly found by a band member on a postcard, the image, subsequently identified as Duane Michaels's "Homage to Puvis de Chavannes" (1949) (Haskins 2014, loc 1086), engages in a similar mode of historical layering: an album from 1980 employs earlier photography which itself references earlier art. Importantly, in this historically oriented engagement, we see not a single, dominant temporality in focus, but rather an eclectic curiosity for an array of references from the distant and near past.

Moreover, on the whole, contemporary album artwork, which itself can be said to be an integral part of the ethos of not only the band and its listeners, but of the broader, ever changing, subculture (Mueller 2008, 130–32), presents a variegated, rather than singular attitude, look, or disposition. From out-of-focus photos of band members to blurred winter images, these visual displays offer fragmented parts, much in keeping with fluidity of the scene, of what will become a more structured aesthetic grammar of gothic subculture. We will see, for example, a typical expression of a gothic mood—a graveyard, an enrobed figure, an allusive title in gothic font and an impending sky—on the album sleeve of the Damned's *Phantasmagoria*, which will appear in 1985. At this time, the contours of a "Gothic medievalism . . . based on an idealized not-here and not-now" (Van Elferen and Weinstock 2012, 29–30) are more readily expressed and discernible.

In the years surrounding 1980, however, articulations not fully formed can be glanced here and there. Within this structure of feeling, the funerary sculpture on *Closer*, together with other artwork from later in the year, such as another image from the Staglieno cemetery for the 12″ of "Love will tear us apart" issued in August 1980 and the cover of *The Black Album* (November 1980) of the Damned, represents a significant elaboration of postpunk aesthetic ideals. The artwork for *Closer*, which appeared in the wake of Ian Curtis's suicide in May of 1980, also helped pair Joy Division in the popular imagination with a fascination for the macabre and facilitated an attendant, retrospective mythologization (Langhorst 2018), even as the band themselves dressed in decidedly drab, mundane, and utilitarian clothing—monochrome button-down shirts with breast pockets and trousers—a style that contrasted markedly with the dramatic makeup, birds-nest hair, and affected styles that will be typically associated with the goth scene.

The early part of 1980 represents a moment of multiple possibilities for the emergent subculture in which the use of the tomb on *Closer* is an important marker. The album artwork itself constitutes only a small element of a wide-ranging visual rhetoric employed by acts associated with gothic in the music press. And the visual, in turn, comprises but one facet of the sensible in an aesthetic that focuses on sound and lyric. Nonetheless, the self-presentation evinced in the album artwork of *Closer* represents a significant set of aesthetic relations and aims. Asserting both the work's timelessness and its timeliness, Saville created an aesthetic apprehension to which many fans, who admire the image for its juxtaposition of classic and modern, have attached themselves. At the same time, as an image from a specific place, abounding in religious iconography and hinting at a sense of the medieval, the artwork further facilitated an ongoing identification with the postpunk gothic and its attendant notions of darkness and the macabre. Looking back from forty years on, we recognize that Saville did indeed create a "classic" object of enduring interest. Yet, the silent medievalism of Paernio's sculpture group represents an important and subsequently perceptible contribution to an aesthetic that continues to draw audiences closer.

NOTE

1. The author thanks Peter Saville for permission to reproduce the artwork for Closer, and for reading and making a number of corrections to this chapter.

WORKS CITED

Altschul, Nadia. 2020. *Politics of Temporalization: The Medieval and the Oriental from the Underside of Modernity.* Philadelphia: University of Pennsylvania Press.

Bibby, Michael. 2007. "Atrocity Exhibitions: Joy Division, Factory Records, and Goth." In *Goth: Undead Subculture,* edited by Lauren M. E. Goodland and Michael Bibby, 233–256. Durham: Duke University Press.

Biddick, Kathleen. 1998. *The Shock of Medievalism.* Durham: Duke University Press.

Bishop, Chris. 2014. "The 'Pear of Anguish': Truth, Torture and Dark Medievalism." *International Journal of Cultural Studies* 17(6): 591–602.

Bohn, Chris. 1980. "Joy Division: University of London Union—Live Review." *Melody Maker.* February 16, 1980.

Carpenter, Alexander. 2012. "The 'Ground Zero' of Goth: Bauhaus, 'Bela Lugosi's Dead' and the Origins of Gothic Rock". *Popular Music and Society* 35(2): 25–52.

Classen, Albrecht. 2007. *The Medieval Chastity Belt: A Myth-Making process.* New York: Palgrave.

Clery, E. J. 2002. "The Genesis of 'Gothic' Fiction." In *The Cambridge Companion to Gothic Fiction*, edited by Jerrold E. Hogle, 21–39. Cambridge: Cambridge University Press.

Corridan, Fiona. 2017. *Texts to Artwork in True Faith. 30 June—3 September 2017*. Manchester: Manchester Art Gallery.

D'Arcens, Louise. 2016. "Introduction." In *The Cambridge Companion to Medievalism*, edited by Louise D'Arcens, 1–13. Cambridge: Cambridge University Press.

Dinshaw, Carolyn. 1999. *Getting Medieval: Sexualities and Communities, Pre- and Postmodern*. Durham: Duke University Press.

Dinshaw, Carolyn. 2012. *How Soon Is Now? Medieval Texts, Amateur Readers, and the Queerness of Time*. Durham: Duke University Press.

Gill, Andy. 1980. "Gothic as a Brick." *New Musical Express*. November 8, 1980: 32.

Goodland, Lauren, and Michael Bibby. 2007. "Introduction." In *Goth: Undead Subculture*, edited by Lauren Goodland and Michael Bibby, 1–37. Durham: Duke University Press.

Grundy, Gareth. 2011. "Peter Saville on His Album Cover Artwork." *The Guardian*. May 29, 2011. https://www.theguardian.com/music/gallery/2011/may/29/joydivision-neworder.

Harriman, Andi, and Marloes Bontje. 2014. *Some Wear Leather, Some Wear Lace: The Worldwide Compendium of Postpunk and Goth in the 1980s*. Bristol: Intellect.

Haskins, David J. 2014. *Who Killed Mister Moonlight: Bauhaus, Black Magick and Benediction*. London: Jawbone Press. Kindle.

Jaeger, C. Stephen. 2010. "Introduction." In *Magnificence and the Sublime in Medieval Aesthetics: Art, Architecture, Literature, Music*, edited by C. Stephen Jaeger, 1–16. New York: Palgrave Macmillan.

Kent, Nick. 1978. "Banshees Make the Breakthrough [Live Review - London the Roundhouse July 23, 1978]." *New Musical Express*. July 29, 1978.

Kornheiser, Tony. 1999. "The Wheels of Death." *The Washington Post*. May 9, 1999. https://www.washingtonpost.com/archive/lifestyle/1999/05/09/the-wheels-of-death/45791d9f-5a5d-4217-bfda-9dc53e3b3036/. Langhorst, Caroline. 2018. "A Northern 'Ode on Melancholy'?: The Music of Joy Division." In *Rock and Romanticism*, edited by J. Rovira, 83–100. Palgrave Studies in Music and Literature. New York: Palgrave Macmillan.

McCullough, Dave. 1980. "Closer to the Edge." *Sounds*. July 26, 1980.

Mueller, Charles Allen. 2008. "The Music of Goth Subculture: Postmodernism and Aesthetics." Phd diss., Florida State University.

Nolan, Maura. 2004. "Making the Aesthetic Turn: Adorno, the Medieval, and the Future of the Past." *Journal of Medieval and Early Modern Studies* 34(3): 549–575.

Rancière, Jacques. 2013. *Aisthesis: Scenes from the Aesthetic Regime of Art*. Translated by Zakir Paul. London: Verso.

Robertson, Matthew. 2006. *Factory Records: The Complete Graphic Album*. London: Thames Hudson.

Rovira, J. 2018. "Introduction: Theorizing Rock/Historicizing Romanticism." In *Rock and Romanticism*, edited by J. Rovira, 1–13. Palgrave Studies in Music and Literature. New York: Palgrave Macmillan.

Shaw, David. 2010. "Closer." *Rock that Font*. June 12, 2010. http://rockthatfont.com /2010/06/closer/.

Spice, Anton. 2016. "You Can Now Create Your Own Joy Division Unknown Pleasures Cover." *The Vinyl Factory*. October 12, 2016. https://thevinylfactory.c om/news/create-joy-division-unknown-pleasures-cover/.

Van Elferen, Isabella. 2012. *Gothic Music: The Sounds of the Uncanny*. Cardiff: Wales University Press.

Van Elferen, Isabella, and Jeffrey Allen Weinstock. 2016. *Goth Music: From Sound to Subculture*. London: Routledge.

Williams, Raymond. 1977. *Marxism and Literature*. Oxford: Oxford University Press.

Wilson, Tony. 1979. Interview for BBC TV. *Something Else*. September 15, 1979. Video, 7:34. https://www.youtube.com/watch?v=QMRZROGtm1Q.

Chapter 2

A Chair Is Not a House

Sepulchral Intimacies in Sharp Objects

Janne Stigen Drangsholt

In recent years, criticism and fiction alike have been concerned with finding a path that leads to the *oikos* (home, or the place of dwelling), in the sense of the site that first helps us onto the earth, then makes us belong to it, and, hopefully, brings us to what Heidegger refers to as "being in the world" (1971, 90). Such a focus can be found in literary texts, such as Margaret Atwood's *The Testaments* (2019); memoirs, such as Joan Didion's *Blue Nights* (2011); nonfiction books, such as Swedish writer Josefin Olevik's *Den Befridde Familien* (2016); and television series, such as HBO's *Better Things* (2016–). What these texts have in common, moreover, is a reading of the *oikos* as manifested in the form of the family. A house is, after all, not a home, and in order to understand the *oikos* we need to comprehend the human interrelations that generate such a sense of belonging that is necessary to become a good citizen and a complete human being.

While crime fiction as a genre has not traditionally been known to explore such complex constellations, there are exceptions. One of these is Gillian Flynn, whose signature trait is to investigate just how the *oikos* can be a site of harm and how it can de-construct rather than con-struct a human being. This is the case with her debut novel *Sharp Objects*, which was published in 2006 and adapted for television by HBO in 2018. While the novel comprises what Stephen King in the blurb refers to as "a relentlessly creepy family saga," the HBO series provides us with a perhaps even sharper focus on the familial relationships. The present essay will comprise an investigation of the representation of *oikos* in the television adaptation of Flynn's text, unpacking the various mechanics of the family as a discursive unit. In other words, we will investigate how the story we tell ourselves of intimate relations that make us belong to the earth is often underpinned by another narrative displaying how we are effectively precluded from bringing ourselves into dwelling, or "being in the world."

Interestingly, moreover, *Sharp Objects* provides us with a particular emphasis on the familial female relations of intimacy, which are often ignored in traditional narratives. In *The Mother/Daughter Plot: Narrative, Psychoanalysis, Feminism*, Marianne Hirsch points out how, in conventional plot structures, men are central while women take on the role of either static objects or obstacles (1989, 2). This is particularly true in narratives that deal with families, which tend to forefront the father figure as a representative of the structures that frame society as a whole. And while Adrienne Rich as early as 1976 alerted us to the silence that has surrounded the most formative relationship in the life of every woman, that is, the one between daughter and mother, it has remained relatively muted in the years that have passed (Rich 1976, 225). In *Sharp Objects*, however, the mother–daughter relationship is not just addressed, probed, and examined, but placed at the very center, rendering it a rare attempt to scrutinize the female figures habitually submerged in narrative plot structures and, more importantly, to problematize the ideologies of maternity embedded in a patriarchal social and cultural community.

INTIMACIES 0: SEPULCHRAL SPACES

In a review in *The New Yorker*, Troy Patterson describes the HBO series *Sharp Objects* as a "domestic thriller with a sultry sense of place" (2018). "Domestic" in this context refers to crime reporter Camille Preaker's (Amy Adams) return to her hometown Wind Gap, Missouri, in order to investigate the murders of two young girls. As with most mother–daughter narratives, the homecoming is occasioned by male intervention, as Camille's editor Frank Curry (Miguel Sandoval) tells her to "get me a story," adding that this is likely to make an impact on readers because it's personal ("Vanish"). Hence, Camille sets out on a quest to procure the holy grail, which naturally is to be found in exactly the point that she left it in the first place—the homestead, which consists of estranged mother Adora (Patricia Clarkson), stepfather Alan (Henry Czerny), and half-sister Amma (Eliza Scanlen), the reunion with whom Curry hopes will help Camille "flush some things out" and get her "back on your feet" (ibid.).

It is not, however, as easy as it sounds for Camille to "flush things out" and get back on one's feet, especially when the "things" at hand are family related. The complexity surrounding this entity is signaled already in the various definitions of the noun, which originates in the Latin *familia* and both means "family servants, domestics collectively, the servants in a household" and, through association, "servant, slave" (*famulus*). To further complicate matters, we have Freud's concept of the uncanny (*unheimlich*), which refers to the sensations of un-familiarity that sometimes occurs at the very center of that which is well known. As is well known, the uncanny both has to do with making things uncertain and with experiencing a sense that things are not as they have come to appear through acquired habit and familiarity.

And just such a sense of uncertainty and (un-)familiarity is clearly visible from the very opening sequence of the first episode, "Vanish," where we are presented with an amalgamated mixture of ambiguous images that are eerily nostalgic and unnerving, and which juxtapose children on swings with pigs gathered in an abattoir, and lush scenery with barbed wire or cords dripping with blood. The sequence, moreover, is musically framed by Franz Waxman's "Dance and Angela," taken from George Stevens's 1951 film *A Place in the Sun*, which heightens the sense of disturbing nostalgia. It is also significant that the opening is held together by Camille Preaker driving, suggesting that the unnerving imagery in some way points back to her feelings toward this homecoming. As viewers, we get a clear sensation of trauma, which is also deepened through the clusters of images. This evokes Roger Luckhurst's *The Trauma Question*, where this kind of emotional shock is, in fact, defined exactly as a knot, or as an assemblage of "tangled objects" that mess up our fundamental categories and prevent us from creating clear boundaries and sharp separations between inside and outside, subject and object (2008, 14). Such a definition also calls forth the tangled relationships that is the family, rendering the sharp objects referred to in Flynn's title an ironic reference to the (potentially harmful) lacking boundaries that domestic intimacy can generate, as well as the more obvious suggestion of the objects that the protagonist habitually uses to carve unsayable words onto her body. What *Sharp Objects* presents us with is a home—and a story—that is not so easily flushed out, but that is closed off, still, and silent, and a place that is not only sultry, but sepulchral, generating tangled images of stasis, sterility, and supremacy.

Most of all, the narrative revolves around the breach between mother and daughter, which holds many similarities to the Greek myth of Demeter and Persephone. As in the mythical narrative, the breach between mother and daughter effectively transforms the space of intimacy into one of sterility and stasis, especially on the part of Demeter. With Persephone no longer there, the goddess refuses to spread her bounty onto the world and will not let the harvests grow. Instead, she presents the earth with stony stasis in the sense of eternal winter. At the same time, the particular relationship mother–daughter relationship in *Sharp Objects* is characterized by attempts to avoid the breach altogether, effectively halting the sequence of events that draws toward separation. Hence, while loss is presented as an inevitable part of the natural sequence of growth in the original myth, the mother figure in Flynn's narrative refuses to accept such circularity and instead conceives a strategy aimed at holding on to her daughter(s) in an intimate space that is exempt from the passing of time.

INTIMACY 1: NOT A STORY TO PASS ON

The term "intimacy" comes from the Latin *intimus*, which means "most inner." It first appears in a Western dictionary in 1632, where it is defined as "inmost or innermost thoughts and feelings" (Yousef 2013, 1). Over the course of modernity, it came to designate both what is closely held and personal, as well as a wide range of relationships that a subject might establish with others. Hence, while it was originally associated with the personal, privacy, individualism, and the domestic realm, it has been broadened to include more fluctuating and flexible associations, both in a physical and nonphysical sphere (Chambers 2013, 41–42). This extension of the space of the intimate has not lessened its importance, however. In fact, the zone of the intimate is today seen as that in which "the self emerges" (Oswin and Olund 2010, 60). Intimacy, Oswin and Olund hold, occupies an elusive space somewhere between a solipsistic "me" and a wholly subsuming "us," and as such provides a topology of self that knows itself in its fullness and authenticity (ibid.). In other words, intimacy is essential to our sense of becoming.

According to Nancy Yousef in *Romantic Intimacies*, intimacy invites a lingering upon the phenomenal fact of proximity between persons, whether sustained over time, as in a relationship between family members, or in fleeting encounters with strangers (2013, 3). As mere proximity, intimacy is without content. It is not until such proximity engenders feelings of closeness and sympathy that content comes into place. While intimacy usually involves a fantasy of attaining mutual recognition, it is typically characterized by asymmetrical and nonreciprocal forms of relation, attention, and appreciation (ibid.). This, perhaps, is particularly the case in relationships between family members, where the proximity over time ensures intimacy, but where the closeness also frequently becomes problematic in many fundamental ways, especially in the relationship between mothers and daughters.

Interestingly, the closeness that is associated with mother–daughter intimacy also creates a challenge in terms of capturing and mediating it in language and as storytelling. In *Of Woman Born: Motherhood as Experience and Institution* Adrienne Rich appropriates the Greek word *cathexis* to explain why this relationship remains the "great unwritten story" (1976, 225). In the original Greek *káthexis* means "holding, retention," but in psychoanalytical terms it has come to define the process of allocating mental or emotional energy to a person, object, or idea. For Rich, however, the term points to the unstable singularity of the mother and the daughter, referred to by Rich as the "flow of energy between two biologically alike bodies, one of which has lain in amniotic bliss inside the other, one of which has labored to give birth to the other" (ibid.). Here, Rich is in line with many other feminist psychoanalytic theorists, who see the daughter as caught in a double bind when it comes to balancing intimacy with a sense of separate selfhood. The same, moreover, is true of the mother, as Julia Kristeva stresses in her essay "About Chinese Women." While the girl, unlike the boy, cannot cut all ties with her mother because her biological likeness prevents her from seeing the parent as a separate "object," the mother is simultaneously made to believe that is because she has a child (Kristeva 1986a, 144). Without the child, in other words, she is nullified. As is the daughter without the mother. But together, it seems, they are equally doomed.

What we see here, then, is a relationship evocative of Luckhurst's concept of "tangled objects," something that both makes it almost impossible to define and—consequently—say. Interestingly, in The Reproduction of Mothering, Nancy Chodorow claims that this problem particularly arises when the mother–daughter connection is in some way characterized by excess (1978, 82). In Sharp Objects, such an excess is first suggested in the imbalance of the family structure. Camille's father is missing from the narrative, and the other father who has stepped in to take his place is incapable of providing the kind of respite and organization required from the paternal protector, and only remains in the periphery of the narrative frame. The periphery, however, is also where we find Camille, who has inaugurated the breach with the mother figure and who is consequently displaced on many levels. When she returns to her childhood home, Adora accordingly greets her with cold rejection, stating that "the house is not up to par for visitors," signaling that there is no natural place for Camille in this domestic sphere ("Vanish"). As the narrative unfolds, moreover, we learn that the reasons for the breach is Adora who, as her name signals, demands excessive subordination in exchange for some semblance of "mutual recognition." Hence, the mother's decision to allow Camille into the house is solely based on adherence to the norms of Southern hospitality, and not on feelings of love and kinship (ibid.). Persephone's choice to disentangle herself from the knot of intimacy, we understand, has resulted in a sepulchral distance between mother and daughter which, as mentioned above, only allows stasis and sterility.

While the narrative of Sharp Objects, then, is on the surface structured as a quest through which the protagonist might reach individuation and autonomy, Camille is really locked in a standstill. And while Curry, who from the very opening adopts the role of the father both on a personal, symbolic, and cultural level, presses Camilla to tell her story, it lacks the kind of linearity that would make it possible to tell. Moreover, it has already been carved into her body in the form of seemingly unrelated and random words, which comprise the only way that she knows how to express that which is fundamentally unsayable. The words are wounds, recalling another word—trauma—which fittingly comes from the Greek word meaning "wound," and which, when it was first used in English in the seventeenth century, referred to a bodily injury caused by an external agent (Luckhurst 2008, 2). In modern medicine it still refers to bodily injury, and the focus on the boundary of the skin in ritual piercing, cutting, or scarification plays with powerful taboos in many cultures. As Steven Connor observes in The Book of Skin, the skin still remains "the visible object of many different forms of imaginary or actual assault" (2004, 65). In other words, the untellable story is there, but as a discourse redolent of Kristeva's concept of the semiotic—the maternal aspect of language that shows the speaker's inner drives and hidden impulses—rather than as part of the symbolic discourse employed by the community as a whole (Kristeva 1986b, 28). Hence, the words carved into Camille's body, such as "vanish," "cherry," "fix," and "milk," name each of the individual episodes—leaving the spectator to decode the symbolic meanings for herself—but do not play any role in the communication between or within the characters. Camille, for instance, does not want to decode any of it. She has many years of training in hiding the story carved into her body and conceals it under long pants and sweaters, while also consuming large amounts of alcohol in order to avoid seeing the words too clearly. Adora, moreover, pulls her weight in keeping the story under the skin by administering sickness and sleep.

Interestingly, silence is also enforced through the use of music in the series. This is signaled already in the title sequence, which opens with a needle descending on a record player. While the accompanying song changes, the music most often remains in the nostalgic vein of Franz Waxman's "Dance and Angela." This is also the kind of nostalgic or placid classical music that Alan and Adora habitually employ to "unwind." In one of the later episodes when Alan starts to worry that something is seriously wrong with Amma, he is told by Adora to "go relax. Play some music" ("Falling"). Hence, he sits down in his chair and puts on noise cancelling headphones that allow him to block out unpleasant thoughts and impressions. As is signaled by the opening image of the needle touching, but not penetrating, the surface, music can insulate the mind and alleviate the pain of the real. When Adora and Allan dance to Engelbert Humperdinck's "The Way It Used to Be," this is almost a sublime manifestation of the human ability to put a lid on unpleasantness and terror.

Camille also employs music to distract and diffuse, together with the above-mentioned alcohol and long drives, although her preference is more in the vein of the pop cultural nostalgia of the late 1960s youth rebellion. In a flashback to when she was admitted to a facility after cutting herself, we see her befriending Alice, another self-harming patient who declares that music helps her "get the hell out of here whenever I want" ("Fix"). We soon realize that the "hell" referred to has nothing to do with Hades, but more with Demeter, and while the stories of the shared experiences cannot be told, music becomes a vehicle for creating an intimate space between the two daughters, allowing them to communicate—and possibly heal—wounds without speaking.

At the same time, this choice of music also functions as yet an ironic layer, as their preferred band is Led Zeppelin, a band of rebellious men who were infamous for their mistreatment of young women (Robinson 2014). What is more, music can only do so much. Later in the same episode Alice cries in bed after a visit from her mother and asks Camille whether it gets "better with your family? Maybe when I'm older, like you?" ("Fix"). Camille's answer is that it does not, you only survive, thus emphasizing the continuing isolation that trauma ensures. There is no easy fix, or even a complicated one. Finally, Alice ends up taking her own life.

The most significant impediment to the saying of Camille's story, however, is, of course, trauma itself, which poses a serious threat to the chronological progression of the narrative through recurrent flashbacks of her sister Marian (Lulu Wilson), who died when they were children. The flashback is an intrusive, anachronic image that throws off the linear temporality of the story and also of the protagonist herself, effectively displacing her in time and place. In the series, it occurs for the first time within the opening 5 minutes of the first episode, revealing Camille's enslavement to a buried traumatic past. While the spectator soon realizes that the flashbacks are intrusive childhood memories, however, the series is more than halfway through before it reveals that they are actually grounded in violent maternal abuse, in the form of the Munchausen syndrome by proxy. It is only after this revelation that the spectator is able to place the seemingly incoherent fragments into a meaningful order and form a story in our heads of what has actually happened in the Preaker household.

At the same time, the presence of Marian isn't purely presented as flashbacks. Rather, she intervenes in a near-physical manner—like a ghost who is scaring and displacing Camille and warning her that something sinister is taking place. As a symbol, the ghost belongs in the category of the uncanny (unheimlich), which is, as mentioned above, irrevocably connected to the hearth in the sense that it is something that belongs to the home (heimlich) yet is terrifyingly other to it (un). The reason why the ghost is uncanny, moreover, is that it, as Jeffrey Weinstock has pointed out, is "neither fully present nor absent, neither living nor dead" (2004, 6–7). In Sharp Objects, such a complex liminality plagues almost of the characters, and is resultingly established straightaway through the voice of Marian asking Camille "what if after you die, part of you goes to heaven, part of you stays here?" ("Vanish"). Marian is also present in the objects that belonged to her, which are kept untouched in her old room. These objects evoke being, but only negatively as absence, emptiness, and pain, as do the "tangled objects" that are the characters themselves.

As Nicolas Abraham notes in his essay "Notes on the Phantom: A Complement to Freud's Metapsychology," moreover, the ghost comprises a "gap in the unconscious of the living" which is produced in us "by the concealment of some part of a loved object's life" (1994, 171). The ghost, we understand, also represents the dark space within the unconscious—or the words carved into the skin—that the characters cannot say or see, and which continues to haunt them for this very reason. In this sense, the narrative also rests on the dynamic of ghostly secrets and the untellable story that cannot be laid to rest.

INTIMACY 2: A POLITICS OF DENIAL

As signaled above, it is not only Camille who struggles to tell her story—it is also a story which is constantly misread by the community as a whole. In order to mediate this problem, the series presents the spectators with a series of red herrings, such as that of the unknown male perpetrator or serial killer. In *Murder: A Tale of Modern American Life* (1998), Sarah Knox argues that dramas featuring demonic serial killers draw attention away from the everyday statistics of murder (1998, 146). The irony in this insight is signaled upon Camille's return to Wind Gap, where there are posters everywhere with photos of the missing girl, Natalie Keene, along with signs telling girls to "Don't be a victim" and to "Stay safe" ("Milk"). The latter also becomes a mantra in the space between the disjointed family, who repeatedly say to each other that "I want you to be safe," ironically and tragically ignoring and occluding the fact that the real danger is actually within the domestic hearth (e.g., "Vanish").

This cultural strategy of denial is perhaps most visible in the stereotypical comprehensions of what it entails to be a woman and girl, mother and daughter. The series as a whole is interested in unpacking how we, as a culture and a society, tend to prefer the communal narratives that represent figures that we can understand and clearly define. In Adora Crellin's case this figure is that of the Southern belle, that is, a beautiful and dignified lady of society dedicated to family and community. Adora also self-identifies as a Southern belle, as she makes plain to Camille before Natalie Keene's funeral, declaring that "it's our family's duty to be involved in the community" ("Dirt"). At the same time, there is also an irony in how this figure simultaneously lays the premise for another, darker figure which comes out of the tradition of the Southern Gothic, with precursory voices in the writings of Tennessee Williams, William Faulkner, and Flannery O'Connor. As such, she is a cliché in the cinematic tradition of *A Streetcar Named Desire* (1951) and *Jezebel* (1938), that all spectators would immediately expect to be something of a monster. The character of Blanche DuBois is, perhaps, the most infamous reference here, as a female character who is unapologetically and self-consciously performative, and who presents female identity as an ongoing negotiation between lack and excess. It is a character who allows room for the coexistence of contradictions, especially in her role as the Angel of Death, through which she simultaneously administers comfort and destruction, salvation and oblivion. Here, there are clear similarities to Adore who, throughout the narrative, withholds comfort and nourishment from her daughters, except for when they are sick. In this sense, the "objects" referred to in the title of the series are her children, who are unbearably sharp and pointed as autonomous and individual beings, and who need to become soft and blurry figures for her to stand them. In this sense, the character of Adora also holds clear likenesses to Flora Goforth in Tennessee Williams's play *The Milk Train Doesn't Stop Here Anymore* (1963), who is visited by Chris, also incidentally known as the Angel of Death, because he has a habit of arriving on the doorsteps of wealthy women who are about to expiate. In one part of the play, however, the tables are turned as Flora Goforth starves Chris in order to force him to comply to her own desires. The perpetual and various states of hunger displayed here make consumption into the foundation of human relations, whether we are talking about alcohol, pills, food, or human beings. In *Sharp Objects* a similar firmament is suggested through the title of the final episode, "Milk," which plays upon Adora's status as giver of both life and death through the (deadly) milk that she administers to all her daughters. Breastfeeding is, of course, the first act of bonding that takes place between mother and infant, securing life on both a physical and psychological level. In the hands of Adora, however, the nectar of life is transformed into its opposite.

In this context, it also makes sense to comment on the links between the figure of the (monstrous) Southern belle and the fairy-tale figure of the queen or the wicked stepmother. This link is clearly established when Amma asks why it is so often the case in stories that girls need to be rescued from witches ("Milk"). The reason for this is that mothering can quickly turn into smothering, and that, at some point, the bond necessarily needs to be severed on both sides of the spectrum—sometimes violently. As Marina Warner points out in *From the Beast to the Blonde*, some of the traditional narrative strategies for forming female identity do take the form of female combat between mother and daughter, for instance, in fairy tales where the young princess must fight against the queen (1995, 220). This is also an approach that Nancy

Chodorow refers to in her book The Reproduction of Mothering, where she
states that "girls in relation to their mothers experience themselves as overly
attached, unindividuated and without boundaries" (1978, 137), which is, of
course, one of the reasons that Rich pointed to for not being able to tell the
mother–daughter story at all.

The fairy-tale mother refuses to let go of her daughter and strives to maintain control, dominance, and power. Hence, it also makes sense that Amma
in *Sharp Objects*, when on the verge of death, dresses up like Persephone.
In her study of motherhood, Adrienne Rich points out that while the loss
of the daughter is one of the great embodiments of the human tragedy, this
narrative has traditionally been met with silence in the canonical works of
literature (1976, 237). While Shakespeare gave us Lear (father and daughter)
and Hamlet (mother and son), he did not give us Demeter. But Flynn gives
us both Persephone and Demeter in all their splendor. And we do not need
Adora to change her attire in order to understand that she inhabits the role of
Demeter, who is freely handing her daughter over to the Underworld so that
she can keep complete mastery over her child. For Adora, it seems, the child
is only manageable in the stillness of death. It is almost as Sylvia Plath writes
in the poem "Edge," that in death each child is "coiled, a white serpent, / One
at each little / Pitcher of milk, now empty" (1981, 272). And the mother, as
signaled above, holds the power to administer the milk of death or life as she
pleases.

In terms of the mythical plot of Demeter and Persephone, the necessary
intervention comes from Hades, who installs time in the lives of the women
who have been caught in a cyclical movement. In *Sharp Objects*, however,
linear time is not recognized, and any intervention of a male figure proves
insufficient to disrupt the cyclical stability that secures the excessive intimacy
and permanent bond that exists between mother and daughter. This is one of
the flaws of society it seems—everything is misread, even the underpinning
rules and regulations that were supposed to secure order. We can for instance
see this in Adora's relationship to her husband Alan, which is so unsatisfying
that it could be seen to comprise an example of what Nancy Chodorow refers
to as "the reproduction of mothering" (1978, 140). Rather than taking on a
role where he can break the cycle, Alan passively becomes part of it. And
although Hades is present in the form of the name-of-the-father, that is, in the
formal restraints of society and culture, this framework is left behind at the
front door in Adora Crellin's house where she is the supreme ruler. Adora is
the unrestrained Demeter, whose hunger for her own child is allowed to grow,
and who would, as mentioned above, rather have her child die than enter time
and become a mature woman.

In the space of the name-of-the-father, however, Adora maintains the face
of the Southern belle, which is a figure whose underside is not recognized

by the communal narrative and can consequently only be inscribed in the daughter's dead body (Marian) or carved into her skin (Camille). As for the daughter who tries to play the same game, that is, Amma, she is represented by an immense ambiguity. In Gillian Flynn's novel, Camille first encounters her half-sister as part of a crowd of generic white girls. She observes "four blonde girls" who sit stiffly on a picnic towel at the site where people are searching for Natalie Keene. Camille does not recognize Amma but describe her saying that she has a "flushed face" with "the roundness of a girl barely in her teens" and hair "parted in ribbons," but that "her breasts, which she aimed proudly outward, were those of a grown woman. A lucky grown woman" (Flynn 2006, 14). This depiction, together with the reader's aware-ness that two young girls have gone missing, is one of the red herrings at work pointing a finger toward an unknown sexual predator and leading us to think that the danger threatening Amma is connected with the male gaze at her grown-up body. A similar portrayal is provided in the HBO series, although here the adult features of the girls are even more emphasized, as they sit on a bench smoking as Camilla passes them ("Vanish"). At the same time, we also learn that there are aspects that do not fit with this master nar-rative. For instance, Ann Nash's father states that it was probably "a faggot. 'Cause he didn't rape her. And the cops say that's unusual" (ibid.). And when Camille returns to her mother's house, she encounters a little girl who wears pretty dresses and plays the role of what Amma herself refers to as a "doll to dress up" (ibid.). Like Pip in *Great Expectations* we are caught in the wrong plot and the narrative is not that of Persephone being abducted and raped by Hades, but of Demeter attempting to keep the first part of the story on repeat.

This unwillingness to read the plot is also visible in the community's deci-sion to overlook the menacing behavior of its youngsters. Girls on swings and girls roller skating in the summer are part of the series' faux-nostalgic opening sequence, and it is also one of the repeated motifs that highlights the dark ambiguity surrounding Amma and her girlfriends. Hence, when Camille in the final episode talks to Mae's mother (Sameerah Luqmaan-Harris) and the latter explains that the two girls have just had their first "little fight" which was probably about "girls' stuff" like "boys or nail polish," the specta-tor suspects that this is probably not the case ("Milk"). The choice of words such as "little" and "girls' stuff" is part of the series' proclivity to ironically counteract the manner in which girls' activities are still viewed as unimport-ant, harmless, and superficial. What is more, when the mother concludes that "I envy the skin, but nothing else about that age," it sums up the series as a whole, in highlighting the conflict and contrast between outside and inside, appearance and actuality, stereotype and reality. Not least as the reference that Mae's mother makes to untouched skin immediately reminds us of

Camille's skin, which has functioned as canvas for expressing her pain since
she was around Amma's age.

In spite of this ambiguity and doubleness, however, we simultaneously
continue to believe in the reality of "girls' stuff" and to be fooled by
appearance. An example of this is to be found in the scenes preceding the
conversation with Mae's mother where Camille and Amma are creating a
life together. Here, we see Amma moving out of the house, getting new
friends, and establishing a space of intimacy that seems to respect boundaries and allow growth. The whole process, moreover, is accompanied by a
sweet, light, and hopeful soundtrack. This goes on until we are struck in the
face with the realization that in the same way that Alan was wrong when
he declared the "story's over" in the beginning of the episode, it is still
not over. Like Adora's house, we understand, Camille's apartment only
seems like a home. And while it has been made snuggly and pretty since
Amma moved in, this too is just a front. In the same way as Amma's toy
dollhouse, which is created as a replica of an ideal home, Camille's apartment is, in fact, filled with dead objects and ghostly figures that are only
human-like. And we learn that, in spite of all our beliefs in success, Amma
is the daughter who was not able to form an autonomous subjectivity, but
who got caught in the fangs of the maternal octopus and ended up as a distorted version of her mother, as was always already suggested in the name
"Amma," which in this context reads like a distorted anagram of the childish denominator "mama."

CONCLUSION

The ending of *Sharp Objects* largely leaves us in despair. According to
Marianne Hirsch, however, female plots are doomed to end this way in the
sense that they act out the frustrations "engendered by these limited possibilities and attempt to subvert the constraint of dominant patterns" by
revising endings, beginnings, and patterns of progression (1989, 8). In other
words—just when you thought you had pinned down the daughter, or when
you thought you had nailed the mother, the narrators pull the rug out from
under your feet and show you that these are only bleak and ghostly figures
produced by a patriarchal structure that has given us a flawed—and insufficient—recipe of what a mother–daughter relationship is, was, and should be.
In her essay "Mothers and Daughters," moreover, Marianne Hirsch states that
female identity must be investigated not only in relation to woman's role as a
daughter of mothers and as a mother of daughters, but also in the wider context of the emotional, economic, and symbolic structures of family and society (1981, 201). Sharp Objects is shaped by the recognition that motherhood

is a patriarchal institution, rendering it a female experience shaped by male structures. The problem, then, is really located in the structures that allow this charade to go on and which continues to push our gaze in the direction of the serial killer or an unknown "they" and who both prevent us from telling and understanding the stories that are out there—the stories that are us.

WORKS CITED

Abraham, Nicolas. 1994. "Notes on the Phantom: A Complement to Freud's Metapsychology." In *The Shell and the Kernel: Renewals of Psychoanalysis*, edited by Nicholas Abraham and Maria Torok, translated by Nicolas Rand, 165–171. Chicago: Chicago University Press.

Chambers, Deborah. 2013. *Social Media and Personal Relationships: Online Intimacies and Networked Friendships*. London: Palgrave Macmillan.

Chodorow, Nancy. 1978. *The Reproduction of Mothering: Psychoanalysis and the Sociology of Gender*. California: University of California Press.

Connor, Stephen. 2003. *The Book of Skin*. New York: Cornell University Press.

"Falling" (Episode 7). 2018. *Sharp Objects*. Written by Gillian Flynn & Scott Brown. Directed by Jean-Marc Vallée. *HBO Nordic*.

"Fix" (Episode 3). 2018. *Sharp Objects*. Written by Alex Metcalf. Directed by Jean-Marc Vallée. *HBO Nordic*.

Flynn, Gillian. 2006. *Sharp Objects*. London: Weidenfeld & Nicolson.

Heidegger, Martin. 1971. *Poetry, Language, Thought*. Translated by Albert Hofstadter. New York: Harper and Row.

Hirsch, Marianne. 1981. "Mothers and Daughters." *Signs: Journal of Women in Culture and Society* 7(1): 200–222.

Hirsch, Marianne. 1989. *The Mother/Daughter Plot: Narrative, Psychoanalysis, Feminism*. Bloomington and Indianapolis: Indiana University Press.

Isherwood, Charles. 2011. "Reaper Arrives? Grab a Kimono." *The New York Times*, January 30, 2011. https://www.nytimes.com/2011/01/31/theater/reviews/31milk .html.

Knox, Sarah. 1998. *Murder: A Tale of Modern American Life*. Durham, NC: Duke University Press.

Kristeva, Julia. 1986a. "About Chinese Women." In *The Kristeva Reader*, edited by Toril Moi, 138–159. Oxford: Blackwell Publishers.

Kristeva, Julia. 1986b. "The System and the Speaking Subject." In *The Kristeva Reader*, edited by Toril Moi, 24–33. Oxford: Blackwell Publishers.

Luckhurst, Roger. 2008. *The Trauma Question*. London and New York: Routledge.

"Milk" (Episode 8). 2018. *Sharp Objects*. Written by Marti Noxon and Gillian Flynn. Directed by Jean-Marc Vallée. *HBO Nordic*.

Olund, Eric, and Natalie Oswin. 2010. "Governing Intimacy." *Environment and Planning D: Society and Space* 28: 60–67. https://journals.sagepub.com/doi/10 .1068/d2801ed.

Patterson, Troy. 2018. "Amy Adams Unravels in 'Sharp Objects'" *New Yorker*, July 10, 2018. https://www.newyorker.com/culture/on-television/amy-adams-unravels -in-sharp-objects.

Plath, Sylvia. 1981. *Collected Poems*. London: Faber and Faber.

Rich, Adrienne. 1976. *Of Woman Born: Motherhood as Experience and Institution*. New York: W. W. Norton & Company.

Robinson, Lisa. 2003. "Stairway to Excess". *Vanity Fair*, February 18, 2014. https:// www.vanityfair.com/culture/2003/11/led-zeppelin-1970s-lisa-robinson.

"Vanish" (Episode 1). 2018. *Sharp Objects*. Written by Marti Noxon. Directed by Jean-Marc Vallée. *HBO Nordic*.

Warner, Warner. 1995. *From the Beast to the Blonde: On Fairy Tales and Their Tellers*. London: Vintage Books.

Weinstock, Jeffrey Andrew. *Spectral America: Phantoms and the National Imagination*. Madison, WI: University of Wisconsin Press.

Yousef, Nancy. 2013. *Romantic Intimacy*. Stanford, CA: Stanford University Press.

Chapter 3

"The Immortal Conception, the Perennial Theme"

Reading the Modern Body in Willa Cather's "Coming, Aphrodite!"

Ingrid Galtung

As the site through which we first organize our awareness of notions such as wholeness and health, rhythm and symmetry, or the interplay of free movement and constraint, the body exists as our original mode of being—the seat of our primordial stories. This essay focuses on the intertwining of literary modernism and the ways in which the body was experienced, thought about, and conceptualized during the first half of the twentieth century. In a time marked by social, political, and economic upheaval, the material body became a key locus through which the experience of rapid change was negotiated, and a state of integrity attempted, reclaimed, and refined. While modernism has often been defined in terms of "an active search for meaning," and a response to the "disorder and fragmentation caused by the modern materialist world" (Friedman 1981, 79), the field of modernist studies has yet to fully elucidate the vital role that the modern human body plays in engendering its new aesthetic forms. The first part of this essay introduces the key role that the body plays in modern individuals' practical and artistic negotiations of their existence. Using Willa Cather's short story "Coming, Aphrodite!" (1920) as a literary example, the second part of the essay continues to investigate how modernists were drawn to the contemporary body's expressivity, endeavoring to encompass and creatively utilize bodily forms, events, and experiences in their artistic quests for meaning.

The first step in exploring the complex relations between the material human body and modernist aesthetics is to clarify entwined notions of "modernism" and "modernity." Broad and viewed by different academic disciplines in different ways, the latter term is most commonly used to denote

31

historical events and world-spanning processes, which, since the start of the sixteenth century, have contributed to speeding up the pace of human life. In his seminal work *All That is Solid Melts into Air* (1982), Marshall Berman describes such processes as "the maelstrom of modern life" (Berman 2010, 16)—a welter of developmental forces that keep the individual in a "state of perpetual becoming" (ibid., 16). In this essay, I follow Berman in seeing "modernity" as referring to the social experience of ongoing change, rather than the social processes of modernization which bring this experience about. "To be modern," Berman argues, "is to find ourselves in an environment that promises us adventure, power, joy, growth, transformation of ourselves and the world—and, at the same time, that threatens to destroy everything we have, everything we know, everything we are. . . . it pours us all into a maelstrom of perpetual disintegration and renewal, of struggle and contradiction, of ambiguity and anguish" (ibid., 15). The experience of modernity, as it is understood here, is characterized by a certain doubleness, encompassing simultaneously the feeling of abundant possibility and an irrevocable loss of tradition and stability. Moreover, those caught up in this conflicting experience often believe themselves to be the first, and perhaps also the only ones to live through it, a feeling which "has engendered numerous nostalgic myths of pre-modern Paradise Lost" (ibid., 15). A heightened awareness of the uprooting experience of modernity is at the forefront of individual and collective consciousness during the late nineteenth and early twentieth centuries, the period in which the contours of our own modern world truly start to take shape.

During this time of unprecedented industrialization, urbanization, and differentiation, the diverse and loosely defined movement of modernism develops in self-conscious response to the experience of navigating an increasingly complex reality. Traditional definitions of modernism often describe its relationship to modernization and modernity in antagonistic terms, regarding the artist as "a seer who would attempt to create what the culture could no longer produce . . . symbol and meaning" (Friedman 1981, 98) or modernism itself, in the words of James Knapp, as "a kind of soul trapped in the gross body of modern industrial society" (quoted in Armstrong 2005, 1). Highlighting instead its interdependence with the materialist world, Berman describes modernism as an abundant variety of "visions and ideas," which seek to "make men and women the subjects as well as the objects of modernization, to give them power to change the world that is changing them, to make their way through the maelstrom and to make it their own" (Berman 2010, 16). Drawing on this definition, I understand modernism as a series of artistic attempts to bring forth and critically utilize the transformative powers that shape the artist's material surroundings and herself as a physical being. It is through the body, after all, that we are present in time and space, and it is inevitably through our physical senses that we actively experience and feel the impact of the maelstrom of modern life. In turn, the artistic practices of modernism must, to a large extent, be thought of as endeavors to articulate and make sense of corporeal events and experiences. In art, the body figures as a site in which modernity and modernism come together, and this is something that the present essay acknowledges and aims to unpack.

Central to this reading of Cather's "Coming Aphrodite!" is the era's fascination with and revival of the Graeco-Roman goddess of Aphrodite/Venus. Aphrodite's figure is at the heart of early twentieth-century body culture, representing an influential ideal that women would strive for. The coming of the modern Aphrodite had begun in the late nineteenth century, as artists, doctors, and dress reformers had come to understand the Graeco-Roman body as the original human form. In an 1883 commentary on the effects of Victorian dress on health, Frederick Treves, an expert in anatomy, explains how in the figure of Venus di Medici "there is a gentle sweep from shoulder to the hip, all parts are in proportion, and the actual outline of the body precisely accords with the principles of beauty. In the modern figure, there is an abrupt constriction of the waist; the shoulders and hips appear ponderous by comparison . . . and, so far as the anatomical eye can view it, the proportions of the body are lost" (quoted in Corrigan 2008, 74). By defining the natural body through an interpretation of classicist imagery, Treves contributes to the initiation of a modernist search for meaning in corporeal terms. His observations identify the Victorian female figure as exhibiting a destructive imbalance of proportions, which, throughout the decades that followed, prompted a desire to recreate the material body through the revival of a corporeal Paradise Lost.

Suitably, Aphrodite's reemergence from the flux of modernity echoes the conditions of her mythical and original birth. In Hesiod's *Theogony*, one of the earliest sources of the becoming of the divine order of Greek mythology, Aphrodite is said to be born from the foam that proliferates from the severed genitals of the sky-god Uranus, which have been thrown into the sea by Cronus, who acts on behalf of his mother Gaia, the Earth Mother. Rising from the chaos this creates—that is, from a liquid mixture of sperm, blood, and seawater—the figure of Aphrodite serves, as Sebastian Goth has argued, to illustrate the appearance of cultural forms from a realm of formlessness: "Not only does the creation myth of Aphrodite depict the very process of aesthetic and material formation; her ideal bodily form can also be understood as a meta-figure of all figuration: as an allegory of artistic form and beauty" (2015, 18–19). Thus, while commonly known as the goddess of love and beauty, Aphrodite is also "a figure of the creative . . . both object and subject of creation" (ibid., 19), which is reflected in the early twentieth century's regeneration of her form.

A quick survey of newspapers and women's magazines of the modernist period shows that columnists, designers, artists, and body culturists proffered the iconic statue of Venus de Milo as the prime template for women's self-creation. Although armless, her figure was celebrated as the epitome of beauty, and through diet, exercise, and beauty treatments, modern women strove to shape their bodies according to her measurements. In a 1916 *Baltimore Sun* article titled "America Grows Big Crop of Venuses," Harrison Fisher reports on the direct impact of the goddess on everyday American body culture, focusing on the era's many regional and national Venus look-alike contests:

> It is a good sign, one that every artist will welcome, that a bigger crop of American Venuses has grown up this year. . . . This sudden outbreak of American Venuses in various parts of the United States is not an accident. It is a sign of the times, a most significant one. It means that our women are preparing a declaration of independence from the rule of Mode. . . . The new fashions . . . are traceable to new ideals of feminine beauty, or rather they are new-old ideals, as the New Thought is the ancient thought of the Stoics applied to modern conditions. (Fisher 1916, 22)

Nourished by the image of Venus's unclothed body, with its "exquisite proportions," and "natural" form, contemporary women were able to break out of confining Victorian body conceptualizations, instigating the birth of a new-old feminine ideal. "The American Venuses who are springing up as unexpectedly and delightfully at different points in the United States as Aphrodite sprang out of the sea are performing a great service to their age and country," Fisher explains, thereby assessing the new-old Venuses as active subjects of modernity (ibid., 22). Yet in framing women's self-creation as a declaration of independence, he fails to acknowledge the restraints brought on by the oft-cited measurements of Venus de Milo's idealized shape, which are also restated as part of his article. It is clear that the template of Venus by no means liberated the modern woman from the "tyranny of fashions" (ibid., 22), but acted upon her body by contributing to her self-evaluation and regulation. Indeed, the period's cultural and commercial preoccupation with restoring and ultimately "normalizing" the body can be said to uphold rather than redeem the experience of loss and imbalance. Nevertheless, the "new-old" Venus was a "sign of the times," and as a sign, her figure connoted modern values such as health, movement, and freedom.

The body's role as a site in which the rhythm of loss and renewal manifests itself visually culminates with World War I, which killed ten million and left eight million bodies broken and disabled (Carden-Coyne 2009, 1). Imbued with values of beauty and symmetry, classicism surfaced in the era of postwar reconstruction as what historian Ana Carden-Coyne terms an "aesthetics of healing," which was "especially conveyed through bodies" (ibid., 2; 4). While modern warfare had fragmented bodies and minds in previously unseen and unimagined ways, living bodies became a medium through which a sense of integrity and coherence could be restored. Above all, the reconstructed body should emanate the ability and muscularity of the bodies of ancient Greece, which "had philosophical and symbolic meanings beyond just beauty. Muscles gave physical expression to the idea of unity and wholeness, at the same time revealing the character of one's soul" (ibid., 164). Moreover, a desire to be slimmer and fitter, and to dress in clothes that revealed the firm body and its implied meanings, became a defining feature of everyday life for both men and women. One of the more significant effects of the experience of war on daily life, Christopher Wilk observes, was the development of "different ways in which the body could be made healthier, or at least, could be made to appear healthier" (Wilk 2006, 252). With the aim of projecting the desired state of dynamism and integrity, the material body was transformed through an active body culture, with activities ranging from boxing and weightlifting to dance, gymnastics, and Greek posing, and commoditized by the rapidly growing beauty and fashion industry. Thus, in applying what Fisher describes as "ancient thought" to "modern conditions" (1916, 22), the first half of the twentieth century shows an acute awareness of the body's malleability and how it lends itself to the generation and telling of individual and collective stories.

An insistent critique of the era's yearning for corporeal and existential integrity surfaces in the poetics of surrealism. The conditions of the modern world—the violence and destruction of World War I and the feelings of estrangement and unhappiness brought on by capitalism—had, according to surrealist opinion, developed from the opposition between humankind's internal desires and the rules and regulations of the social realm. In his surrealist pavilion titled *Dream of Venus* designed for the 1939 New York World Fair, Salvador Dalí challenges Enlightenment notions of selfhood and self-construction by unleashing the latent life of Venus's iconic form. Visitors would enter the underwater-themed pavilion through a gigantic pair of women's legs, and overlooking the entrance was a large cutout of the Venus figure from Sandro Botticelli's *The Birth of Venus* (1484–1486). Dalí's reworking of the iconic painting is interesting, particularly if one approaches the figure of Aphrodite/Venus as "a meta-figure of all figuration" (Goth 2015, 18). Whereas Botticelli's painting depicts the emergence of her ideal bodily shape from water and into the exterior world, Dalí instigates a reverse birth into a realm of unbounded life (Debenedetti and Elam 2019, 270–71). Inside the pavilion, visitors would encounter a nude Venus, sleeping on an elaborately decorated bed surrounded by surrealist imagery and installations. In large adjacent aquariums, semiclothed dancers, some with crustacean features, staged underwater performances, the inhabitants of erotically tinted dreams-capes. By evoking the semiotic chaos that precedes and makes the emergence of Aphrodite possible, the pavilion reminds the visitor of the perpetual avail-ability of alternative realities and the possibility of formal renewal.

Thus, both materially and aesthetically, the bodies of the modernist era contribute to the primary rhythm that undergirds modern experience, cease-lessly articulating a loss or rejection of form and its subsequent retrieval. To truly make one's way through what Berman terms "the maelstrom of moder-nity" (Berman 2010, 15) requires a capacity to navigate between and integrate the two contrasting spheres: the suppleness and energy of Dalí's realm of potentiality on the one hand, and the strength and integrity of Fisher's popu-larized ideal on the other. Finally, as these examples have served to illustrate, early twentieth-century modernity is permeated by a return to the body, the nexus through which we most immediately develop our ability to stay com-posed while in motion, and by extension, our ability to ground ourselves in a world of flux.

Cather's short story "Coming, Aphrodite!" narrativizes the relationship between corporeality and modernism by tracing the passionate relationship between Eden Bower, an aspiring opera singer, and Don Hedger, a New York-based modernist painter. Featuring two different types of artists, whose conflicting artistic views eventually draw them apart, Cather's story invites a discussion of the nature of art: Whereas Hedger detests the idea of "becoming a marketable product," devoting himself to formal innovation by "groping his way from one kind of painting into another" (Cather 1999, 9), Eden yearns for fame and commercial success. At the end of the story, Eden has succeeded in her endeavor, as she triumphantly returns from her expatriate existence in Paris to New York to star as Aphrodite in the same-titled opera. While the story critically considers the "many kinds of success" an artist might pursue (ibid., 44), it also shows Hedger's modernist aesthetics as decidedly inter-twined with, and also partly deriving from, Eden's popular performance of Aphrodite. Exploring their developing relationship through five significant scenes, I read "Coming, Aphrodite!" as an inquiry into modernist creation.

The first time Eden appears in the story, Hedger observes her at a distance as she arrives in Washington Square, where they will soon become next-door neighbors. Described as "young and handsome—beautiful, in fact, with a splendid figure and good action" (ibid., 8), Eden merges with the vibrancy of the urban scene, which, filtered through the sensibilities of the modernist painter, is conceived in terms of ongoing change: "Looking up the Avenue through the Arch, one could see the young poplars with their bright, sticky leaves, and the Brevoort glistening in its spring coat of paint, and shining horses and carriages—occasionally an automobile, mis-shapen and sullen, like an ugly threat in a stream of things that were bright and beautiful and alive" (ibid., 7–8). In line with Berman's modern individual, who finds herself in an environment that promises "adventure, power, joy, growth, transformation of ourselves and the world" (Berman 2010, 15), Hedger interprets Eden as being welcoming of her new surroundings. "You're gay, you're exciting," he imagines her addressing the city, "you are quite the right sort of thing" (Cather 1999, 8). With her youth and "good action," Eden, too, is "the right sort of thing," projecting the vitalist current that Hedger endeavors to make visible through his art. Subscribing to a modernist sense of homelessness, Hedger is introduced as a man "travelling about without luggage, like a tramp, and . . . chiefly occupied with getting rid of ideas he had once thought very fine" (ibid., 9). While embodying a modernist attitude of critique, ceaselessly pushing beyond the purview of accepted forms and practices, his attraction to modern life is nonetheless marked by an awareness of the ambiguity of change, and its power to, as Berman puts it, "destroy everything we have, everything we know" (Berman 2010, 15). During what is "almost the very last summer of the old horse stages on Fifth Avenue" (Cather 1999, 7) Hedger describes the occasional automobile, a future symbol of modernity, as "mis-shapen and sullen, like an ugly threat" (ibid., 8). To be modern, Hedger's observations imply, is not to seek out the strictly contemporary, but to capture the underlying and continuous stream of life that brings change about. In life and in art, Hedger searches for an interplay of mobility and stability—a dynamic yet grounding cadence that he eventually discovers in the gestures of Eden's "splendid figure."

The first time the two meet, Eden is "caparisoned for the bath" (ibid., 13)—on her way to the common tub of their adjoined apartments "carrying various accessories" and dressed in a flowing dressing gown that "fell away from her marble arms" (ibid., 12). The reference to Eden's "marble arms" calls attention not only to the whiteness or pureness of her exposed skin; it also evokes the cool, smooth, and durable surfaces of classical Greek statues. The scene as such bears resonance to the archetypal Greek scene of Aphrodite at her bath, which typically portrays the goddess naked, crouching down with one arm attempting to cover her breasts and her head turned over her right shoulder as if surprised by an onlooker. Shortly thereafter, Hedger also adopts the role of voyeur, as he discovers a knothole in their shared wall which allows him to watch Eden undress:

he had never seen a woman's body so beautiful as this one,—positively glorious in action. As she swung her arms and changed from one pivot of motion to another, muscular energy seemed to flow through her from her toes to her finger-tips. The soft flush of exercise and the gold of afternoon sun played over her flesh together, enveloped her in a luminous mist which, as she turned and

twisted, made now an arm, now a shoulder, now a thigh, dissolve in pure light
and instantly recover its outline with the next gesture. Hedger's fingers curved
as if he were holding a crayon; mentally he was doing the whole figure in a
single running line, and the charcoal seemed to explode in his hand at the point
where the energy of each gesture was discharged into the whirling disc of light,
from a foot or shoulder, from the up-thrust chin or the lifted breasts. (ibid., 14)

Critics tend to focus on Cather's blunt portrayal of sexual passion and the
merging of Hedger's art and physical sensation—his actions, as noted by
Sharon Hamilton, being "suspiciously evocative of masturbation" (Hamilton
2013, 860). More important in this context, however, is the way in which
Hedger's imaginary drawing of Eden adds to the theme of artistic genesis,
which permeates the story. Echoing the trajectory of Aphrodite, who emerges
from a chaos of sperm and seawater, Eden, too, appears as both "object and
subject of creation" (Goth 2015, 19). As she rises from her bath and reveals
her full figure, her corporeal self-fashioning both triggers and is accentuated
by Hedger's voyeuristic and erotically charged representation.

    Thus, at the narrative center of Cather's story is Eden's process of modern
self-formation. A female version of F. Scott Fitzgerald's Jay Gatsby, Eden
has migrated from the Midwest to New York, where she is now developing
her identity and career, awaiting her chance to travel onward to Paris. On
the advice of an admiring music journalist, she has changed her name from
"Edna Bowers" to "Eden Bower"—a name "he felt would be worthy of her
future" (Cather 1999, 19). The theme of creation is clearly present in Eden's
first name, whose biblical resonance gestures to a meaning of "originality" or
a pure beginning. Her last name also recasts the Garden of Eden in feminine
terms, entwining two poetic meanings of the word "bower": that of "a place
closed in or overarched with branches of trees, shrubs, or other plants," and
that of "a lady's private apartment; a boudoir" (*OED*). As Hedger surveys
Eden exercising in the nude in the comfort of her private room, he peers into
a modern Garden of Eden, witnessing what Fisher describes as the birth of
"new ideals of feminine beauty," a "declaration of independence" from previous notions of femininity (Fisher 1916, 22). The notion of independence
also echoes in Eden's full name, borrowed from the refrain of Dante Gabriel
Rosetti's "Eden Bower" (1869), a ballad of Lilith, who in Jewish mythology
is the first wife of Adam, preceding Eve.[1] Aware that she and Adam were
both created from the dust of the earth, Lilith resists the inferior position
assigned to her, fleeing the Garden of Eden as Adam rejects her demand for
equality. Appearing "so tall and positive," and moving with a "free, rov-
ing stride" (Cather 1999, 12; 13), Eden embodies not only Lilith's beauty,
but also her confidence and self-determination. When prior to her bath she
confronts Hedger about his use of the tub to wash his dog, he describes her

with reverence as "fairly blazing with beauty and anger. He stood blinking, holding on to his sponge and dog-soap, feeling that he ought to bow very low to her" (ibid., 12). Remembering how in Greek mythology the mortal Actaeon was turned into a stag and later killed by his own dogs, all because he had intruded upon the goddess Artemis's "bath of beauty" (ibid., 12), Hedger leaves Eden feeling "vanquished" (ibid., 13). Thus, in a story of art and artists, Eden's bath and boudoir, more so than Hedger's adjoining studio, surface as the primary sites of creation.

The nature of Eden's corporeal transformation also speaks to her status as both object and subject of modernization. Whereas women's participation in sports and exercise had been relatively uncommon prior to the early 1900s, Eden's gymnastics routine testifies to the 1927 observation of German polymath Wolfgang Graeser that "from America to Australia, from Europe to Japan" "[s]omething new had appeared. It could be called a movement, a wave, a fashion, a passion, a new feeling for life . . . It had no name but was called by a hundred old names and a hundred new ones . . . Body culture, gymnastics, dance, cult dances, the new corporeality, the new physicality, the revival of the ideals of antiquity" (quoted in Wilk 2006, 256). Hedger, who himself "practiced with weights and dumbbells" (Cather 1999, 10), is clearly drawn to this new corporeal ideal. In contrast to his past nude models, most of whom had "flaccid bodies" (ibid., 24), Eden embodies beauty and symmetry—and with her slenderness and muscularity, early twentieth-century modernity. Bathing in "a pool of sunlight," a "golden shower . . . pour[ing] in through the west windows," the sun that "play[s] over her flesh" seems to awaken not only Eden's body, but also, more abstractly, the strength and dynamism of classical sculpture (ibid., 15; 14). With her "up-thrust chin" and "lifted breasts" Eden invigorates the mythical scenes of the bathing Aphrodite or Artemis, she is "in action" rather than concealing herself from view: "there was nothing shy or retreating about this unclad girl,—a bold body, studying itself quite coolly and evidently well pleased with itself, doing all this for a purpose" (ibid., 16). Later in the story, Eden even reveals her awareness of Hedger's knothole, which recasts her seemingly private exercise as a self-directed mock performance, and her voyeur as an intended audience to her self-formation.

However, whereas Eden is set on her process of formation, Hedger is attuned to the life that emanates from and through her form. The listing of Eden's various body parts, and the iterative repetition of the word "now" underscores the immediacy of the body's shapeshifting action, the rhythm through which her bodily contours "dissolve in pure light and instantly recover" (ibid., 14). Carefully pivoting from one movement to the next, emitting a flow of muscular energy, Eden seems to emit an original capacity for renewal—or what Hedger retrospectively describes as "a primitive poetry of motion" (ibid., 10).[2] In contrast to the other women of Hedger's Washington Square neighborhood, whom he describes as being pure objects of modernization, "artificial and, in an aesthetic sense, perverted . . . enslaved by desire of merchandise and manufactured articles, effective only in making life complicated and insincere" (ibid., 17), Eden's modern body appears to Hedger as a meta-figure of art: "for him she had no geographical associations; unless with Crete, or Alexandria, or Veronese's Venice. She was the immortal conception, the perennial theme" (ibid., 17). With "no desire to know the woman" (ibid., 17), Hedger's interest is with the bare movement of her supple form, preserved by his imaginatively drawing her in a "single running line" (ibid., 14).

Hedger's spare, dynamic line aligns his poetics with what Peter Nicholls sees as modernism's general transition from "representational" to "transformative" art (Nicholls 1995, 71). Alongside Berman, who comments on modern individuals' attempts not only to make their way through the maelstrom of modernity, "but to make it their own" (Berman 2010, 16), Nicholls describes how the modernist would "seek to harness the transformative energies of the modern to his own project of self-renovation" turning a sense of "impasse and decline" into "a moment of decisive change" (Nicholls 1995, 71). In Cather's story, the modern world's "transformative energies" are unleashed by Eden's body—"the energy of each gesture . . . discharg[ing] into the whirling disc of light" (Cather 1999, 14). To express an experience of her renewed form, Hedger's drawing suggests, means to capture not the body as such, but its power of transformative becoming—a power indispensable to his own endeavor of shaping a world of flux.

Considered in itself, however, Eden's performance appears transformative only in the sense that it reaches for the representational. "Eden Bower," the narrator explains, "was, at twenty, very much the same person we all know her to be at forty, except that she knew a great deal less. But one thing she knew: that she was to be Eden Bower" (ibid., 21). By contrast, Hedger "had already outlived a succession of convictions and revelations about his art" (ibid., 9). The difference between their artistic goals can be summed up by the tension between commodity and art. Elisabeth Grosz sheds light on this distinction by explaining that material production is "directed to the accomplishments of activities, tasks, goals, or ends," which often generate "pre-experienced sensations" (Grosz 2008, 4). In turn, art offers more than a product by "enabl[ing] matter to become expressive, to not just satisfy but also to intensify—to resonate and become more than itself" (ibid.). Whereas Hedger's "running line," although invisible, challenges Eden's spectacular image by extending beyond the contours of her form, Eden endeavors to be recognizable, which demands that she repeats and refines her visual image.

The two different approaches to Eden's process of formation emerge as Hedger invites her on an outing to Coney Island, which proves an ideal arena for her self-configuration. With its beachside and amusement parks, Coney Island figured in the early twentieth century as a microcosm of modern life, offering its visitors a multisensory, body-engaging experience of modernity's perpetual novelty and seemingly endless possibility within a controlled realm. Coney Island, as Ann Sally puts it, "reconfigured the dizzying effects of urbanism, modernity and the capitalist machine as entertainment, inviting pleasure seekers to experience the shock of modernity as fun" (Sally 2006, 293). Not only did the resort immerse its visitors in the speed, lights, and thrill produced by modern machinery; it also made them part of a living spectacle of corporeality. At Coney Island, the bodies displayed in freak shows, beauty contests, and acrobatic performances mingled with those of everyday beach-goers, making visible the body's capacity to resist, challenge, and adapt to form. This spectacularization of the body is highlighted in Cather's story, where the intended purpose of Hedger and Eden's excursion is to see Molly Welch, one of Hedger's artist's models, do a trapeze act suspended from a hot air balloon. Gliding over the beach, Molly appears as a "figure in green tights . . . gracefully descend[ing] through the air, holding to the rod with both hands, keeping her body taut and her feet close together" (Cather 1999, 26).[3] More than her daring deed, it is Molly's body that captures the audience's attention, causing them to "murmur . . . admiring comments upon the balloonist's figure. 'Beautiful legs, she has!'" (ibid., 26). Eyeing a chance to advance her own spectacular becoming, Eden convinces Molly to let her take over the night's final act, in which she is to ascend wearing a full evening dress. Unknowing of Eden's scheme, Hedger becomes a passive onlooker, with Molly as Eden's accomplice and director: "She's coming down on the bar. I advised her to cut that out, but you see she does it first-rate. And she got rid of the skirt, too. Those black tights show off her legs very well. She keeps her feet together like I told her, and makes a good line along the back. See the light on those silver slippers,—that was a good idea I had" (ibid., 28). Shedding her traditionally female costume as she descends expertly on the trapeze, Eden flaunts her well-trained body, whose shape and action Hedger has previously admired. This time, however, his reaction to her appearance is one of vexation rather than awe, "his mouth . . . full of the bitter taste of anger and his tongue . . . stiff behind his teeth" (ibid. 28). While Hedger's anger remains unarticulated, it responds to the manner in which Eden's vigor is now channeled into an entertainment product for the masses. In Hedger's view, Eden is "the perennial theme" (ibid., 17), original in the sense that she carries with her traces of an undivided potentiality. However, in the spectacular context of Coney Island, she performs to satisfy the expectations of a given script, which aids her visibility at the cost of her vitality. To be apprehended as an image, the scene gently warns, involves an incarcerating repetition or reinscription of the same, as is underscored when Eden later attempts to take as a souvenir the plastic flowers she was awarded after her performance. "I give 'em to you for looks, but you can't take 'em away," she is told by the show's page, "They belong to the show" (ibid., 29). "Oh, you always use the same bunch?" Eden replies, having failed to fully see how the flowers, rather than lauding the singularity of her impulsive act, serve to imbue it with a false veneer of newness (ibid.).

While the show casts Eden's body not as a vehicle of self-realization but a commodity in an economy of mass production, her balloon descent is nonetheless simultaneously, by way of Hedger's artistic sensibility, framed as an authentic moment of becoming: "Though Hedger was sulking," the narrator notes, "his eye could not help seeing the low blue welter of the sea, the arrested bathers, standing in the surf, their arms and legs stained red by the dropping sun, all shading their eyes and gazing upward at the slowly falling silver star" (ibid., 28). With the toss of the ocean as a backdrop, Eden arrives on the seashore like the mythical Aphrodite, whose birth, as Goth puts it, "depict[s] the very process of aesthetic and material formation" (Goth 2015, 18). While in Botticelli's iconic painting, the goddess emerges on a seashell assisted by the wind god Zephyr and is helped ashore by the goddess of spring, Eden is carried to shore by a modern parachute, with "Molly Welch and the manager [catching her] under the arms and lift[ing] her aside" (Cather 1999, 28). Although as Hedger's critical stance suggests, Eden appears as an object of modernization, she also actively takes part in her own creation. Her landing on the beach at Coney Island can be seen as encapsulating her ongoing emergence from the new wealth of opportunity offered by the flux of modernity. "[L]ooking down over the sea of upturned faces" (ibid., 28), Eden appears as an emerging star on the horizon, her arrival foreshadowing the success that will eventually land her the role of Aphrodite.

Finally, Eden and Hedger enter into a romantic liaison, having "somehow taken hold of each other" (ibid., 29). Upon their return from Coney Island, Hedger feels "as if they were enveloped in a highly charged atmosphere" (ibid.), whose tension parallels and intertwines with their opposing views of art. Over dinner, he struggles to explain to her his painterly principles, his trying "to get away from all that photographic stuff" (ibid., 30) "When I look at you," he tells Eden, "I don't see what a camera would see, do I?" (ibid.), his question revealing his fascination not primarily with her spectacular image, but with its ability, to borrow Grosz's turn of phrase, "to resonate and become more than itself" (Grosz 2008, 4). However, with her unwavering commitment to the recognizable image, Eden remains uncomprehending of Hedger's poetics. When introduced to his favorite sketches from the French countryside, she rejects them as simply unfinished, or to use Hedger's photographic metaphor, underdeveloped, concluding that "these landscapes were not at all beautiful and they gave her no idea of any country whatsoever" (Cather 1999,

20). Eden nonetheless experiences the effect of Hedger's modernist eye, his impulse to touch what remains on the periphery of the known. As he relates to her a Mexican fertility myth which has inspired a recent painting, a tale of sexual promiscuity and moral transgression, Eden knows that "Nobody's eyes had ever defied her like this. They were searching her and seeing everything; all she had concealed from . . . the millionaire and his friends, and from the newspaper men. He was teasing her, trying her out" (ibid., 33). Because Hedger is attuned to the "everything" concealed beneath her curated surface, a realm reminiscent of the eroticized chaos visualized by Dalí's *Dream of Venus*, Eden later declares him to be "the only one who knows anything about me" (ibid. 36). In turn, because Eden embodies an ideal interplay of force and form, her figure maintaining a relation to an originary whole from which she seems to have only recently emerged, she enables Hedger "to explain all his misty ideas about an unborn art the world was waiting for . . . explain them better than he had ever done to himself" (ibid., 38). Simultaneously complementing and opposing one another, the two facilitate each other's becoming, and in what appears as an ekphrastic echoing of Hedger's modernist style, the narrator describes their anticipated union:

> Standing against the black chimney, with the sky behind and blue shadows before, they looked like one of Hedger's own paintings of that period; two figures, one white and one dark, and nothing whatever distinguishable about them but that they were male and female. The faces were lost, the contours blurred in shadow, but the figures were a man and a woman, and that was their whole concern and their mysterious beauty,—it was the rhythm in which they moved, at last, along the roof and down into the dark hole. (ibid., 35)

Drawn with Hedger's "running line," the lovers' contours blur and fleetingly disintegrate, their individual faces lost to what he has previously, in relation to Eden's body, described as "a primitive poetry of motion" (ibid., 10). The tension between dark and light, male and female, imbues the scene with rhythm, a fluctuation of contrasting elements. Their embrace, in other words, is characterized by dialectical interdependency rather than a unifying harmony, which includes them into the story's articulation of "a stream of things that were bright and beautiful and alive" (ibid., 8).

However, undulating to a rhythm of renewal and dissolution, Eden and Hedger's constellation dissolves as abruptly as it has come into being. Their final encounter takes place as Eden returns from visiting the studio of Burton Ives, a commercially successful painter. Impressed by Ives's "beautiful" paintings, "the kind of pictures that people can understand" (ibid., 37), Eden suggests that Hedger should request his mentorship. Wounded by Eden's rejection of his bounding line, the realization that in her eyes, he is "only an

unsuccessful Burton Ives" (ibid., 38), Hedger leaves for Long Island, decid-
ing to stay "until things came right in his mind" (ibid., 39). Upon his return
to the city, he finds that Eden has vacated her apartment, having seized an
opportunity to go to Paris. Leaving her practice performances in New York
behind, Eden emerges into the wider world, and like a modern incarnation of
a Greek goddess, she is ready "to be admired and adored" (ibid., 29).

The difference between Eden's and Hedger's modes of artistic production—one affirming the individual by fulfilling desires; the other desiring to
reach beyond the status quo—is revisited in the story's final scene, in which
a mature Eden has returned to New York to star in the role of Aphrodite:
"Leaning back in the cushions, Eden Bower closed her eyes, and her face,
as the street lamps flashed their ugly orange light upon it, became hard and
settled, like a plaster cast; so a sail, that has been filled by a strong breeze
behaves when the wind suddenly dies. Tomorrow night the wind would
blow again, and this mask would be the golden face of Aphrodite" (ibid.,
44). The "gold of the sun" which in the past enveloped Eden's naked body
is now replaced by mundane streetlamps, flashing their "ugly light" upon
her features. The vibrant contours of her youth have given way to a "hard
and settled" face—resembling the plaster casts which in the eighteenth and
nineteenth centuries were used to produce inexpensive copies of classical
sculptures. Each night, her mask-like face turns golden, temporarily revived
under the stage-lights, yet the simile of the cast frames Eden's performance
of Aphrodite as unoriginal. Although "the wind would blow again," continuing to carry her to shore, Eden has lost her connection to the vast beginning
from which she originates. Having already arrived at her "spectacular success" (ibid., 42), the energy that once "seemed to flow through her from her
toes to her finger-tips" (ibid., 14), giving life to her movements like wind to
a sail, is gone.

As an inversion of Eden's settledness and lack of forward movement,
Hedger is described by Eden's driver as having become "a great name with
all the young men, and . . . decidedly an influence in art. But one can't defi-
nitely place a man who is original, erratic, and who is changing all the time"
(Cather 1999, 44). Embodying change, Hedger evades definition, and his art,
as opposed to Eden's, is thereby perceived as "original"—a quality he first
encountered in Eden's figure. On a beach in Long Island, "watching the moon
come up out of the sea," Hedger arrives at the insight that "there was no wonder in the world like the wonder of Eden Bower. He was going back to her
because she was older than art, because she was the most overwhelming thing
that had ever come into his life" (Cather 1999, 39). The rising moon evokes
the memory of Eden's emergence, which in turn echoes that of Aphrodite,
whose origin story, as Goth argues, articulates the very process of formation
(Goth 2015, 18–19). Finally, Eden is "older than art" in the sense that she

embodies a "poetry of motion" (Cather 1920, 10), the primary principle that underlies Hedger's art, which subsequently serves to illustrate how the transformative practices of modernism reflect, utilize, and depend upon the nature and knowledge of the modern body.

NOTES

1. "It was Lilith the wife of Adam: *(Eden bower's in flower.)* / Not a drop of her blood was human, / But she was made like a soft sweet woman" (Rossetti and Alighieri 1949, 18–23).

2. The line "he had seen a woman emerge and give herself up to the primitive poetry of motion" (10), is found in Cather's first version of the story, "Coming, Eden Bower!" published in *Smart Set* 62.4 (August 1920).

3. Molly's act echoes those seen in turn-of-the-century advertisements for the Barnum & Bailey Coney Island Water Carnival, where female acrobats, often dressed in green costumes, dive from great heights or descend by parachute over the beach (Frank et al. 2015, 32).

WORKS CITED

Armstrong, Tim. 2005. *Modernism: A Cultural History*. Cambridge, MA: Polity.

Berman, Marshall. 2010. *All that Is Solid Melts into Air: The Experience of Modernity*. London: Verso.

Carden-Coyne, Ana. 2009. *Reconstructing the Body: Classicism, Modernism, and the First World War*. Oxford: Oxford University Press.

Cather, Willa. 1920. "Coming, Eden Bower!" *Smart Set* 62(4): 3–25.

———. 1999. "Coming, Aphrodite!" In *Coming, Aphrodite! and Other Stories*, edited by Margaret Anne O'Connor, 5–44. London: Penguin Books.

Corrigan, Peter. 2008. *The Dressed Society: Clothing, the Body and Some Meanings of the World*. London: Sage Publications.

Debenedetti, Ana, and Caroline Elam. 2019. *Botticelli Past and Present*. London: UCL Press.

Fisher, Harrison. 1916. "America Grows Big Crop of Venuses." *Baltimore Sun*, March 12, 1916.

Frank, Robin Jaffee, Charles Denson, Joshua Glick, John F. Kasson, and Charles Musser. 2015. *Coney Island: Visions of an American Dreamland, 1861–2008*. New Haven, CT: Yale University Press.

Friedman, Susan Stanford. 1981. *Psyche Reborn: The Emergence of H. D.* Bloomington, IN: Indiana University Press.

Goth, Sebastian. 2015. "Venus Anadyomene: The Birth of Art." In *Venus as Muse: From Lucretius to Michel Serres*, edited by Günter Blamberger, Hanjo Berressem, and Sebastian Goth, 15–40. Leiden: Brill Rodopi.

Grosz, Elizabeth. 2008. *Chaos, Territory, Art: Deleuze and the Framing of the Earth.* New York: Columbia University Press.

Hamilton, Sharon. 2013. "Breaking the Lock: Willa Cather's Manifesto for Sexual Equality in 'Coming, Aphrodite!'" *Women's Studies* 42(8): 857–885. https://doi.org/10.1080/00497878.2013.830875.

Nicholls, Peter. 1995. *Modernisms: A Literary Guide.* Basingstoke: Macmillan.

Rossetti, Dante Gabriel, and Dante Alighieri. 1949. *Poems & Translations, 1850–1870: Together with the Prose Story "Hand and Soul."* Oxford: Oxford University Press.

Sally, Lynn. 2006. "Fantasy Lands and Kinesthetic Thrills." *The Senses and Society* 1(3): 293–309. https://doi.org/10.2752/174589206778476289.

Wilk, Christopher. 2006. "The Healthy Body Culture." In *Modernism: Designing a New World: 1914–1939*, edited by Christopher Wilk, 249–296. London: V&A Publishing.

Chapter 4

Not Reading the Signs in Nick Drnaso's *Sabrina*

Jena Habegger-Conti

We are generally comfortable with the age-old idea that to see is to know. The field of visual literacy in particular is based on the belief that visual texts hold information that can be seen, decoded, and comprehended. In a textual world increasingly governed by images, the fast and accurate transmission of a message requires that the codes through which images speak be familiar and agreed-upon. However, the field of hermeneutics has aimed at better and more comprehensive understanding and given little attention to misreadings and the ethical ramifications of inaccurate assumptions. This chapter will thus discuss a work that exposes the inaccuracy and futility of the practice of reading for codes, not only in literature but also in our readings of every-day texts like images, online news, emails, blogs, and chats. Nick Drnaso's graphic novel *Sabrina* (2018) questions our familiar patterns of interpretation and demonstrates how our familiarity with visual signs can lead to falsehoods that enable deep misreadings. I will also explore the possibility of remedying these misreadings by altering our method of decoding visual texts, namely, to *see* rather than to *look*, and to *listen* rather than to *hear*, a practice that entails paying attention to what is absent rather than concretely present in the visual text.

This chapter takes its starting point first in a quote from Jean-Luc Nancy who, in a philosophical exploration of listening, writes: "Perhaps we never *listen* to anything but the non-coded, what is not yet framed in a system of signifying references, and we never *hear* (*entend*) anything but the already coded, which we decode" (2007, 35). Nancy's point cleverly plays on the French homonym *entend* which means both "hear" and "comprehend." The question in this context is whether we read a text to listen to what it says, or whether we read to hear/comprehend the message that we already know. A second point of departure is my analysis of Marjane Satrapi's graphic memoir

Embroideries (2003) in which I counteract readings of difference that other-ize with a practice of reading that seeks out moments of direct eye contact between the reader and the characters of the story, which I will briefly recount here.

Embroideries is a story that ostensibly allows readers an intimate and privileged peek at the hidden lives of women in post-Revolution (1980s) Iran through its recounting of an after-dinner conversation between women only in the home of Satrapi's grandmother. Although much of the critical debate surrounding the work has challenged the ethics of Satrapi's choice to depict the sexual encounters and desires of these women to a Western readership still tethered by history and art to the fantasies of the exotic Orient, I argue that the loudness of the coded (e.g., the pose of Grandma Satrapi's which recalls Ingres's *La Grande Odalisque*) can act as a distraction from other aspects in the text, such as the relationship that the text seeks to initiate with the reader through its use of visual direct address. Briefly, visibility relies on presence, but invisible aspects, such as sight itself, are worth paying attention to. The vast majority of images in *Embroideries* rebuke and refuse otheriza-tion by depicting strong, independent females in positions of demand. Female characters are shown from the shoulders or chest up, with a full-face view, eyes out to the reader, portrait style. In the field of visual literacy, a full-frontal view with eyes gazing out toward the reader is understood as a form of direct address that yields power to the person represented. The women thus refute the visual codes through which the "Orient" has been portrayed. Visual direct address disrupts the subject–object relationship and dissolves the role of the spectator, creating a positive environment for acknowledging equal subjectivity. The symbolic contact with another human being afforded by visual direct address may also generate empathic engagement, offering the reader an opportunity to stand subject to subject with the represented other. I term these instances of visual direct address "seeing eye to I" (Habegger-Conti 2019).

Nick Drnaso's graphic novel *Sabrina* (2018) initially appears as a stum-bling block to this approach. How might we apply the concept of "seeing eye to I" to text in which the reader and characters *never* make eye contact in the entire course of the narrative? Not only does *Sabrina* enact the very opposite of visual direct address, many of the images in *Sabrina* are long shots, posi-tioning the reader at a distance, if not completely outside the field of commu-nication (see figure 4.1). More frequently than not, the characters are depicted with their faces turned away from the reader or even with their backs to the reader. At times the distancing effect is so great that it is difficult to determine which character is which. Baggy bodies defy gender codes, black button eyes stare elsewhere, and blank doughy faces void of any distinguishing character-istics mask what the characters might be thinking or feeling.

Figure 4.1   Many of the Images in *Sabrina* Position the Readers at a Distance (Drnaso 2018, 3). *Source*: Used with permission from Granta (London) and Drawn & Quarterly (Montreal).

Briefly, *Sabrina* tells the story of a missing young woman and those devastated by her disappearance. It is also a comment on the current information age, the deluge of "facts" that surround us but offer neither knowledge nor truth. I will also show that at its core, the story is about the absence of trust and meaningful human connections. For all of its efforts to distance its readers, *Sabrina* is the first graphic novel to be long-listed for the Man Booker Prize, and has received critical acclaim from reviewers, authors, and fellow comics. How, then, might we engage "eye to I" with a visual narrative when a symbolic connection between the reader and the characters is never established? And more generally: How might reading practices lead to affective involvement *despite* visual distancing, and *despite* instances in which the visual text positions the reader as spectator? Through an analysis of the visual texts in *Sabrina* I will explore how visual indeterminacy and an aesthetics of the nondescript overturn common assumptions about how readers engage with images, and challenge our practices of looking and knowing. I will also demonstrate how reading absence through faces, similar to reading the invisible in direct eye contact in *Embroideries*, can help readers to see and listen to others, and offer an alternative to the "meaning" arrived at through an interpretation of the images and written text.

IMAGES, POSITIONING, AND INTERPRETATION

The degree to which the visual text positions the reader to participate in the image and in meaning production is grounded in looking practices and interpellation—the reader's sense of whether or not s/he is precisely the subject to whom the text directs its message. *Sabrina* appears to offer no entry point for getting to know, or relating to the characters represented. In the first section, the reader must rely on variations in clothing and hair to distinguish between the characters, but when the story moves to an army base and everyone wears the same camouflaged, service uniforms and caps, visual interpretation becomes much more challenging. Adding to the visual indeterminacy is the spectacularly nondescript visual style of *Sabrina*. The bare rooms drawn in unmodulated greens and browns with low saturation produce scenes that cause the eye to see entire pages as gray in tone. The images are mundane to the point of signifying "there is nothing at all to see here."

As a central rule of thumb in visual semiotics, when viewers do not meet the gaze of someone else, they gain power in the role of spectators. Kress and Van Leeuwen claim that when someone looks at the viewer from within a picture "something is symbolically 'demanded' from the viewer (sympathy, respect, etc). If this is not the case the picture simply 'offers information' about what is represented" (Van Leeuwen 2016, 107; Kress and Van Leeuwen 2006). This would thus imply that distancing not only cedes power to the reader, but enables the reader to comb the text for the information it offers, simultaneously supplying information to fill in any gaps.

How we receive and interpret this "information" has much to do with our learned schema for organizing and confirming new visual stimuli according to what we already know. Neil Cohn calls this a "shared visual vocabulary" (2013, 27) that arises from systematic, cognitively stored patterns. We read *into* images with information we have already stored; visual recognition takes its point of departure in prior knowledge, in customs and preconceptions, and makes predictions (inferencing) based on prior experiences both from the real world, and from other texts. To express graphically that a character is young, old, fat, thin, Asian, Islamic, male, female, and so on requires a common cultural understanding stored in the minds of both the comic and the reader. These signs, however, can often function as a shorthand, paving the way to stereotyping. Spectatorship may thus involve a breach of ethics if the viewer collapses or reduces the other through quick decoding practices that operate on the level of naming, practices produced by our predetermined beliefs and prejudices (Habegger-Conti 2018).

My reading of Drnaso's *Sabrina* is not intended to undermine the powerful role that representation and visibility have in interpellating the reader and subsequently changing systems of belief. Comics and other forms of visual representation have become an extremely popular form in recent years through which minorities and oppressed peoples have gained recognition, empathy, and acceptance. Anthologies such as *Multicultural Comics from Zap to Blue Beetle* (2010) and the body of works by comic artists like Joe Sacco and Alison Bechdel attest to this, as do celebrated television shows like *Star Trek*, *Mary Tyler Moore*, and *Modern Family* which helped Americans acclimate to newness and difference regarding race, women, and sexuality. These works in general may be said to alter both how we see and what we see by giving visibility to otherwise invisible members of a society, or by pointing to the very limits of what can be represented visually and verbally. *Sabrina* does, however, illuminate the limits of interpretation when decoding visual texts, and our tendency for reading *into* comics through our socially agreed-upon norms. Because images are, to a certain extent, open vessels for meaning, comic artists often rely on written texts to point readers in the right direction. For example, in Alison Bechdel's *Fun Home* (2006) what would commonly be interpreted as a "masculine-looking" character because of the person's clothing and haircut, Bechdel informs the reader through the written text that the character is actually a woman (118). Bechdel's clarification reveals the ease with which it is possible to misread characters by incorrectly interpreting visual codes that lack further written explanation.

Drnaso's text refuses to offer clues for how to read certain scenes, and thus actively hinders the reader in the very acts of recognizing and knowing that could limit a character's identity. The images in *Sabrina* do not operate according to Barthes's notion of anchoring/relaying the message of the written text, neither do they offer supplementary information, nor ironically contradict its meaning (Baetens and Frey 2015, 147). *Sabrina* is not a work without visual codes, but the fact that visual codes cannot be confirmed by a written text to guide the reader in how s/he should interpret or contextualize them, frustrate familiar patterns of recognition, providing us with no signifying references that would allow us to comprehend anything for certain about the characters and their world. *Sabrina* exposes the ways through which readers come to know a character through both the visual representation of the character and their environments by disrupting some of the more typical signifying codes that help readers navigate and process both the drawn and the real world: facial expressions, the style of clothing someone wears, how a character decorates his/her home, to name a few.

Before going further it is important to acknowledge that visual indeterminacy in *Sabrina* succeeds because its characters are all white (with the exception of one black man in a grocery store), middle class, and easily recognizable as "normal" or "average" in the American culture from which Drnaso writes. Even so, Drnaso's ability to break down the false familiarities within our system of visual recognition can help readers to question the ease with which they can claim to know anyone or anything through the information given by visual or linguistic codes.

DRNASO'S AESTHETICS OF THE NONDESCRIPT

Drnaso's text seems to delight in an aesthetics of the nondescript with one-point perspectives, lack of shading, and an overuse of vanishing points that intensify the flatness of *Sabrina*'s world and contract the reader's level of engagement. Nothing in the opening pages is remarkable, captures interests, or draws the eye to it. The first two chapters begin with a series of visual stills in which the amount of information conveyed is so scant that they challenge the reader's ability to read a narrative through images alone. Because images in the comics genre tell part of the story, rather than simply illustrating it, the opening scenes of *Sabrina* allow readers to question whether the ordinariness or mundanity communicates something larger, more significant. The reader may easily slide into the role of detective, or even conspiracy theorist, while trying to find something of significance.

In comics the background of each frame is generally referred to as "the environment," but in *Sabrina* the level of engagement between the characters and spaces they inhabit is limited to such an extent that the chairs, couches, and other items appear as an inconsequential background. Little would change in the narrative if the characters were drawn against a monochrome square. The color palette lacks depth and seems to underscore the emotional void of the characters. The green of a bedspread is only a tad lighter than the green of the bedroom walls. The brown floor of the bedroom is distinguishable from the brown nightstand only by the black outlines marking off its edges. The flat, unmodulated colors are given low saturation so that every hue seems a shade away from beige or gray. In one home the kitchen is drawn as an L-shaped arrangement of tan boxes, resembling a computer model kitchen before personalization. The walls are entirely bare. Drnaso leaves out bookshelves, photos, artwork, or any other item that could provide the usual clues about the type of people who inhabit the rooms.

The event of Sabrina's disappearance itself is "non-descript," communicated to readers in script nineteen pages after the reader last sees Sabrina. Furthermore, the casual conversation in which this information is revealed—mentioning it only indirectly and without naming Sabrina—does not transmit the seriousness of the event.

> "So what happened today? You said you have an old friend staying with you who's going through some kind of crisis of his own?"
> "Yea, my old friend from Illinois. It's a weird thing. His girlfriend is missing." (29)

The delayed information about Sabrina's disappearance sheds light on the otherwise uncontextualized previous seventeen pages, which now appear ripe with clues. After the first section focusing on Sabrina in her home, we see someone named Calvin meeting someone named Teddy at a train station. After learning of Sabrina's disappearance, we can reread the first two sections of the book as connected: Teddy is the boyfriend of the missing Sabrina. He has traveled from Chicago to Colorado Springs to stay with his old high-school friend Calvin in order to not be alone.

Initially it may seem that the visual text requires the written text about Sabrina's disappearance to make sense, and that a rereading of the opening scenes is necessary for more knowledge about Sabrina and her disappearance. Sabrina is last pictured writing a note and leaving her parents' home with a backpack on, leaving the reader to wonder: Is this note her last message to the world? Does it say that she is running away? Is it a suicide note? The frames depicting the night before her disappearance might now also be read differently with the new information of her disappearance: Is her blank face sad, or merely pensive as she brushes her teeth? Does she look worried as she lies in bed with her eyes open? What is she thinking as she sits in silence with her cup of coffee the next morning, just before she writes the notes on the kitchen counter? The images now offer the potential for signifying differently than they did before, but Drnaso gives no answers to the multitude of questions that arise.

The desire to go back and correct earlier readings when more information is procured draws parallels to the reader of literature, or perhaps more accurately, the academic reader of literature who learns the practice of underlining and noting anything suspected of value in a larger context of meaning: theme, characters, symbols, motifs. With the belief that a "deeper meaning" exists in the text, we set about finding it. Sometimes we assume that the author intends for us to notice all of these clues that s/he dropped, only to read in an author interview that the author had something else in mind entirely. Drnaso's text illuminates the similarities between the reader and conspiracy theorist, and the faulty lines along which the practice of "close reading" and literary analysis in general are formed.

The experience of futile wondering about what the images could mean is more often the case than not when reading *Sabrina*. The reader is placed in a similarly hopeless situation later in the novel when Calvin and Teddy cannot remember when they last saw Calvin's cat. The cat is shown so seldom, and without remark, that its disappearance unsettles the reader's prior knowledge: *Was there ever a cat in this house?* Forty-eight pages before Teddy asks Calvin when he has last seen the cat, the cat is drawn in his final appearance in a single frame, its gray form huddling in the dark against a gray wall, barely noticeable.

"When is the last time you've seen him?"
"I don't know. He hides sometimes." (159)

Maybe the cat has not gone missing and we can find it hiding in these pages? The cat never reappears in the story and it is impossible to determine what happened to the cat. The effect of Drnaso's aesthetics of the nondescript is strengthened by visual indeterminacy in which scenes show but do not tell, or tell but do not show.

VISUALLY INDETERMINATE FACES

In visual media like comics, faces convey textual clues about what a character is thinking or feeling, and also provide quick and condensed information
about character traits, often based in common stereotypes. For example, a
face with the corners of the mouth turned down and V-shaped eyebrows
is generally perceived as "untrustworthy" (Oosterholf and Todorov 2008).
Drnaso draws most of the faces in *Sabrina* with a degree of abstraction so
that they convey little or no information. Their flatness also masks gender
and age. That the images offer none of the usual markers of character or emotion is underscored by a superficial dialogue which masks what characters
are thinking or feeling, and a lack of narrative voice on which readers could
rely for background or explanatory information. This matters greatly to our
ability to read and interpret the actions and motivations of the characters. For
example, late one night (the time of day is signaled by the darker atmosphere
of the frames and a frame depicting Teddy in bed), Calvin smokes a cigarette
outside and stares off into the distance. He goes back inside, picks up a box on
the floor, walks into the laundry room, climbs up onto the washing machine,
and opens a small panel in the ceiling. When he is placing the box into it,
Teddy surprises him from behind: "Calvin?" This clearly startles Calvin, who
responds, "Jesus Christ! You scared the shit out of me!" (56). When Teddy
asks what Calvin is doing, Calvin responds, "I thought I heard a rat in the
attic." "A rat?" Teddy asks. "Yea. I didn't see anything."

Prior to this point the images and written text have provided some basic
information about Calvin: he is an army officer, separated or divorced (his
wife and child live in Florida), he has a cat, and he likes to wear a Snuggly
at night but does not want anyone to know about it. In addition, the "Mental
Health Survey" he completes daily at work reveals that, with a few variances
in stress and sleep levels, Calvin reports his own state of being as average in
every way: he gets an average amount of sleep, drinks an average number of
beers, and his overall mood and stress level are average (23). None of this
information seems relevant to what Calvin might be hiding in the attic, or
why he needs to lie to Teddy about it. There are only two ways to interpret the
scene: (1) it is entirely *irrelevant* to the story; (2) it is entirely *relevant* to the
story and Calvin should be treated with suspicion. Drnaso offers no answers
to the reader who asks the question: What type of person hides things in the
attic and lies about them?

That the characters' faces in *Sabrina* are generally rendered as emotionally neutral also frustrates attempts at interpretation (thin straight lines for
mouths, black circles for eyes, and no definition to muscle or bone structure). The recognition of basic emotions is crucial for activating emotional
responses and empathy in real life and facial expression in particular is one

of the primary ways in which we have learned to detect emotions in others. Perceived facial expressions also signal approachability and the possibility for connecting or disengaging with others: expressions of happiness are interpreted as approachability, while expressions of anger can distance us.

The expressionless faces add to the reader's confusion about which emotion the author intends to convey. Affect studies have shown that feelings such as "bored" and "miserable," "aroused" and "alarmed" can be better understood along an axis of "pleasure–displeasure," "activation–deactivation" (Russell 1980). Because certain expressions resemble others along the same access, it is easy to misrecognize miserable for bored, and alarmed for aroused, sleepy with peaceful, and so on, without some type of linguistic confirmation. Mona Lisa's smile is a case in point: her facial articulation appears ambiguous, mysterious even, because of the way our brains process visual input. Her nearly expressionless face allows us to imagine what emotion we think we see, read it into her face, and then see it appear (Blakeslee 2000). Misreading faces does not always mean incorrectly reading the codes, but it can mean reading predetermined ideas *into* faces.

Sabrina is full of "Mona Lisa" moments that both confuse and give rise to what Eve Kosofsky Sedgwick has called "paranoid reading" (2003, 123): the practice of needing to unveil what we perceive as hidden from us in a text. With the knowledge of Sabrina's disappearance, it is no longer possible to read every face as neutral or "bored." One of the more disturbing blank-face moments occurs when Teddy screams in the middle of the night, waking Calvin. Calvin grabs a gun and runs to Teddy's room, where he sees Teddy, wearing only his white underwear, backed into a corner and screaming. Calvin shakes him awake and tells him he is only having a nightmare. He places his hands on Teddy's shoulders and tells him, "Teddy. Lay down. Relax" (46). Teddy, who has just woken up, experiences this moment with paranoia, as a sexual advance. He responds with panicked (surprised?) eyes, telling Calvin: "No. . ." In previous, though infrequent, scenes of interaction between Calvin and Teddy, Calvin's actions appear to be no more than those of a friend. Calvin has invited Teddy to stay in his home, has given him some clothing, and has tried to feed Teddy when he refuses to eat on his own. Against this background, we might infer that the fear in Teddy's response stems from something akin to night terrors in the wake of the trauma of Sabrina's disappearance and is not related in any way to Calvin's actions.

In the next frame, Teddy is back in bed, lying flat in a spread-eagle position, face up with eyes closed. Calvin kneels beside him on the mattress. His knees are bent, feet turned inward, and both hands are positioned in the region of his pelvis. He is positioned with his back to the reader, but his gaze is toward Teddy (see figure 4.2).

Figure 4.2   Teddy Screams in the Middle of the Night, Waking Calvin (Drnaso 2018, 46). *Source:* Used with permission from Granta (London) and Drawn & Quarterly (Montreal).

It is uncomfortable to interpret Calvin's actions as masturbation because nothing in the narrative up to this point has suggested that Calvin has any sexual feelings for Teddy. This may be why I read *Sabrina* through twice before even noticing this scene. On the one hand, the visual indeterminacy of this scene allows us to skip over it; on the other it may offer us a chance to reflect on the way that we have decoded the scene and categorized Calvin: *What type of person masturbates over a friend? A deranged person? A closeted homosexual? A lonely person?* And perhaps most importantly: Must all of Calvin's actions so far add up to a knowable, identifiable "type"?

The two subsequent frames show a close-up of Teddy's emotionless face (relaxed, sleeping?) and a close-up of Calvin's awake, but emotionless face (thinking what?). Eight frames later, when Calvin utters "Jesus" (notably punctuated with a period and not an exclamation mark), again positioned with his back turned toward us, there is no certain way to interpret the expletive. If the scene does not depict masturbation, the utterance of "Jesus" could refer to Calvin's exasperation with his life situation in general, or with the fact that the sun is already coming up and he has not slept. If the scene depicts

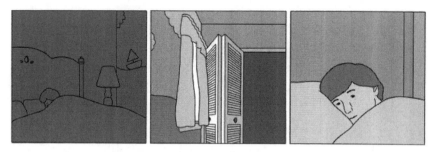

Figure 4.3   Sabrina's Bedroom (Drnaso 2018, 11). *Source*: Used with permission from Granta (London) and Drawn & Quarterly (Montreal).

masturbation, the motivation behind Calvin's earlier scenes of kindness toward Teddy (e.g., when Calvin comments that he likes Teddy's hair when first meeting him at the train station, or when Calvin plays an old mix-tape of songs that Teddy gave him for his twelfth birthday) could be interpreted as clues to Calvin's secret sexual affections for Teddy.

Drnaso employs visual parataxis to the same effect, offering an opportunity for readers to create links, while struggling to make meaning out of them. Two frames on page 11 appear first to establish an aspect-to-aspect transition, allowing the reader's eye to wander from a slightly ajar closet door in Sabrina's bedroom to a close-up of Sabrina's face against the pillow (see figure 4.3). With the information received later about Sabrina's disappearance these two may be related: the open closet door, with an interior that is represented as a solid black cavity, gives rise to a sense of paranoia. Perhaps Sabrina chose to sleep with the closet door open for fear of someone hiding in the dark? Sabrina's restful face on the pillow might, on second read, be interpreted as fearful rather than calm.

Because of the ways in which our eyes are trained to quickly perceive, identify, and link visual patterns, the potential for parataxis expands with the juxtaposition of frames that contain similar shapes and/or colors. On page 49 three dark objects are placed centrally in individual frames that form a column on the page: a dark gray cat, a dark gray mobile phone, and a dark gray gun (see figure 4.4). The eye reads these as a column on the page instead of following the left-to-right motion of reading because of their visual coherence, and the layout invites consideration about whether these items, which all belong to Calvin, are somehow also related in the disappearance of Sabrina. At another point in the text, when Calvin speaks to his daughter via his computer, the thematic tones of the individual frames (rose-colored for Calvin's daughter and tan-colored for Calvin) cohere in a downward pattern, rather than across the page. Thus, the flow of the visual narrative is against the flow of the written narrative, inviting a different type of reading that emphasizes the lack of connection between Calvin and his daughter.

Figure 4.4 A Gray Cat, a Gray Mobile Phone, and a Gray Gun (Drnaso 2018, 49).
Source: Used with permission from Granta (London) and Drawn & Quarterly (Montreal).

Nonsequitur frames also question the flow of the visual narrative and frustrate comprehension. Drnaso redraws three pages from the children's books that Teddy reads (on pages 53, 146, 147) but offers no explanation or comment to help the reader understand why he has included them in the story. If they offer clues about Teddy, Calvin, or Sabrina, the onus is on the reader to draw these conclusions.

READING SILENCES AND ABSENCES

Sabrina makes our search for answers futile, and indicates that information is never knowledge, despite the fact that the text offers an abundance of news and documentation in every form. Frame after frame in *Sabrina* reproduces internet texts, emails, the speeches from talk radio, photographs, and TV news reports. The amount of information on offer in *Sabrina* is suffocating, and yet none of it leads the reader any closer to understanding what happened to Sabrina Gallo. The deluge of news reports, blog musings, email accusations, and police questioning lure the reader to read within the conventions of the true crime genre, reading and interpreting everything in *Sabrina* as a possible clue, or, quite literally, as a sign. *Sabrina* never allows the ease of identification in visual media that readers have become comfortable with; it never confirms the meaning we attach to the signs it gives. One of Drnaso's themes might consequently be formulated thus: in the information age readers have become too adept at reading signs and are too quick to connote what the message is. Without a practice of slow critical reading—not *close* reading, but reading that is critically aware of the practice of making meaning—we fall prey to culturally agreed-upon norms of communication and lose our ability to imagine the world, or a character, another way. Gathering information has become our predominant method of navigating the digital world, but *Sabrina* demonstrates that information is what prevents us from truly seeing each other.

In *Sabrina* the entire system of visual communication is turned on its head: the texts in *Sabrina* do not communicate only through the visible or audible, but also through what is presumed to be invisible, silent, and absent. What I have termed as Drnaso's "aesthetics of the nondescript" may also echo a wider movement to impede decoding practices and the public's desire to "know" by concealing personal or distinguishing characteristics through practices of "anti-visibility" such as masks, hoodies, and other disguises (Habegger-Conti 2019, 150). A 30-second YouTube ad for Calvin Klein by American pop singer Billie Eilish addresses the problem head-on. Titled "Billie Eilish Speaks Her Truth," and published online in the spring of 2019, the seventeen-year-old American singer stands in front of a mirror and explains the baggy clothes that define her style:

> I never want the world to know everything about me. I mean, that's why I wear big baggy clothes. Nobody can have an opinion because they haven't seen what's underneath, you know, nobody can be like, ah, "she's slim-thick," [laughs] "she's got a flat ass," "she's got a fat ass." No one can say any of that because they don't know. [laughs] I speak my truth in my Calvins. (Billie 2019)

In *Face Politics* Jenny Edkins expresses similar views on visibility and recognizable characteristics: "Once we recognize people, we can 'flatten' them—pigeonhole them, slot them into a category, track them down, capture them" (2015, 127). Preventing others from "knowing" has also become common practice among political activist groups on both the far right and far left who don masks of various types to prevent "doxing"—a term coined to reflect the gathering of documents, personal information about someone in an effort to discover pieces of identifying information and publish them online. A new web app called "Nondescript" aims to keep anonymous authors safe when publishing internet texts by removing any traces of a writer's personal style, looking for stylistic features such as sentence and word length and the repeated use of synonyms or unusual words.

While our distinguishing characteristics and unique personalities may make us vulnerable, they also enable us to engage and empathize with each other as humans. The visually flattened characters in *Sabrina*, and its palette of almost indistinguishable colors, its distancing angles and plethora of seemingly irrelevant information work to position the reader from engaging emotionally with the text and its characters. Yet this may also be one of *Sabrina*'s greatest strengths in helping us to avert misreadings. "If we don't 'recognize' [people]," Edkins writes, "we have to listen to what they tell us, and listen afresh each time" (2015, 127). Edkin's sentiment corresponds to Jean-Luc Nancy's remarks on listening that I quoted earlier in this chapter: "Perhaps we never *listen* to anything but the non-coded, what is not yet framed in a system of signifying references, and we never *hear* (*entend*) anything but the already coded, which we decode" (2007, 35).

Reading and focusing on the content of *Sabrina* distracts us from listening to and seeing absence. I wrote in the introduction to this essay that the visual text in *Sabrina* does not seek to establish a connection between the readers and the characters in the way that *Embroideries* does, and I would like to revise that view slightly here. The very first image in *Sabrina* is a human face. The very first spoken words in *Sabrina*, spoken to a cat hiding under the bed, are: "There you are!", "Why were you hiding from me?" "Look at that face." Taking this as a directive for reading *Sabrina*, I flip through the pages again, trying to listen to the images of faces, seemingly absent of any emotion, rather than the loud visual codes of "clues." I notice how most frames contain only one, solitary person. I notice that the faces no longer appear blank, but lonely. Even when the characters communicate with each other, they do so, by and large, locked up in separate frames. The absence of any real, human connection in this graphic narrative speaks loudly on page after page: the final words of *Sabrina* are uttered while a man stands outside a closed-door shouting, "Hey, let me in." Reading the signs may make us suspicious of the ulterior motives of this man. Reading the absence of another human in the frame highlights the inability to connect with each other despite all of the ways we claim to "know" each other.

At the beginning of this essay I also questioned how our reading practices might lead to affective involvement *despite* visual distancing, and *despite* instances in which the visual text positions the reader as spectator. Precisely because of its visual distancing, *Sabrina* is a story that has the potential to reroute our readings for content and comprehension through the habitual processes of decoding with which we have become all too familiar, to an engagement with the other through the conscious act of listening to and seeing what is absent. "To be listening," Nancy writes, "is thus to enter into tension and to be on the lookout for a relation to self" (2007, 12). Nancy uses the present progressive form to underscore the unending moment of listening, and the "self" he envisions is not only *my* self, but that of others as well: "listening is passing over to the register of presence to self" (ibid.). "Self" is not what is available, or present on the page, but what is enacted in an ongoing process of interaction with others, also in the act of reading. Textual absences, indeterminacies, and visual silences present opportunities, openings between the reader and the text, and between the reader and the world.

WORKS CITED

Baetens, Jan, and Hugo Frey. 2015. *The Graphic Novel: An Introduction*. Cambridge: Cambridge University Press.

Bechdel, Alison. 2007. *Fun Home: A Family Tragicomic*. New York: Houghton Mifflin.

Billie Eilish. 2019. "Billie Eilish Speaks Her Truth in #MYCALVINS #CALVIN KLEIN." May 14, 2019. Video, 0:30. https://www.youtube.com/watch?v=-nJ loNKdtgo.

Blakeslee, Sandra. 2000. "What Is It with Mona Lisa's Smile? It's You!" *The New York Times*, November 21, 2000. https://www.nytimes.com/2000/11/21/science/ what-is-it-with-mona-lisa-s-smile-it-s-you.html.

Drnaso, Nick. 2018. *Sabrina*. London: Granta.

Edkins, Jenny. 2015. *Face Politics*. London: Routledge.

Habegger-Conti, Jena. 2018. "Transcultural Literacy: Reading the 'Other,' Shifting Aesthetic Imaginaries." In *Emerging Aesthetic Imaginaries*, edited by Lene Johannessen and Mark Ledbetter, 49–64. Lanham, MD: Lexington Books.

Habegger-Conti, Jena. 2019. "Reading the Invisible in Marjane Satrapi's Graphic Memoir Embroideries." In *Invisibility in Visual and Material Culture*, edited by Asbjørn Grønstad and Øyvind Vågnes, 149–164. Cham, Switzerland: Palgrave Macmillan.

Kress, Gunther R., and Theo Van Leeuwen. 2006. *Reading Images: The Grammar of Visual Design*. London: Routledge.

Nancy, Jean-Luc. 2007. *Listening*. Translated by Charlotte Mandell. New York: Fordham University Press.

Oosterhof, Nikolaas, and Alexander Todorov. 2008. "The Functional Basis of Face Evaluation." *PNAS* 105(32): 11087–11092. https://doi.org/10.1073/pnas .0805664105.

Russell, James A. 1980. "A Circumplex Model of Affect." *Journal of Personality and Social Psychology* 39(6): 1161–1178. https://doi.org/10.1037/h0077714.

Sedgwick, Eve Kosofsky. 2002. *Touching Feeling: Affect, Pedagogy, Performativity*. Durham: Duke University Press.

Van Leeuwen, Theo. 2016. "A Social Semiotic Theory of Synesthesia?—A Discussion Paper." *Hermes: Journal of Language and Communication in Business* 55: 105–119. https://doi.org/10.7146/hjlcb.v0i55.24292.

Chapter 5

Apprehensive Figurations

Monuments in "Site-Specific Performances"

Lene M. Johannessen

Abbeville is a small town in southern South Carolina with a population of about 5,000 people, near evenly divided between African American and white. It is mostly an agricultural and forestry town, and most times one visits it is also a quiet town.[1] Its quaint historic court square is lined by a Court House, an old Opera House, the old Belmont Inn, and other nineteenth-century commercial buildings, now repurposed. It is a quite lovely square with trees and benches that naturally and peacefully marks the town's center. Like in most such squares around the South, the one in Abbeville is also home to a Confederate monument, an obelisk of some stature near one end of the little park that commemorates the approximately 350 men who died in the Civil War. Unlike most such town squares, however, the one in Abbeville also hosts another and a very different kind of memorial. This is a plaque placed diagonally across the square from the Confederate monument in front of the Opera House, just a little to its side. The inscription on the black plate abruptly and unexpectedly disrupts the familiar presentation of the court square: This is a memorial to the lynching of Anthony Crawford in 1916.

In this essay I am interested in "reading" the Abbeville court square as a sited, citing, and situated "text" of extraordinarily webbed complexity. In a revision of the common phrasing, "the stories we tell," this is instead a case of "the *places* we tell." Evoking Wallace Stegner's well-known words, that "[n]o place is a place until things that have happened in it are remembered in history, ballads, yarns, legends, or monuments. Fictions serve as well as facts" (1986, 4), the Abbeville square stands before us as a dramatization of local history that extends well beyond its concrete locality. The remembering that happens through monuments and memorials does however not resort to fiction; this is instead a site-specific "performance" of an all too real history. By approaching the site as a kind of text with participants engaged in dialogue and with an audience present, we are able to grasp in the complex figuration of relationality a comprehensive staging of the contemporary as the history of now. The alteration of the space, where the Confederate monument and the Crawford memorial are placed, can furthermore be more closely analyzed by the help of site-specific performance theory in combination with that of chorography, simply stated the "representation of space or place" (Rohl 2011, 1). In its subdued yet violent "staging" of the past, the significance of the "performance" on this one square brings to acute presence what has been ominously absent and silent.

Anthony Crawford was a planter, father, and husband who owned more than 400 acres of land and whose success as cotton farmer enabled him to make important contributions to the African American community. On October 2, 1916, a white businessman approached him, wanting to buy cottonseed from him below price. Crawford refused to sell, and this led to an argument and his subsequent arrest. As the plaque explains, "a few hours later, 300 white men seized him from jail and dragged him through town behind a buggy. Finally stopping at the fairgrounds, the mob stabbed, beat, handed, and shot Mr. Crawford over 200 times—then forbade the Crawford family to remove his hanging body from the tree" (Equal Justice Initiative n.d.). Realizing that Abbeville was no longer a safe home, the Crawford family and numerous other members of the black community left Abbeville to go North. When the plaque was unveiled in 2016, several of Crawford's descendants returned to partake in the commemoration, and a painfully belated closure.

The plaque in Abbeville is one of many which the Montgomery-based nonprofit organization Equal Justice Initiative (EJI) has put up around the country, the vast majority of them in the South. EJI was founded in 1989 and are dedicated to "ending mass incarceration and excessive punishment in the United States, to challenging racial and economic injustice, and to protecting basic human rights for the most vulnerable people in American society" (Equal Justice Initiative n.d.). Many will recognize the organization from the Legacy Museum established on the site of an old warehouse in the former slave market in Montgomery, and the now very famous National Memorial for Peace and Justice nearby, sometimes referred to simply as the Lynching Memorial. Apart from offering legal counseling and documenting racial injustice in films, websites, museums, and outreach programs, EJI also a few years ago began a mission to commemorate individual victims of lynchings. This work involves putting up markers or plaques like the Crawford plaque to memorialize lynchings that have gone silenced, and to mark the concrete places where the many victims were murdered. In EJI's own words, this work is about

the power of "truth and reconciliation" to address oppressive histories by helping communities to honestly and soberly recognize the pain of the past.

As more communities join in this effort to concretize the experience of racial terror through discourse, memorials, markers, and other acts of reconciliation, more are overcoming the shadows cast by these grievous events. (Equal Justice Initiative n.d.)

On one side of the plaques is typically a text telling in detail what happened to the specific individual, while the other side gives a broader context for the particular state's role in what many refer to as a national scheme of terror. The narration in both cases resonates in a sober tone, and effectively imparts on the reader the harrowing history without sentimentality to detract from a starkness of facts that needs no further embellishing.

As of 2019, EJI has documented more than 4,400 lynchings between 1877 and 1950, 4,084 in twelve Southern states alone, and markers have been put up in many of the places where the atrocities took place. Wherever they are placed, they change that space, creating new sites for and transformed perceptions of remembering and reflection. Sometimes a plaque will appear on the side of a road, to be passed, quickly and en route, the sudden swiftness of its appearance echoing the willed obliviousness and non-notice that for so long befell these histories of lynchings. The glimpse of individual fate and the history that the marker in that flash mobilizes into presence transforms the space it inhabits, and it is the modification that results, and the implications this may have to a futurizing potential of remembering that I am most interested in here. The plaque in Abbeville will consequently be the main focus because it seems to me that its companionship with the Confederate monument as well as with certain other markers in its immediate proximity, which I shall come back to, raises some compelling questions related to apprehension as well as a kind of apprehensive remembering. The resulting site also goes directly to the problem of history's perpetual "untelling" and the absences left in its wake.

Pressing from the edges of history to claim its place in the center of remembrance, the Crawford plaque disrupts the hitherto familiar presentation of the past on the court square, inviting contemplations on a number of questions. One of these is concretely related to the monument debates in the United States, where the modified space of the Abbeville square offers a mode for reckoning that is different from other such modes currently "circulating." This is in turn intimately connected to what we may think of as a performative element that reconfigures the square in a (involuntary) staging of history which potentially invites to a space of understanding, if not reconciliation. The "performance," if you will, understood here in terms of constellation and perception, not entertainment, depends absolutely on the movement that inheres in the plaque's mobilizing of remembering. I use the word remembering here instead of memory to emphasize the dynamic of presencing that is involved on the "stage" as it activates an element of history in dialogue with other elements engaging the flow of now. It is consequently different from how we perceive and are engaged in a museum, where objects are relegated to a definite past and the spectator's gaze correspondingly fixed. In place, on site, we are drawn into the surfacing of the past–present in site-specific performance's triad of site–work–audience.

This relatively little-known piece of Abbeville's history adds to the poignancy of its square and the monument and memorial it hosts: the town is commonly referred to as birthplace *and* deathbed of the Confederacy. It was where several thousand South Carolinians gathered for the first secession rally after Lincoln was elected president, and it was where Jefferson Davies and his cabinet announced that the Confederacy was dissolved. As participant in the larger, national discourse about monuments, memories, and place, the small town of Abbeville consequently comes to that conversation with a historical record of unusual swag and lends itself well to a chorographic reading. To understand where the court square stands in relation to other squares, memorials, and debates, let us for instance turn to the speech Mayor of New Orleans, Mitch Landrieu, gave after his city removed the Robert E. Lee, Jefferson Davis, and P. G. T. Beauregard statues in 2017. In the morning following the first removals, when cranes had lifted the statue of Lee off of its pedestal at night and placed it in storage, Landrieu explained the unusual maneuver in a 17-minute speech. Among other things he said that "While some have driven by these statu[es] every day and either revered their beauty or failed to see them at all, many of our neighbors and our fellow Americans see them very, very clearly. Many are painfully aware of their long shadows, their presence cast not only literally but figuratively" (Landrieu 2017). Landrieu's speech reminded people that stones and markers are not innocent, that their presence and insistence on holding certain memories in place implies the negation of other memories. For the long shadows are indeed long, and the tragic events that would transpire in Charlottesville, VA, later in that summer of 2017, when the demonstrations of the Unite the Right Rally ended in the killing of a young woman, made evident just how long they are. The Charlottesville tragedy was the result of deeply polarized positions in relation to the debate of what to do with the statues of Robert Lee and Stonewall Jackson which figure prominently in that town.

In the aftermath of the violence, the two statues were covered in black tarp but were unveiled again following the ruling of Judge Richard E. Moore in the Virginia Circuit Court the following February. In October of 2019, the same judge ruled it unlawful to remove the statues. This is a stance repeated across the South; Alabama, Kentucky, North Carolina, and Georgia are only some of the states where interfering with Confederate monuments and memorials is punishable by law. The situation leads to a challenge for those who would see commemorations associated with the Confederacy and its history removed from publicly condoned spaces. Barring removal, towns and cities, first and foremost across the South, are consequently looking for alternate ways of dealing with the countless monuments. The first city to do so, Atlanta has found a different solution. They are putting up what they call contextual markers next to or at the base of some of the city's monuments, and it means, as Sheffield Hale, president and CEO of the Atlanta History Center explains, that

> the panels will serve as an example to other communities grappling with their own Confederate monuments and will help foster discussions and learn how to best address them. "If you remove the statue, you remove the conversation," Hale said. "For me and many historians, they provided that ability to spark a conversation and put it in our face that we did not have a perfect past—far from it, in the South." (Andone 2019)

The Atlanta solution is interesting and may be more effective in relation to addressing collective memory than simple removal is. And yet, Hale is only partially right, I think. Removing the monuments does not necessarily equal removing the conversation; you risk forcing it elsewhere. This is also quite literally happening, with monuments in some instance being relocated to privately owned ground. The context that the Atlanta markers add may on the other hand be so forceful, that despite often being dwarfed by the size of the monuments they comment on, the myopic outlook they stand for may not be able to withstand the added perspectives.

Atlanta's idea may also be more transferable to other sites, for the list of contested monuments and memorials is long, very long. In fact, it is so long that their handling also potentially becomes a practical question: Would it even be feasible to purge the nation of all monuments and memorials? Traveling around just the one state of Georgia makes for a daunting prospect: Where would one begin? And what about markers elsewhere, for instance, the one in the corner of Hyde Park in Chicago, the largest Confederate memorial outside of the South which commemorates between 4,000 and 7,000 Confederate prisoners who died in Camp Douglas? Its removal has been called for, but since it is also a burial ground there are complications.

It is in relation to questions such as these that the Abbeville town square stands out. It stages for its visitor a very different kind of argument than those represented by New Orleans and Atlanta and constructs a third approach to selection and remembering. By bringing into a silent, spatial dialogue two incommensurable figures of memory, the square creates what can be "read" as a figure for thinkability, an aesthetic very much of apprehension and hesitation, yet also perhaps signaling the promise of a potential for alternate

Figure 5.1   Equal Justice Initiative, Crawford Memorial Plaque, Abbeville, SC. *Source*: Private photo.

discourses of and on historical and cultural memory. To draw out this reading, let us now look at the actual "staging" in more detail.

Context in the image in figure 5.1 takes on a different value and function than it does in relation to the contextual markers in Atlanta. Context, the connection that emerges from the fabric of meanings woven together, is here a result of association rather than explicit direction. There is no explicitly intentional relation between the Confederate monument, the obelisk that we see in the background and the plaque closest to us, and this is not only due to the camera angle. There is in fact no conceivable way that the two could be brought into more immediate proximity, as is the case with the Atlanta contextual markers and the monuments they comment on. Here, instead, we "see" a dialogue that arises into its singular form as the result of historical trajectories; the figuration that results may seem coincidental, but when we consider context again, it is in fact the only logical outcome. The reason is this: On the one hand, what the obelisk in the background reminds us of is in a historical sense inextricable from what the plaque reminds us of; namely the lynching, which is the direct result of an ideology that would manifest in the desire to commemorate the confederacy on the other side of the square. The placement is similarly the result of the sequence of arrest and mob justice—the courthouse right next to the plaque is the site of Crawford's initial incarceration. The distance and angle between the two "participants" on this stage of remembering is also weirdly appropriate: Marking a spatial rupture, it falls on the spectator to invest that distance and relation with meaning. In this image we also notice the clock next to the plaque. I shall come back to its role on the site in more detail a little later; for now, suffice it to say that it, too, has a function to the problem of remembering, and apprehension. With these preliminary comments in mind, let us turn to what insights from site specificity and site-specific performance can bring to our reading.

Tate Gallery of Modern Art describes site-specific installation art as being distinguished from "sculpture or other traditional art" in that it "is a complete unified experience, rather than a display of separate, individual artworks" (*Tate Art Terms* n.d.). Citing artist Ilya Kabakov, the description goes on to note that "[t]he main actor in the total installation, the main centre toward which everything is addressed, for which everything is intended, is the viewer" (ibid.). As with all site specificity, the audience/spectator is an essential component of the artwork itself, for the potential of the work in place can only be realized through what performance artist and scholar Mike Pearson describes as the "reading of site . . . [where] a complex overlayering of narratives, historical and contemporary, [creates] a kind of saturated space, a scene of crime, where [. . .] everything is potentially important" (quoted in Kaye 2000, 43). The saturation Pearson refers to is inseparable from the concrete specificity of the place the artwork inhabits, and this will sometimes include geographic, historical, and cultural coordinates and significance. Reading and seeing the Abbeville square in this framework consequently have unexpected and thought-provoking consequences, for let us now consider this: What are those two memorials and their angular, distanced juxtaposition but precisely the invitation to a dialogue of layered narratives and rememberings? The square is quite *literally* the scene of a crime that Kaye describes above, the plaque a synecdochic trope which holds in it only a small part of an impossibly large whole. The spatial relationship between it and the rest of the "works" on the square is furthermore and ultimately addressed to the viewer in an insistent invitation to reassessments of relations and responses.

Sites, places, and locations can in this description be fabrics of signification not unlike a text, invariably carried in narratives, in stories. Similarly, too, to the text, site can be "readerly" released from the shackles of what Chimamanda Adichie calls the "the danger of the single story" (2009). Such release depends, however, wholly on the availability of what Jacques Rancière calls "figures of the thinkable" (2010, 17), for the "thinkability" of said figures resides resolutely in a sense of history that carefully selects from among a register of collective memories. The bridge from memorials on a town square into the reading of them as site-specific installation thus goes via aesthetics: In Rancière aesthetics relates to the "re-configuration of sensible experience," the relation between a "power that provides a sensible datum and a power that makes sense of it" (15). However, in the relation between "sense and sense" the concept of power cannot be separated from the modalities of inscribed memories, and this is where the Abbeville square inserts itself as a possible interruption of the long shadows of "original" monuments. The addition of the Crawford memorial forces onto the court square *cum* stage a relationality with its other that compels the spectator to partake in the complexity that this "dialogue" drives to the surface. This fact in and of itself makes for a poignant contribution to a climate that is currently often obfuscating alternatives to increasingly polarized positions. The potential disruption of the hitherto familiar thus gestures to the spectator that they address relations so far obscured, or silenced, and create a figure of thinkability that emerges in the context of what we can perhaps think of as a kind of chorography. That is to say, filtered through the spectator, the staging of the emerging dialogue produces a script of emplaced history that lets place and memory speak in unison.

In geographer Darrell Rohl's straightforward words, chorography can be described quite simply as the "representation of space or place" (2011, 1). There is, however, a lot more to this ancient tradition, testified to by the interest chorography has attracted in the past few decades and across several disciplines, and by its general participation in the spatial turn. That coinage can be conceived of in Denis Cosgrove's depiction as "a shift away from the structural explanations and grand narratives that dominated so much twenti-eth-century scholarship, with its emphasis on universal theories and system-atic studies, and a move toward more culturally and geographically nuanced work, sensitive to difference and specificity, and thus to the contingencies of event and locale" (2004, 57). What lies at the core of the spatial turn is consequently a de-privileging of time over place, a reorientation toward the pivotal role played by actual locales, and by actual situatedness and relational emplacement as the generator of spatiality, hence time.

Questions of place such as these moreover come trailing questions of val-ues and traditions, a further complication of Stegner's earlier quoted sense of place: "No place is a place until things that have happened in it are remem-bered in history, ballads, yarns, legends, or monuments" (1986, 4). Place and story are inseparable, and hence the claim to place is also the claim to narrative, and the history that makes it. Chorography records place in all its hues and colors, and Pearson's summary of its reach is here worth quoting at some length:

The nature of chorography is to distinguish and espouse the unique character of individual places. At particular scales of apprehension, it identifies and differentiates sites of significance as, potentially at least, places to visit within a given region. Chorography attends to the local: it concerns specificities, particularities and peculiarities. . . . [Chorographies] involve the systematic description of a region's natural and man-made attributes, its emplaced things. Its scenic features. Its inhabitants, their histories, laws, traditions, and customs. Ancient sites and relics. Property rights, and the etymology of names. (2010, 31, emphases in original)

Chorography consequently engages methods of explorations from a range of different disciplines, long, long before the concept of the trans- or inter-disciplinary had been conceived.

I make a stop here to emphasize that in the case of Abbeville, there is of course no actual composer, no chorographer present. Or, in one sense it is the viewer who takes that role in the attempt to read the square and the fig-ures its performance produces. More importantly, however, and as I briefly mentioned above, I think in some ways the chorography of the Abbeville square manifests in the "script" that the dialogue between obelisk and plaque, between monument and memorial, *itself* creates, and which transpires from the internal workings of layered stories and memories allowed to speak on the same site. In other words, the conglomerate of all what Pearson lists above congeals into a new kind of "text" that may now be read again. Attention to some of the elements that define chorography is helpful to see how this works. Aside from the basic point about how chorographies represent space/place, Rohl also lists more concrete elements, among them how they see *time as a feature of place*; how they emphasize the *interconnection* of the human and its environment; how they reorient received perceptions of center and periphery ("the particular place or region . . . to which all roads lead"); how they are concerned with "real emplaced experiences"; and the sedimentation of meanings into stories about place (2011, 6). *Seeing time as a feature of place* is the fundamentals of any monument and memorial—the remember-ing itself that we are asked to do—already temporal—is tied indelibly to location, their very meaning derived from their emplacement. And, as we saw, the concreteness of that emplacement, the angular distance between the monument and the plaque on the square, creates an ambiguous relation of proximity from afar. From this follows the *interconnectedness of the human with its surroundings*: the signifying power of the Confederate monument and Crawford's memorial is embedded in the very fabric of the site of Abbeville itself. The recollection of the town's role in the Civil War and its aftermath presses ominously on the stage, amplifying the meta-commentary on and of the spatial confines. From this we now arrive at *the reorientation of periphery and center*: The monument was established as the one and only center until now, with the Crawford memorial from hitherto margins interrupting the one story and literally redirecting our gaze into a differently framed reception of the fabric of relations. Finally, from this follows now also the unearthing of sedimentation of meanings not only related to Abbeville, SC, but by extension entire regions.

With this in mind, we do well in looking again to what performance studies scholars say about site. Pearson reminds us that performances on site "rely upon the complex superimposition and coexistence of a number of narratives and architectures, historical and contemporary. These fall into two groups: those that pre-exist the work—of the host—and those which are of the work—of the ghost" (quoted in Turner 2004, 374). One can hardly imagine a more appropriate vocabulary for the "installation" on the site in question: Here is in a sense the return of the ghost, a presencing of silenced stories brought onto the stage as a host in its own right. I must emphasize again that site specificity in the case of the Abbeville square is not technically a site-specific performance in the tradition that Pearson describes. The nature of the citations on the site is however such that it lends itself meaningfully to that vocabulary for a fuller comprehension of the drama and trauma which compose it. In his writing about the Welsh performance company Brith Gof, Nick Kaye lists some elements the company's cofounder Clifford McLucas considers central in relation to what he calls "placeevent." Rather than emphasizing a synthesis of elements between performance and site, McLucas suggests a coexistence of different architectures where the site can offer one or more of the following elements to the installation: "a particular and unavoidable history; a particular use (a cinema, a slaughterhouse); a particular formality (shape, proportion, height, disposition of architectural elements, etc.); a particular political, cultural or social context" (quoted in Kaye 2004, 53). Reading the Abbeville site with the first and last of these elements in our minds provides a framework for seeing differently that I suggest moves it from a static distribution of stone and marble into a living space that vibrates with what Toni Morrison calls rememory: "[h]istory versus memory, and memory versus memorylessness. Rememory as in recollecting and remembering as in reassembling the members of the body, the family, the population of the past" (Morrison 2019). Another look now at the plaque and its immediate surroundings from a different angle brings out the depths of an eerie performance of the history of now.

While the plaque is positioned in front of the Opera House (right), its immediate neighbor, as we see in figure 5.2, is a standing clock, and to the far left in the picture, a stone marker, located more precisely in the space between the Court house and the Opera House. The stone marker commemorates the law offices nearby belonging once to John C. Calhoun, a name that to most evokes the staunch defense of slavery and views on states' rights. In the address "The Positive Good of Slavery" he gave to the Senate in 1837, Calhoun stated that "I hold then, that there never has yet existed a wealthy and civilized society in

Figure 5.2 Equal Justice Initiative, Crawford Memorial Plaque, Abbeville, SC. *Source*: Private photo.

which one portion of the community did not, in point of fact, live on the labor of the other. Broad and general as is this assertion, it is fully borne out by history" (1837). To Calhoun, the institution of slavery was inseparable from the survival of the South as a region, as civilization, and it is perhaps not without reason that he is sometimes referred to as the man who started the Civil War. The marker that commemorates his presence on the Abbeville square can consequently be read in anticipation of the war that would lead to the monument across from it, and to the plaque recalling its devastating results.

It is furthermore appropriate that between the Calhoun marker and the Crawford plaque is a clock. It is taller than any of the other markers in the space, and works in its function as meter of temporality, ambiguously both reminding and warning. If the marker, plaque, and monument all serve as measures of spatiality, of history and remembering wrapped into the space of a small-town square, then the clock is all temporality. Loosened from the confines of emplaced happening, the clock's relentless measuring of time brings to the "installation" a compelling signal of the urgency of remembering and reckoning.

Such, then, are the essentials of the chorography—and choreography—that Abbeville's court square presents as installation on site: it is a writing of place that is impossible to turn away from. The square also speaks poignantly to the very nature of memorials and monuments in and of themselves. In her book *Memorials Matter: Emotion, Environment and Public Memory at American Historical Sites* Jennifer Ladino reminds us that even if monuments and memorials are sometimes conflated, they are different. Often, she writes, "monuments refer to built structures on a grand scale . . . which tend to (but don't always) celebrate dominant national narratives and reinscribe official histories. Memorials, by contrast, can be as simple as a plaque and tend to mark sites of grief or trauma. Memorials recognize a messier past and give expression to American publics that are 'diverse and often stratified'" (2018, xiii). The distinction Ladino makes bears on the Abbeville square in my viewing it as chorographic site-specific installation. It also applies to the many other places where plaques have been added to existing commemorations of one story only. If the monument holds its place as the safe keeper of a sphere of historically and culturally agreed-upon memories, then the plaque as memorial brings rupture, emphasizing the warning that resides in the Latin root, *monere*—to remind *and* to warn. The ambiguity of temporal orientation at play adds to the complexity of the Abbeville installation: the relationship between the monument and the memorial is spatially and dialogically bound in a simultaneous leaning toward the past as well as future, the expression of an impulse to re-member as well as *de*-member, to protect as well as to destroy. What the chorography ultimately invites to is consequently an open display of a national haunting that resides in what is not resolved or reconciled.

By way of conclusion I want to return to Rancière, for, having now assessed as best as we can what actually goes into the site we are looking at, what is it, aesthetically speaking, that transpires? The question relates closely to all of the conceptual challenges residing in the title of this volume: *Aesthetic Apprehensions: Silence and Absence in False Familiarities*. In the chorography that the installation on the Abbeville square presents, the command on sensing that aesthetics places on us is, as we have seen, difficult to turn away from. The problem of false familiarity, one borne of what has not been expressed, seen, and brought into contemporaneity, moreover resonates with something Rancière says about the ethical order in relation to aesthetics. The ethical order, he notes, is "a whole organization of the visible, the thinkable, and the possible, determining what can be felt, seen, thought, and done by this or that class of beings, depending on its place and occupation" (2010, 17). The description fits the nature of the town square before the Crawford memorial came up all too well, and synecdochically so, that of an entire region. The impact of the Abbeville work, so to speak, as it stands before us today, is an instance of precisely what Rancière goes on to call an aesthetic heterotopia, a rupture with the ethical order that opens up a space for sensing differently. It is however not entirely heterotopic, if by that we mean other in an absolute sense, because the Abbeville square and its installation is conditioned by the specificities, in all their complex layeredness, which pertain to its site and which precede its current form.

To conclude, let us recall chorography's emphasis on "real emplaced experiences" (Rohl 2011, 6) and the sedimentation of meanings that transpire into stories about place. Long silent and invisible, the stories and sedimentations that enshroud the town square have not been *absent*; instead their veiled presence marks the very conditioning of the figure the square has made. This is an example of how the ethical order, the distribution of the sensible, helps create false familiarities: the shadow cast by the sole monument perpetuating an agreement on absence that does not allow for the surfacing of its already and conditioned, embedded presence. When the EJI plaque is introduced onto this stage, it disrupts the agreement and produces an aesthetic effect that can be linked to what Rancière describes as redistribution:

> What is at issue is the configuration of the sensible landscape in which a community is framed, a configuration of what it is possible to see and feel, of the ways in which it is possible to speak and think. It is a distribution of the possible which also is a distribution of the capacity that these or those have to take part in this distribution of the possible. (2010, 24)

The quote goes to the heart of the rupture and the resulting performance of the Abbeville square and its chorography: here is the possibility of staging differently, and of seeing differently, and it is the possibility of this possibility that marks the installation as radically different from other responses to the monument debates. Central to this possibility is the role of the audience, the mandate that site specificity places on us to engage with the work in order to realize its potential; it is in the relation between the audience and the work that Rancière's redistribution of the sensible emerges, again, as the possibility of possibility, and which is precisely where fabrics falsely familiar unravel. Aesthetic apprehensions amplify as the depths of the site unfold before us, and perhaps this is the potential that the staging of spaces of memory the Abbeville "installation" opens for.

NOTE

1. A section of this essay appears in revised form in *Site-Seeing Aesthetics: California Sojourns in Five* Installations (Brill 2020).

WORKS CITED

Adichie, Chimamanda. 2009. "The Danger of Single Story." *TEDGlobal*, July 2009. https://www.ted.com/talks/chimamanda_ngozi_adichie_the_danger_of_a_single_story/transcript.

Andone, Dakin. 2019. "Georgia Law Prohibits Removing These Confederate Monuments. So Atlanta Is Adding Context." *CNN*, August 2, 2019. https://edition.cnn.com/2019/08/02/us/atlanta-confederate-monuments-context/index.html.

Calhoun, John C. 1837. "Speech on the Reception of Abolition Petitions, Delivered in the Senate, February 6th, 1837." In *Speeches of John C. Calhoun, Delivered in the House of Representatives and in the Senate of the United States*, edited by Richard R. Cralle, 625–633. New York: New D. Appleton, 1853. https://www.stolaf.edu/people/fitz/COURSES/calhoun.html.

Cosgrove, Denis. 2004. "Landscape and Landschaft." *Bulletin of the GHI Washington* 35(Fall).

Equal Justice Initiative. https://eji.org.

Kaye, Nick. 2000. *Site-Specific Art: Performance, Place, and Documentation*. Milton Park/New York: Routledge.

Ladino, Jennifer. 2019. *Memorials Matters: Emotion, Environment, and Public Memory at American Historical Sites*. Reno: University of Nevada Press.

Landrieu, Mitch. 2017. "Speech on removing confederate monuments in New Orleans." *The Times-Picayune*, May 23, 2017. https://www.nola.com/news/politics/article_ef299e19-761d-51a4-91f0-aafb2e43e833.html.

Morrison, Toni. 2019. "I Wanted to Carve Out a World Both Culture Specific and Race-Free." *The Guardian*, August 8, 2019. https://www.theguardian.com/books/2019/aug/08/toni-morrison-rememory-essay.

Pearson, Mike. 2010. *Site-Specific Performance*. London: Palgrave Macmillan.

Rancière, Jacques. 2010. "The Aesthetic Heterotopia." *Philosophy Today* 54: 15–25.

Rohl, Darrell J. 2011. "The Chorographic Tradition and Seventeenth- and Eighteenth-Century Scottish Antiquaries." *Journal of Art Historiography* 3: 1–18.

Stegner, Wallace. 1986. *The Sense of Place*. The University of Wisconsin-Madison: Silver Buckle Press. http://www.pugetsound.edu/files/resources/7040_Stegner,%20Wallace%20%20Sense%20of%20Place.pdf.

Tate Art Terms. n.d. "Installation Art." https://www.tate.org.uk/art/art-terms/i/installation-art.

Turner, Cathy. 2004. "Palimpsest or Potential Space? Finding a Vocabulary for Site-Specific Performance." *New Theatre Quarterly* 20(4): 373–390.

Chapter 6

Apprehending the Past in the National Parks

False Familiarities, Aesthetic Imaginaries, and Indigenous Erasures

Jennifer Ladino

With its Smokey Bear hat, bison-embossed gold badge, and militaristic green-and-gray color scheme, the NPS ranger uniform is an icon of tradition and American nature preservation. When I took a job with the NPS the summer after college graduation, I wore the uniform proudly, though I initially had little intellectual interest in the agency or its history. I was much too busy making my way to the top of the jagged summits in Grand Teton National Park. Over the course of the thirteen summers I spent as a seasonal ranger, however, I became inspired to think and write about the NPS in connection to national identity, public lands, and the strong affective attachments that visitors form in connection to park rangers and the sites they manage.[1]

As manager of over 400 sites that attract millions of visitors each year, the NPS plays a leading role in shaping a collectively imagined national identity. This essay extends fieldwork I did for my book *Memorials Matter: Emotion, Environment, and Public Memory at American Historical Sites* (2019), which tracks how the physical environment shapes tourists' emotions at seven historical sites managed by the NPS. While the literature circulating both virtually (e.g., on NPS websites) and in person—trail maps, brochures, park newspapers, and such—shapes our visits, the physical features of particular sites also make strong impacts. In *Memorials Matter*, I explore how both built structures and natural landscapes have "affective agency," which I theorize as "matter's capacity to generate felt impressions on other bodies even while remaining recalcitrant" (Ladino 2019, 38). I suggest that the environmental features and the texts visitors encounter at NPS sites are often in tension, generating what I call *affective dissonance*, an unsettling sensation of hold-ing mixed or conflicting emotions in one's body simultaneously (ibid., 22).

This essay foregrounds a different, though no less significant, impact on visitors' emotional encounters with NPS sites: the *aesthetic* associated with the NPS, visible in the familiar ranger uniforms, the "natural" look of the (often wood or faux wood) signage, and the nostalgic tone of the "parki-tecture" that characterized early NPS visitor centers (Frankenberger and Garrison 2002). I am using the word aesthetic as Jacques Rancière defines it, as "a form of experience, a mode of visibility and a regime of interpretation" (2010, 24). This essay is also informed by the idea of what Ranjan Ghosh calls an "aesthetic imaginary":

> Mostly undetermined, indeterminate, and capacious, aesthetic imaginaries aggregate around dwellings in culture, social practices, characters of imagina-tive reconstruction, and affiliations with religious and spiritual denominations and preferences. The aesthetic imaginary is built inside the borders of a nation, a culture, a society, a tradition, or an inheritance; but, it disaggregates and reconstructs itself when exposed to the callings and constraints of cross-border epistemic and cultural circulations. (2017, 449–50)

What I am calling the NPS aesthetic imaginary refers to an aesthetic aggrega-tion that is experienced affectively, textually, and corporeally by tourists on the ground at NPS sites. A sense of tradition is a cornerstone of the agency. Hence the uniforms that remain relatively unchanged since 1916 and the endurance of the distinctive "Park Service Rustic" architecture, a style based on the principle that the "natural setting comes first and the man-made ele-ments must blend into the surrounding context" (Frankenberger and Garrison 2002). While newer buildings tend to reflect more modern architectural trends, for the NPS itself, "Tradition is sacred: a zealously guarded truth in its exfoliation and trajectory is pinned down to an immovable wholeness . . . breeding a community of believers, inculcating a stability in high seriousness and sovereignizing a communitarian unity" (Ghosh 2017, 455). Visitors to NPS sites become part of a "community of believers" that typically under-stand themselves as loyal patriots. To paraphrase Cindy Spurlock's reading of Ken Burns's *The National Parks* documentary, tourists certify themselves as "park supporters and good citizens" just for showing up (2012, 263). In *Memorials Matter*, I refer to members of this community with the phrase "implied tourist," the visitor to whom a site's rhetoric is addressed (Ladino 2019, xvii). The NPS aesthetic imaginary, while always open to disruption, disaggregation, and reconstruction, remains strongly determinative of con-temporary tourists' experiences, and I will suggest it tends to elegize as much as it commemorates.

Indigenous peoples are the biggest casualties. Too often, NPS sites either obscure Indigenous presence or render it past tense via an imperialist nostalgia (Rosaldo 1989). In what follows, I consider three NPS historical sites: San Juan Island National Historical Park (NHP), along the US–Canada border; World War II Valor in the Pacific National Monument (which contains Pearl Harbor and the USS *Arizona* Memorial); and Sand Creek Massacre National Historic Site, in eastern Colorado. All three inadvertently encourage tourists to apprehend Indigenous peoples as absent, despite efforts to represent their historical and ongoing uses. At San Juan Island NHP, the colonial story of the peaceful joint occupation of the island by American and English troops overtakes and silences the story of Coast Salish tribes who use the region. At Pearl Harbor, stories of Kanaka Maoli (Native Hawaiians) are told in the past tense, making their traditions seem antiquated and folklorish, and eliding ongoing sovereignty movements. And at Sand Creek Massacre NHS—despite efforts to center Indigenous peoples' stories and images—contemporary tribes' voices are still hard for non-Native visitors to hear when framed within the powerfully felt NPS aesthetic imaginary that encompasses their stories.

In *The National Park to Come*, Margret Grebowicz calls for a "new cartography of affects" at NPS sites (2015, 58). And as Ghosh points out, "affectivity" is an element of the aesthetic imaginary that "we cannot fully ignore" (2017, 454). By looking closely at these three NPS sites, my essay draws out the affective dimensions of this aesthetic imaginary and emphasizes apprehension of historical sites as an *affective* as well as a cognitive, narrative, and ideological process. NPS historical sites prescribe a specific "mode of attunement" (Grebowicz 2015, 58) that is predominantly nostalgic and patriotic. The aesthetic imaginary also reinforces a false familiarity with the NPS. For most tourists, the agency feels like a trusted friend, a democratic and neutral entity promising the false comfort of American patriotism and national belonging. Most NPS sites invite tourists to feel a sense of patriotic loyalty, in which historical violence is an anomaly in an otherwise progressive chronology of events, and in which most visitors can easily insert themselves as the good citizen, on the right side of history. Despite recent efforts to chronicle a wider range of histories, the NPS is constrained by an ossified aesthetic that tends to historicize culture, silence present-day political concerns, and render the most unsettling aspects of the American past unthinkable.

SAN JUAN ISLAND NATIONAL HISTORICAL PARK

Most people who take the ferry to San Juan Island are not thinking of San Juan Island NHP as their primary destination; in fact, only half of park visitors are even aware that it exists.[2] The implied tourist is unlikely to know much about the history this site commemorates, but they will quickly learn about the "Pig War," an almost-war that (the site mentions repeatedly) was staved off when level-headed leaders chose "peace *over* war." The 1846 Oregon Treaty had left the San Juan Island boundary unclear. By 1859, much of the island was occupied by the British and their Hudson's Bay Company, which had begun raising sheep and other animals on the island. But there were American squatters there too. One of them, Lyman Cutler, killed one of the Hudson's Bay Company's pigs, and war nearly broke out over possession of the island. Largely due to the "cooler heads" of the British, most NPS signs suggest, the two nations instead managed to coinhabit without conflict by setting up camps on opposite ends of the island, for twelve years, until a German Kaiser ruled that the island would go to the Americans.

San Juan Island NHP was designated in 1966, when the Vietnam War was at its height, but it is a peaceful place to visit. In its written rhetoric, the site tells a story of nineteenth-century United States developing in opposition to England, an old colonial story with a new, less violent twist. Whether or not visitors have heeded the San Juan Islands Visitors Bureau website's suggestion to "relax and imagine yourself in a simpler time,"[3] the minimalist NPS signage, the dated displays, and the dilapidated trailer that functions as a visitor center set a historical tone. The binary setup of the two camps—on either end of the island—naturalizes two dominant environmental imaginaries: the frontier, identified with American camp and its scrappy squatters, and the pastoral, encapsulated in English Camp's restored garden landscape. The aesthetic imaginary here encourages an affective mix of frontier nostalgia, American patriotism, and a sense of peace, all of which smooth over the impacts of colonization on Indigenous inhabitants of the region.

In his book-length account of the Pig War conflict and subsequent joint occupation, historian, veteran, and park ranger Mike Vouri speculates that the Royal Marines who arrived on the island in 1860 "must have been struck by the irony of this peaceful setting" (2004, 1). Surely this place was too lovely for war. Perhaps more ironic was the fact that they erected their camp "on the ruins of a native village amid mounds of clam shells, bleached white by sun and resembling drifts of snow" (ibid.). Native peoples are represented primarily by the remains of this shell midden and a few scattered signs explaining their traditional fishing in the area. The colonial story of the peaceful joint occupation of the island by American and English troops overpowers the story of Coast Salish tribes who continue to use the islands.

The textual celebration of peace generally works in harmony with the island environment, especially since most tourists visit during fair weather. Of its roughly 310,000 annual visitors, most come to San Juan Island NHP to recreate.[4] Hiking is a popular activity. Psychological research suggests recreational hiking enables a kind of temporary peace when it exposes us to "natural stimuli which produce soft fascination," engages our default mode network, and has "emotionally positive and low-arousing" impacts on our bodies (Atchley et al. 2012, 2).[5] Hiking is usually satisfying, calming, and rejuvenating, but here at this historical park these feelings risk precluding engagement with the history: the narrative display signs disrupt soft fascination by challenging us to read and think historically. It's tempting to want to ignore or skim over the signs if your goal is recreation rather than education.

Figure 6.1 NPS Display Sign Overlooking English Camp, San Juan Island. *Source:* Photo: Jennifer Ladino 2016.

If one does stop to read the aging displays at English Camp, one might see signs such as "Making the Island Home" (figure 6.1). This story tells of how Royal Marines pitched their tents, cleared the shore of trees, then built a storehouse, fenced vegetable garden, cooking house, barracks, officers' quarters, and finally constructed the commanding officer's house atop the terraces that rise from the main parade grounds. The frontier narrative may sound quintessentially American, even Turneresque, but the physical environment—especially the recreated garden—feels distinctly British. As another sign puts it, "Victorian England had arrived on San Juan Island." While there are plenty of displays describing the process of colonial homemaking, one would have to look online for information about how the island is the ancestral homeland of Coast Salish tribes, and how some, like the Lummi, are working to reestablish their traditional uses today.[6]

On the other end of the island lies the far less manicured landscape of American camp. A humble double-wide trailer serves as the only visitor center, more generic than rustic with its nondescript, boxy design. Walking the trails from there, one quickly encounters the open, windswept prairie landscape that characterizes American camp. The restored Laundress Quarters and Officers Quarters buildings are presented by signs showing historical renderings that give us a sense of how these buildings used to look. The scant wayside displays reflect the NPS's familiar aesthetic of wood materials and simple fonts. The signs appear tiny against the vast grasses. The effect is that the prairie itself seems infected by the historicity of the buildings that are rebuilt and re-presented as traditional and authentic. The landscape becomes a kind of relic in its own right, as "historical" as the park itself. Once you cross the prairie you come to an overlook with two more wayside displays, offering context for visitors who pause to gaze on South Beach below (figure 6.2).

One sign, titled "National Park View," celebrates that, from this "sweeping view" we can see four other NPS units, all part of the "American legacy of preserving and protecting landscapes and historic places for the enjoyment and benefit of people" and touting the diversity of those landscapes ("from mountain peak to seashore, from glacier to desert, and from Liberty Bell to battlefield"). Ironically, the sign just to the right of it tells a very different story. "Fishing Traditions" provides a brief history of the net technologies used to catch salmon on South Beach—technologies that trace back to American Indian reef netting over 2,500 years ago. An attentive close reader might detect a celebration of sustainable fishing techniques used by Indigenous people and a condemnation of corporations like Pacific American Fisheries, who made the process so efficient that they were catching "up to 37,000 fish per day" and had their operations "outlawed" due to the

Figure 6.2 Two NPS Signs Overlooking South Beach in American Camp, San Juan Island. *Source*: Photo: Jennifer Ladino 2016.

"decimation of sockeye salmon populations." Still, the fact that NPS sites like this one displaced, and sometimes violently removed, the Indigenous peoples who used the resources that are now "protected . . . for the enjoyment and benefit of people" is omitted in the narrative itself.

Inside the cramped visitor center is a display titled "What was it like to live here 2000 years ago?," which compounds the past-tense problem. With a collection of arrowheads and other objects presented in a glass case, the display highlights the uses of the Coast Salish, especially their more transient hunting and fishing practices and affirms that they "*lived* throughout the San Juan Islands, traveling during different times of the year to collect the bounty of the season."[7] The tense quickly switches back to present: the tribes "still live nearby today," and they "share the island's natural bounty with other island residents and visitors." The implication is that they're content, "despite drastic changes" to their "lifeways," to "share" the area. There is no mention of where they were during the Pig War or what they're doing now to reclaim these islands.[8] "History" implicitly begins in the nineteenth century, with the Pig War and joint occupation; everything else is ancient history, a long, fuzzy precursor to Manifest Destiny.

WORLD WAR II VALOR IN THE PACIFIC
NATIONAL MONUMENT

World War II Valor in the Pacific National Monument is similar to San Juan Island NHP in several ways. First, the monument takes an approach to history that positions Native uses of the island in the distant past. Second, tourists who visit the San Juan Islands and the Hawaiian Islands are likely influenced by environmental imaginaries in which islands are peaceful refuges of "prelapsarian innocence and bliss, quarantined by the sea from the ills of the continent" (Tuan 1974, 118). Third, like visitors who stumble upon English and American camp while recreating on San Juan Island, most people stop by Pearl Harbor as part of a longer vacation to Oʻahu. Finally, at both sites progress narratives are inflected with patriotic nationalism that reinforces an association of American identity with whiteness and casts Indigenous peoples as romantic relics, effectively rendering them absent, despite efforts to represent their historical uses on display signs.

Unlike the history of the Pig War, Pearl Harbor's story is well known in its broad strokes, and the World War II Valor in the Pacific NM is a place where tourists can both learn more details about the war and grieve the loss of lives on the USS *Arizona* Memorial. There is an affective trajectory that the built environment encourages us to follow, and it parallels the NPS's interpretive theme "from engagement to peace." The implied tourist should move through the museum galleries and watch the orientation film, where we learn about the attack and the war itself; then shuttle to the USS *Arizona* Memorial, where we solemnly honor (and ideally, grieve for) the soldiers who died (figure 6.3); and finally, return to the "Contemplation Circle" back on shore, where we achieve the cathartic "peace" of knowing the nations are now reconciled.

Thomas Patin suggests that "national parks are essentially museological institutions, not because they preserve and conserve, but because they employ many of the techniques of display, exhibition, and presentation that have been used by museums to regulate the bodies and organize the vision of visitors" (2012, 270). What is interesting about the Pearl Harbor complex is how the implied tourist's *emotions* are "regulated" and "organized" at Pearl Harbor. As an ex-military friend of mine who visited put it, our feelings are "compartmentalized." The NPS aesthetic imaginary organizes our affective apprehensions of the site and its history at every step, both inside and outside the museum galleries.

In *Memorials Matter*, I highlight how the sun, breeze, tropical birds, swaying palm trees, and other features of the more-than-human world threaten to disrupt visitors' emotional engagement, including complicating the grief we're meant to feel at the USS *Arizona* Memorial. I personally felt an unsettling sense of affective dissonance, and I imagine some visitors simply have

Figure 6.3 Tourists Visit the USS *Arizona* Memorial, Pearl Harbor. *Source*: Photo: Jennifer Ladino 2015.

a hard time mustering the grief they think they're supposed to feel and sense instead an "affect imposter syndrome"—a feeling of "not getting it" or not having the authentic experience of a site (Ladino 2019, 24). The micromanagement of our bodies becomes a "place ballet," to borrow David Seamon's term for how a sense of place is created by the movements of people who use it, that is, specific to tourism. At San Juan Island NHP, hikers dance along marked trails, pause at overlooks and display signs, or sit and contemplate on a designated bench. At Pearl Harbor, the ballet is more of a regimented shuffle, with diligent pauses to read historical text, while yielding a polite amount of space and time to other members of the crowd so they can do the same. The NPS aesthetic imaginary provides a sense of comfort, steering us with familiar fonts and historical images toward feelings of peace and patriotism.

Visitors who don't quite feel the "valor" this site is meant to promote might be called "affect aliens," Sara Ahmed's term for a person whose emotions are out of synch with the dominant affective norms—usually optimistic ones. At Pearl Harbor and elsewhere, Indigenous peoples are among those who might fit this description. Not only might Native peoples feel mixed emotions about the NPS—an institution of settler colonialism—but their presence could be seen by some as "an unwanted reminder of histories that are disturbing, that disturb an atmosphere" (Ahmed 2010, 50). Today, Kanaka Maoli are likely to see Pearl Harbor as a thoroughly militarized space. "Pu'uloa," as they've traditionally called it, is part of an *ahupua'a*, a traditional landscape division structured by natural boundaries, called Hālawa, one of twelve in the 'Ewa district.[9] Its story is a declensionist one of a ruined paradise that has gone, to cite the title of one gift shop book, "from fishponds to warships." As historian and musician Jon Kamakawiwo'ole Osorio explains, it is "a landscape so altered as to seem alien," "forbidding" to many Kanaka Maoli—"unless they join the armed services or the large corps of civilian workers at Pearl Harbor" (2010, 14; 4). They are liable to detect what geographer Kyle Kajihiro describes as a "paradox": Pearl Harbor is at once "hypervisible as a war memorial and tourist attraction, yet forbidden and mysterious," a landscape in which "something important [is] being concealed, something more than classified secrets or critical military facilities" (Kajihiro 2014, 1–2).[10] The aesthetic imaginary contributes to that concealment.

Despite Pu'uloa being an ancestral homeland with a long history, very little of that history is represented at the current NPS site. Stories of Kanaka Maoli are, just as at San Juan Island NHP, told mainly in the past tense, making their traditions seem antiquated and folklorish, and eliding ongoing sovereignty movements. There are a lot of displays at the complex, but I counted only two devoted to Indigenous perspectives. The first is a sign toward the entrance, "A Home To Many Peoples," which splits its rhetorical space between multicultural and Indigenous histories and features a multiethnic population pie chart along with black-and-white photos of immigrants and Native peoples. Native Hawaiians, the sign notes "had steeply declined" in number in the 100 years prior to 1940. At that time, "only 15 percent of the islands' population was Kanaka Maoli . . . and sacred areas were being lost to large-scale sugar and pineapple plantations, new construction and military use. Access to land and water was important to traditional Hawaiian customs, practices and beliefs." The sign cites Jon Osorio, who puts it this way: "It is not that the ships and armed soldiers themselves are menacing, so much as it is the sense that they belong to this place and we do not."

This quote is the most direct mention of the way Native Hawaiians respond to the contemporary site. The NPS is clearly making an effort here to emphasize the damage to the landscape and loss of culture that Osorio himself sings, writes, and teaches about. But the past-tense rhetoric feeds into dominant nostalgic narratives about Indigenous peoples and their cultures as always already disappearing, and so undermines the power of Osorio's words. Access to land and water still *is* important to Kanaka Maoli; it should be discussed in the present tense. The sign's rhetoric also verges on a problematic form of multiculturalism, one that prioritizes "the cultures of Hawai'i *since* the colonization of Hawai'i" and so continues to marginalize Indigenous history (Sumida 2002, 109).

The other display, titled "Bountiful and Revered," describes Native Hawaiian uses of the fertile landscape and oyster-filled waters, beginning by telling us Pearl Harbor has always "been valued" as a "place of immense worth." The fact that these waters "were" home to various Hawaiian gods and goddesses renders the culture past tense, along with the once "abundant" fish and pipi (pearl oysters) that are no longer so abundant. The story of the *kupuna* (respected elder) and the "warning from Ka'ahupāhau," the shark goddess, reads as a superstitious tale that, together with photos of fisherpeople on the undeveloped shoreline, come across as a "folkloric remnant of a vanishing culture, a fragile artifact of knowledge to be preserved" (Kajihiro 2014, 19). Kajihiro explains that this *mo'olelo* has been mobilized by the US Navy and the media to legitimize military presence on the island and "represent itself as her successor in the role of benevolent chief and vigilant guardian" (2014, 39). Even while the NPS display probably intends to let Native voices tell the story, Ka'ahupāhau risks being appropriated as "a cultural artifact of colonial nostalgia" (ibid., 115) by the aesthetic imaginary through which the narrative is filtered.

Figure 6.4 Military Technology Onshore with USS *Arizona* Memorial in the Distance, Pearl Harbor. *Source*: Photo: Jennifer Ladino 2015.

This and other NPS display signs are overshadowed by the dominant tone of the Pearl Harbor complex, exemplified in the torpedoes and other military objects collected on shore (figure 6.4), surely meant to signify progress, military strength, and what I call in *Memorials Matter*, techno-patriotism: "an affective state marked by pride in a country understood as exceptionally tech-savvy, inventive, and forward-looking" (Ladino 2019, 148). Political ceremonies held on the USS *Arizona* Memorial reinforce the narrative of peace and reconciliation that this NPS site wants to tell, a narrative that casts the United States as the generous player in a relationship of "forgiving" Japan for the attack. But this narrative is incomplete without reconciliation with Native Hawaiians, whose ancestral connections to Pearl Harbor disrupt this story with attention to a much longer historical record. In *Memorials Matter*, I encourage the NPS to invite young Kanaka Maoli to the harbor to give talks, much like the veteran survivors of the attack (nearly all of whom have passed on now) have traditionally done. Such a move would create an opportunity to disrupt the false familiarity of the aesthetic imaginary at this "valorous" site.

SAND CREEK MASSACRE NATIONAL HISTORIC SITE

Sand Creek Massacre National Historic Site is situated 175 miles southeast of Denver, on a remote stretch of Colorado's high plains, in the southeast corner of the state. This quiet, out-of-the-way place can feel a bit desolate, especially in winter. With its shortgrass prairie and scrub, low moisture and relatively high elevation, the Colorado plains are known for extreme temperatures, tornadoes, and near-constant wind. Historian Ari Kelman cleverly describes the landscape at Sand Creek Massacre NHS as looking "like the NPS had made a bulk buy of olive-drab scenery at a local army-navy surplus store" (2013, 1). The natural environment complements and compounds the familiar NPS aesthetic. The ranger uniform blends perfectly with the landscape (figure 6.5).

As traumatic events tend to do, the story of the massacre keeps coming up; I must have read about it, or heard it told, five or more times while visiting the site. The short version goes like this: On November 29, 1864 (just five years after Lyman Cutler shot the pig on San Juan Island), a Colorado regiment of 675 men massacred 230 Arapahoe and Cheyenne people, two-thirds of whom were women and children, all of whom were camped peacefully. Chief Black Kettle had raised a white flag and was also flying the American flag at the time.

The NPS works closely with tribal descendants of the victims to commemorate this traumatic history. Some parts of the site—like the repatriation area—remain sacred to the tribes and are clearly designed for them; the display here is written mostly in the Arapaho and Cheyenne languages. But the majority of the interpretive talks and displays at Sand Creek Massacre NHS

Figure 6.5   Ranger Next to Display Sign, Sand Creek Massacre NHS. *Source*: Photo: Jennifer Ladino 2015.

are in English and assume an implied tourist who is non-Native, who's come to understand, and perhaps even to atone for, what happened here. Part of my reading of this site aligns with what Greg Dickinson, Brian Ott, and Eric Aoki say about the Plains Indian Museum: that it fosters "a rhetoric of reverence" that encourages visitors to "adopt a respectful, but distanced observational gaze" (Dickinson et al. 2006, 27). This "rhetorical mode," they argue, lets non-Native viewers off the hook, "absolv[ing] Anglo-visitors of the social guilt regarding Western conquest" (ibid., 29, 27). At Sand Creek Massacre NHS, this is a big risk, which is compounded by the NPS aesthetic imaginary.

The aesthetic of the signage makes it easy to overlook the gruesome details. One exception is a display sign just next to the parking lot, on which survivor George Bent describes a "terrible sight: men, women, and children lying thickly scattered on the sand, some dead and the rest too badly wounded to move." The sign shows a painting by a descendant of one of the massacre's survivor's, Eagle Robe Eugene J. Ridgely, Sr. In it, a soldier holds up either a scalp or, more likely, a slain Indian's genitals; the body lies at the soldier's feet, naked from the waist down, legs spread, a bloody hole at its middle. It's a horrifying image. This is one moment where the aesthetic imaginary feels momentarily disrupted. But I think most non-Native tourists would quickly move past this display to identify with others that taut the event's non-Native heroes: Silas Soule and Lieutenant Cramer, who did not follow Colonel Chivington's orders. Their stories are championed, including on a display called "Conscience and Courage" located just behind the one with the devastating painting. Black-and-white or sepia-toned portraits of the men involved feature prominently around the NHS, contributing to an overall historical aesthetic that mutes the violence, making it hard to imagine the graphic details of the massacre and even harder to conjure the emotions we're meant to feel.

The environment itself also complicates the "reverent" mode at the site. On one hand, the quiet, understated landscape, combined with the NPS's minimalist approach to management, is ideal for contemplation. A series of benches overlooking the creek where the massacre took place welcome visitors to sit and think. But American tourists are used to more spectacle. Some struggle with conceptualizing the violence. In NPS surveys, one tourist wrote: "We actually could not view the encampment site nor the sand creek. So we could not visualize in our minds the actual slaughter. The limited view was a great disappointment. Cutting down some foliage or erecting a tower would have greatly helped."[11] I suspect the aesthetic imaginary of NPS tourism strongly influences this response. Seasoned tourists to NPS sites are accustomed to having more guidance, more signage, more engaging visual depictions of the history, than this minimalist site provides.

Many of the signs that do exist feature close-ups of human faces, and those can come across as confrontational. For instance, a display bearing a close-up image of Cheyenne chief War Bonnet, who was slain at Sand Creek shortly after visiting President Abraham Lincoln in Washington, D.C., seems to beg for visitors' consideration and compassion (figure 6.6).

And yet, the signage itself is so unobtrusive, so subtle, so historical in tone, that it can be easy to pass by, to skim over, and to distance oneself from emotionally. It is insightful here to consider how our aesthetic judgments become "disinterested." Rancière engages Kant's "Analytic of the Beautiful" to describe this process as one in which "We withdraw [an aesthetic object] from the hierarchical distribution linked with matters of needs and desire" (2010, 18). In the case of the NPS, an institution of settler colonialism, that

Figure 6.6 NPS Display Featuring Close-Up Image of Cheyenne Chief, Sand Creek Massacre NHS. *Source*: Photo: Jennifer Ladino 2015.

hierarchical distribution is almost always rendered invisible, unthinkable, by the aesthetic imaginary. Sand Creek Massacre NHS is trying to make visible that hierarchy; this isn't a case of "deliberate mystification," nor it is an "ignorance about the reality of those hierarchies" (Rancière 2010, 18). Rather, there is something affective at work for the non-Native visitor, a felt allegiance to the nation that the aesthetic itself encourages. Even when Native peoples are the main subject of a site and partners in its creation, the aesthetic imaginary and the false familiarity of the NPS can render them invisible, absent, or romanticized. At Sand Creek Massacre NHS, the landscape and the elegiac NPS aesthetic work together to make it very difficult for people to see Arapaho and Cheyenne peoples as present-day inhabitants of this region with strong and ongoing ties to it.

CONCLUSION: DISRUPTING THE AESTHETIC IMAGINARY

At these and other NPS sites, even narratives of traumatic historical events can be coated in a nostalgic patriotism. The false familiarity many visitors feel for the NPS reinforces a cultural literacy in which tourists are by definition good patriots, and our country is a democratic, progressive one. Grebowicz draws on Lauren Berlant's formulation of "cruel optimism" to argue that NPS sites participate in a consumer-oriented affective economy, perpetuate an exclusionary "wilderness affect" that obscures history, and foster "fantasies of our [national] coherence" (2015, 66; 15; 55). The national inheritance imagined at NPS sites is consistently a non-Native one. Its "coherence" excludes other people of color as well. The NPS will continue to struggle to remain relevant, attract a diverse audience, and live up to its democratic goals unless it can learn to anticipate and manage tourists' affective responses in ways that disrupt the aesthetic imaginary and the false familiarity that plague it.

How, in an agency to which tradition has always been sacred, does one achieve these goals? It helps to remember that "Tradition is much more than what it thinks it is: not always wary of the wires that interweave, for interweaving is not always a conscious activity" (Ghosh 2017, 457). Indeed, here is where attending to affect matters. While affect does sometimes crystallize into an identifiable emotion, affect is more often than not an *un*conscious activity. But it nevertheless shapes NPS tourism (and our embodied experience of any environment) in profound ways. Affective responses among individual tourists are one of the unpredictable ways that tradition "unmoors . . . teetering on the cusp of stability, relationality, possibility, tangentiality and transgression" (Ghosh 2017, 460).[12]

Because affect aliens are always threatening to transgress the expectations of NPS sites—including compulsory patriotism—increased diversity in visitor demographics means greater potential for disrupting the aesthetic imaginary. In her important book *Black Faces, White Spaces: Reimagining the Relationship of African Americans to the Great Outdoors*, Carolyn Finney reflects on how public land management agencies are trying to overcome a long history of overshadowing, silencing, or erasing the stories and contributions of people of color, including African Americans. She warns that good intentions aren't enough: "building relationships across difference means you have to do the internal work, both within the organization and within oneself," to assess one's limitations, before one is able to "'meet someone else with honesty and clarity'" (2014, 132). The NPS must cultivate an honest intercultural and intertribal dialogue that guides interpretation and management of the present-day sites.

Not just dialogue but, ideally, some form of comanagement would be helpful in expanding the "topography of the thinkable" (Rancière 2010, 24) to include the historical and ongoing relationships Indigenous peoples and people of color have to public lands managed by the NPS. An "aesthetic subversion of the ethical order" can only occur when those who have been rendered invisible reappropriate the aesthetic in a way that "produces a disruption of the ethical circle within which they have been enclosed" (ibid., 19). When I suggested in *Memorials Matter* that Indigenous peoples play a stronger role in NPS leadership, this is the kind of appropriation I had in mind. Tribal nations and their ongoing concerns break apart the tenuous borders of the nation inside of which the NPS aesthetic imaginary was formed and make visible the histories of exclusion in which the agency is complicit, creating space for the honesty and relationship building that Finney and others rightly demand.

New technologies at historical sites, including more interactive exhibits and audience centered engagement strategies—which treat visitor stories as important contributions to making meaning at NPS sites—also have the potential to help create a more heterotopic aesthetic. If we understand a heterotopia as "a certain way of thinking of the 'heteron' or the 'other': the other as the effect of a reconfiguration of the distribution of places, identities, and capacities," then a heterotopia can be generated when there's a "disruption in the relation between a concrete place in space and a place in the ethical order of the community" (Rancière 2010, 20–21). For the NPS, the relationship between the concrete places, the sites themselves, and the ethical order on which those sites were created—the history of violent expulsion and the ongoing legacy of settler colonialism—must be made visible. A revolution in the aesthetic realm is one place to start.

NOTES

1. I explore representations of park rangers in more detail in my essay, "Labor, Leisure and Love of Country: Rangering in the Age of the Alt-NPS" (forthcoming in *Planet Work: Rethinking Labor and Leisure in the Anthropocene*, Ryan Hediger, ed., Bucknell UP).

2. The NHP is the primary destination for only about 20% of the island's visitors. This data is from the most recent NPS survey, taken in 1995. Margaret Littlejohn, "San Juan Island National Historical Park Visitor Study," University of Idaho Park Studies Unit. US Department of Interior (1995, iii).

3. https://www.visitsanjuans.com/islands/all-san-juan-islands/history. Accessed 22 March, 2017.

4. They reported 316,122 in 2016; at its heyday in the late 1970s, annual visitation topped 1,000,000. https://irma.nps.gov/Stats/SSRSReports. Accessed 17 March, 2017.

5. For another definition of soft fascination, see Peter Aspinall, Panagiotis Mavros, Richard Coyne, and Jenny Roe, "The urban brain: analyzing outdoor physical activity with mobile EEG," *British Journal of Sports Medicine*, vol. 49 (2015): 272–276. Accessed 22 May, 2017. Although research on the default mode network is still in its infancy, it is linked to creativity, memory, and "restful introspection" (Atchley et al. 2012, 2).

6. The San Juan Island NHP webpage "The First Ones" links to a slideshow of photos from a July 2014 event in which Lummi Nations members canoed and camped on English Camp's shoreline, "probably for the first time since the 19th century." https://www.nps.gov/sajh/learn/historyculture/the-first-ones.htm. Accessed 23 March, 2017.

7. This quote comes from the NPS website page called "The First Ones," which provides a more detailed account of how Coast Salish tribes used the islands. https://www.nps.gov/sajh/learn/historyculture/the-first-ones.htm. Accessed 23 March, 2017.

8. Vouri's books suggest they were mostly involved as buyers for illegally sold whiskey and prostitution, and the threats posed by their raids were used for political leverage in the England–US border drama.

9. For a history of this ahupuaʻa, see Klieger, P. Christian, "Nā Maka O Hālawa: A History of Hālawa Ahupuaʻa, Oʻahu" (Honolulu: Bishop Museum Technical Report 7, 1995).

10. Kajihiro's genealogy of Pearl Harbor demystifies that "something" by historicizing the harbor as a "lost geography," in which an ideologically neutral view of the place as "simply a beautiful portal" through which bodies, products, and military forces can move at will masks the ways in which it has been "conscripted to do the work of imperial formation." Kajihiro suggests the memorial site reinforces ideals of American innocence and exceptionalism and rewrites the role of the United States in World War II as a defensive and reactionary one, rather than an imperialistic one.

11. *Sand Creek Massacre NHS Visitor Survey Card Data Report* (Pacific Consulting Group, 2015).

12. It seems significant that Ghosh is invoking Karen Barad here, a citation that implicitly invites more scholarship at the confluence of aesthetics and material ecocritical theory.

WORKS CITED

Ahmed, Sara. 2010. "Happy Objects." In *The Affect Theory Reader*, edited by Melissa Gregg and Gregory J. Seigworth, 29–51. Durham: Duke University Press.

Atchley, Ruth Ann, David L. Strayer, and Paul Atchley. 2012. "Creativity in the Wild: Improving Creative Reasoning Through Immersion in Natural Settings." *PLoS One* 7(12): 1–3.

Bergman, Teresa. 2012. "Can Patriotism Be Carved in Stone?" In *Observation Points: The Visual Poetics of National Parks*, edited by Thomas Patin. Minneapolis: University of Minnesota Press.

Dickinson, Greg, Brian Ott, and Eric Aoki. 2006. "Spaces of Remembering and Forgetting: The Reverent Eye/I at the Plains Indian Museum." *Communication and Critical/Cultural Studies* 3: 27–47.

Finney, Carolyn. 2014. *Black Faces, White Spaces: Reimagining the Relationship of African Americans to the Great Outdoors*. Chapel Hill: University of North Carolina Press.

Frankenberger, Robert, and James Garrison. 2002. "From Rustic Romanticism to Modernism, and Beyond: Architectural Resources in the National Parks." *Forum Journal: The Journal of the National Trust for Historic Preservation*. http://forum .savingplaces.org/viewdocument/from-rustic-romanticism-tomodernism. Accessed May 26, 2020.

Ghosh, Ranjan. 2017. "Aesthetic Imaginary: Rethinking the 'Comparative.'" *Canadian Review of Comparative Literature* 44(3): 449–467.

Grebowicz, Margret. 2015. *The National Park to Come*. Palo Alto: Stanford University Press.

Kajihiro, Kyle. 2014. "'Becoming Pearl Harbor': A 'Lost Geography' of American Empire." Master's thesis, Department of Geography, University of Hawai'i.

Kelman, Ari. 2013. *Misplaced Massacre: Struggling over the Memory of Sand Creek*. Boston: Harvard University Press.

Ladino, Jennifer K. 2019. *Memorials Matter: Emotion, Environment, and Public Memory at American Historical Sites*. Reno: University of Nevada Press.

Osorio, Jon Kamakawiwo'ole. 2010. "Memorializing Pu'uloa and Remembering Pearl Harbor." In *Militarized Currents: Toward a Decolonized Future in Asia and the Pacific*, edited by Setsu Shigematsu and Keith L. Camacho. Minneapolis: University of Minnesota Press.

Patin, Thomas. 2012. "America in Ruins: Parks, Poetics, and Politic." In *Observation Points: The Visual Poetics of National Parks*, edited by Thomas Patin, 267–290. Minneapolis: University of Minnesota Press.

Rancière, Jaques. 2010. "The Aesthetic Heterotopia." *Philosophy Today*: 15–25.

Rosaldo, Renato. 1989. "Imperialist Nostalgia." *Representations* 26: 107–122.

Rosenberg, Emily S. 2004. *A Date Which Will Live: Pearl Harbor in American Memory*. Durham: Duke University Press.

Seamon, David. 1979. *A Geography of the Lifeworld*. London: Croom Helm.

Seiden, Allan. 2001. *From Fishponds to Warships: Pearl Harbor: A Complete Illustrated History*. Honolulu: Mutual Publishing.

Spurlock, Cindy. 2012. "America's Best Idea: Environmental Public Memory and the

Rhetoric of Conservation Civics." In *Observation Points: The Visual Poetics of National Parks*, edited by Thomas Patin, 247–266. Minneapolis: University of Minnesota Press.

Sumida, Stephen H. 2002. "A Narrative of Kuki'iahu and its Erasures." *Pacific and American Studies* 2: 101–110.

"The First Ones." https://www.nps.gov/sajh/learn/historyculture/the-first-ones.htm. Accessed March 23, 2020.

Tuan, Yi-Fu. 1974. *Topophilia: A Study of Environmental Perception, Attitudes, and Values*. Englewood Cliffs: Prentice-Hall, Inc.

Vouri, Mike. 2004. *Outpost of Empire: The Royal Marines and the Joint Occupation of San Juan Island*. Seattle: Northwest Interpretive Association.

Chapter 7

The Garrulous Eye

Allegorizing Rape in Djuna Barnes's Ryder

Helle H. Lapeniene

While the silence of rape is a common trope for the suppression of experiential accounts, it also points to the muted subject, whose voice is continuously replaced by discourses that speak of rape's allegorical and sociopolitical significance. Rape becomes a malleable configuration that is traced and talked around—outlined, but with no way of access. At the same time, rape is invisible as an inner experience, and cannot be visualized (Bal 1994/2006b, 44–45), even though its re-presentations abound in Western literature and visual arts. Arguably, we cannot "see" rape but we see allusions to displacements and replacement narratives. The combination of sense perception and critical discussions on the historical contextualization and understanding of rape—as sexual assault, abduction, or seduction—mitigate the image that frequently appears in myths, paintings, and poems. Its invisibilization in exegeses affects how and where we look when we read "rape."[1] Looking (away) and explaining (away) converge in a critical act.

Reading re-presentations of rape as allegory replicates mechanisms that characterize the re-presentations themselves, reframing and displacing the act. Allegorization modifies disparate elements and subsumes them under one reading. In allegory, the subject is dispensable and their attributes rather speak to their function in the story—the subject thus becomes a figure with the status of an object, as some*one* becomes emblematic of some*thing*. When this happens, the figure also takes on similar properties of an emblem—the visual and the textual elements coincide in one image that speaks to the significance of the story. Allegorizing a display is also a metonymic displacement: the eye that sees becomes the voice that explains. Culturally and critically, descriptions further shape the contours of a figure and our ability to *see* something in the figure of a body and reading it as a cluster of signs. To name what one is seeing when reading rape imagery, to describe some*thing*, potentially refigures what we are looking at.

The focus on (re)description highlights how aesthetic apprehensions form(ulate) the content. As such, form *is* content. The modernist author and artist Djuna Barnes, like many artists, had a fraught relationship with criticism, seeing it as "so often nothing more than the eye garrulously denouncing the shape of the peephole to access hidden treasure" (quoted in Levine 1991, 32). The image of the garrulous eye also points to description as an evaluative act, where seeing is displaced as text and creates a metaphoric conflation of two modes. The paradoxes of rendering the invisible and reading images as text create gaps that are bridged metaphorically and analogously. As an extended metaphor, allegory elaborates an initial comparison already displaced, where the tension of the formal paradox is dissolved and replaced by a unity of expression.

Barnes's 1928 illustrated novel *Ryder* begins with a parody of biblical exegesis, foregrounding its hermeneutic influence, but also speaks to aesthetic exegesis in general. As the story of the Ryder family unfolds in a mixture of pastiche, parody, and allusions, the novel interrogates earlier trends in visual and narrative re-presentation of volatile themes, such as rape, gender relations, and family interactions. Tyrus Miller argues that the text, which is interspersed with Barnes's own drawings, is still at the periphery of Barnes's critical reception, despite nuanced readings (2019, 162). The text–image relationship is even further sidelined and often subsumed by the text. However, this gesture points to *Ryder*'s textual primacy and authority over images and allegorization in visual representations. The very term "illustrated novel" must be scrutinized as the text and drawings create metonymic displacements, where one mode influences or alters the other. Irene Martyniuk argues that what the novel really "illustrates" is the dual literacy of reading text and pictures required to communicate the unspeakable (1998, 79). The novel's own parallel layers of text and images parody assumptions of visual and textual cohesion, interrogating this dual literacy through layering and displacement of visual and textual sources. The disjunction of verbal and visual narratives, of two stories that do not add up, is a critique of an allegorical mode of reading that explains away how form impacts our perception.

Ryder's chapter "The Beast Thingumbob" reframes the question of whether we are reading rape as sexual assault or abduction in visual arts by staging an allegorization of rape as love. While critics note that the chapter depicts the gendered trope of women sacrificing themselves in childbirth, this gesture toward reading rape imagery is largely unexplored.[2]

The chapter obliquely alludes to the myth of the Rape of Proserpina, although the word "rape" is never mentioned. Its absence from the title and the story is noteworthy since it appears in a previous chapter, "Rape and

Repining," that shows how numerous community voices eclipse the victim's voice. In *Images of Rape: The "Heroic" Tradition and Its Alternatives*, Diane Wolfthal argues that the juxtaposition of rape images and text in the 1758–1760 edition of Cesare Ripa's *Iconologia* exemplifies how the text indicates a "'proper' reaction" to the images of the violent attack on the Sabine women since it explains that "the barbaric theft brought about happy results" (1999, 27). She indicates that such interpretation of the aftermath influences word choices when describing rape imagery; while rape appears in the title, descriptions vary from abduction, and pursuit to love, which veils power relations and abduction for sexual purposes (ibid., 28–9). The Rape of the Sabine Women is justified since it establishes a new nation, and "medieval allegorisation . . . verges on a romance narrative" (Saunders 2001, 153).

"The Beast Thingumbob" reframes the question of semantics in its allusion to Ovid's version of the myth of the Rape of Proserpina in which Jupiter redefines Pluto's Rape of Proserpina as an act of love, presented *after the fact*. Barnes's reframing of the myth questions how readings of rape are based on notions of what happened before and after the event, and by staging rape as an ellipsis it replicates its absence in allegorizations of rape as love that obscure the difference between rape as abduction or as sexual assault. The title of the chapter, "The Beast Thingumbob," plays with the disjuncture between title and description, where the placeholder name, "thingumbob," alludes to some*thing* or some*one* that has been forgotten. While the name is tied to the figure of the beast, it also points to descriptive words influencing the content and steering the eye. To be an *object* of love in Barnes's version configures an axis of being seen and described, as relative to other elements. By withholding "rape" from the title and the text, Barnes re-presents the displacements in discussions as a parody of shifting definitions depending on perspective, emphasizing diegetic focalization both inside and outside the display. The chapter takes familiar interpretations and makes them into the story itself, as if asking if we recognize what we see.

The chapter is a narrative digression, a story-within-a-story, and appears as a curiosity within the context of Ryder family relations, and as representative of Wendell Ryder's misogynistic views. According to Wendell's story to his children, the Beast Thingumbob desperately wants a companion and is burning with desire when he sees Cheerful, the creature who came to earth for harvest. The two fall in love, she dies in childbirth, and her self-sacrifice is romanticized with Cheerful's alleged claim that she wanted to die. However, the metadiegetic re-presentation of her voice creates an impossible reading of her sacrifice; the figure in the image lacks a mouth and facial expression and is rendered through the Beast's desiring gaze. Moreover, the story is narrated by Wendell whose fragmented ideology is pieced together throughout the novel to justify his polygamous lifestyle and fantasies of repopulating the earth. The

Figure 7.1   The Beast, Ryder, c. 1928, by Djuna Barnes. Series 8, Box 5, Folder 1, Item with the cap- 3.41. Djuna Barnes Papers. Special Collections, University of Maryland Libraries. © Authors League Fund and St. Bride's Church, as joint literary executors of the Estate of the List of Djuna Barnes.

impossibility of Cheerful's voice is reflected in the disparate elements that are rearranged in "impossible," hybrid ways, yet unified in allegorization. As the visual and textual re-presentations do not add up, a sense of unease becomes the driving reading force and the "evidence" of what happened unravels.

The layers of signification that the chapter creates stage the allegorization of rape as love as an expository gesture,[3] that points to tendencies in rape narratives in general—the focus on brutality as an isolated event, followed by childbearing as a "happy ending," is tied to notions of motherly sacrifice read through the female form. The text and the drawing (figure 7.1) resituate pre-texts that inform visual interpretation and, as a result, the figure in the drawing becomes a visualization of the description in the story.

SENSE AS *SENSE*: THE CRITICAL EYE/I

Barnes's references to the critic/reader in textual and visual terms can inform how we regard source material in reading art as a re-presentation of experience. In a letter to Emily Coleman, discussing exposure, Barnes argues that "in art [the secret] is lifted back into its own place again, given back to itself, tho [*sic*] also given to *the reader, the eye*. Only the best reader will understand it, like initiation, which is not for everyone" (quoted in Caselli 2016, 195, n13, emphasis added).[4] The complexity of re-presenting experiences is given "back to itself" in art: a realm that facilitates enigmatic expression and recreates a fundamental displacement of experience as one interprets and expresses one's own. While the comment on the reader's ability to understand what they are given seems typical of modernist elitism that demands a highly educated reader, the "understanding" that the comment refers to more abstractly highlights the creation of a new displacement when *the reader, the eye* meets the work, creating a new experience. Contrasted with the garrulous eye of a highly informed critic, Barnes's appeal to an artwork's ability to initiate can also indicate a moment when one is trying to figure out what is happening. As such, it plays with notions of knowledge as already knowing, and *Ryder*'s parody reframes and rearranges familiar elements so that they require a knowing again.

The image of the reader as the "eye" is elaborately played with in *Ryder*. The notion of sense as *sense* that carries an expectation of correlation between sensing and knowing is upset, especially in terms of vision and truth. Vision has its own ideological and aesthetic history and framework but its sheer ubiquity is reflected in the novel's treatment of the primacy of vision in sense-making. The novel's opening chapter can serve as a case in point. Its overall conflation of vision and (biblical) visions, to see and have a vision, presents an array of images that fall into hierarchical systems of knowledge because "all things are not equal about His feet" (Barnes 1928/2010, 4), satirizing gender relations and values. The play with the visionary tradition and the iconoclastic opposition of images as artificial is reflected through a set of admonitions, such as "Reach not beyond the image" (ibid., 3). The ironic closing statement at the end of the chapter repeats the parody of vision and knowledge: "These things are as the back of thy head to thee. Thou hast not seen them" (ibid., 5). Whether we are talking about religion or aesthetics, the idea of the visionary interpreter having direct access to truth is undercut from the first chapter. Knowing without really looking creates an endless repetition of dogmatic thinking that subsumes and organizes elements in hierarchical frameworks, whereas the abject can be incorporated through sublimation—a refiguration and recontextualization.

The novel's play with relations of body parts as sense-making signs and images also interrogates allegorical relations in aesthetic apprehensions that occur in reading text and image. What we "see" when we look at things, and how they are illuminated through renderings of vision(s) into language, appeals to the elevated mode of allegory. As such, the novel sheds light, to use the visual metaphor, on the processes of an allegorical reading/seeing mode that obfuscates details at the behest of appealing to "grander" themes.

Parts of the novel and several of its drawings were considered too obscene and censored before publication. Lost in the spectacle of obscenity trials in the early twentieth century, *Ryder*'s impact as an example of a censored modernist work has been minimal. Its provocation is contained within its pages, where Barnes marked the censored passages with asterisks and included a foreword warning that the work had been "murdered" (ibid., vii). While some of the lost drawings were reinstated for the 1979 reprint, "The Beast" drawing was not reinstated until 1990.[5] In the middle of visual references to popular images, medieval woodcuts, and marginalia, "The Beast" drawing stands out with its surreal elements. The text in this chapter was not censored and the description of Cheerful appears in full: "Her feet were thinly hoofed, and her hair was many coils. And her face was not yet, and her breasts were ten" (1928/2010, 119). The chopped-up description starts with her feet but does not produce a linear carnivalesque description from bottom to top. It neatly passes the face as unfinished and creates a collagistic syntax that disintegrates bodily coherence but emphasizes its function in the allegory. After Cheerful dies, "Thingumbob rose up in the dawn and plucked his sons from her belly" (ibid., 121), which is not shown in the drawing. The drawing re-presents description and renders action ambiguous, thus questioning how description influences our reading of the events in the story. While the text describing Cheerful remained unscathed, the censure of the drawing ironically exemplifies the erasure that the chapter interrogates. As a drawn representation of all her virtues and idealized function as mother—as if she were drawn from description alone—the image of Cheerful is too violent, too grotesque, and too sexual when visualized.

READING LINE BY LINE

While texts offer descriptions, images offer lines. The composition of the drawing presents an assemblage of images emblematized by the sacred heart of Jesus with the inscription, "THE BEAST," introducing dichotomy, paradox, hybridity, and a patchwork of iconographic features that relate ideal love to sacrifice. The reading modes of the emblem, allegory, and the metaphor create a triangle that (re)positions *the reader, the eye* in-between the drawing, the story, and their interdependency. The chapter composes an aesthetic of blind spots through visual image and text, from which the word rape is absent but appears between the lines. The blind spots suggest assumed links between the female figure as a representative of fertility, sacrifice, and virtue, which influence discourses of how experience is read and understood once appearing *in the figure of* a woman. The drawing and the text inform the story in different ways, and a denouncement of form—the visual versus the textual re-presentation—negates their equivocation in the chapter. By extension, the chapter stages a reading of false familiarities between text and images that depend on tropes of depicting, and imagining, experience.

In his essay on drawing, art critic and artist John Berger likens the process of drawing to discovery. But it is not easily separated into a perceived object and stored information (memory), nor is it a process that has a linear beginning and an end analogous to inspiration and final product. The "platitude in the teaching of drawing," he says, "is that the matter lies in the specific process of looking. A line, an area of tone, is not really important because it records what you have seen, but because of what it will lead you on to see" (1953/2001, 10). The double meaning of picturing—to depict and to imagine—oscillates in Berger's example of lines on a page. One line leads or feeds into the other while a simultaneous process occurs in the imagination.

The image of Cheerful's body brings allegory into play by way of short lines. The body as a hermetic form is split open, and falls between two images of the woman-creature: one of continuous curvature and smooth lines, and another of the "cavernous" female body. While the vulva is shaded, as is common in nude paintings, the added anatomical detail of the line is replicated in and directs attention to the rest of the short lines on the body—the eyebrows and the split goat hooves. Reading anatomical details of the female figure as representative of her function amplifies the connection between female anatomy and metonymy. Together, the lines all point to the more troubling aspects of the narrative that question how she can have agency when her voice-qua-mouth is erased and we read signs from her body. Cheerful's body is on display with her ten breasts and the hooves, alluding to her animality and status of a sacrificial animal. But an animal does not sacrifice itself, it is sacrificed for the communal good. As Wendell explains it later in the novel, "[W]omen . . . are equal, until one dies in child-bed, then she becomes as near to saints as my mind can conceive. Why is that? you ask; because they died at the apex of their ability" (1928/2010, 202). The trope of a mother's sacrifice has transmogrified Cheerful's body into that of a sacrificial animal that bolsters the ambiguity of agency. The triangle that her horizontally displayed body forms with the ram-beast's raised wing as its "apex" re-presents a pyramidal configuration of unity. However, Cheerful at the apex of her "ability" is aligned with the horizontal plane, the base. Linda Nochlin identifies the formal means by which nineteenth-century artists re-presented the abject by displaying fragmented bodies horizontally as opposed to vertically (1994, 20), the vertical line, according to Rosalind Krauss, being representative of formal coherence and beauty (quoted in ibid., 21). By re-presenting Cheerful horizontally as a result of the apex of her ability, where body and purpose meet, the drawing rejects any appeal to an elevated status as "saint" that reads beauty in her sacrifice and sublimates it into communal ideals. The angel wings instead appear on Thingumbob, whose gaze frames Cheerful in the text, ironizing the perspective of such an interpretation.

The issue of sacrifice is connected to woman as an image of fertility that Cheerful embodies in a grotesque symmetry between body and purpose. While the grotesque is often characterized as a form of asymmetry—a distortion of the ideal—the drawing parodies this assumption and shows the grotesque in the ideal. The iconography of the multiple breasts evokes Diana of Ephesus—the Great Mother and fertility goddess whose image fell from Jupiter. The important part here is not so much her likeness to the Diana figure, but the deployed iconography. Body and purpose are presented in a grotesque symmetry where the number of breasts stands for the number of children, ten in total. Mary Russo problematizes the female grotesque and its valorization of "traditional images of the earth mother, the crone, the witch" and the "natural connection between the female body (itself naturalized) and the 'primal' elements, especially the earth" (1995, 1).[6] The iconographic irony in this drawing points to the image eternal, of the earth mother, connecting the female body, fertility, and natural elements. While the figurations and personifications of fertility change, the image remains.

Wendell Ryder subscribes to a patriarchal view of fertility and aims to be the "Father of all Things" (1928/2010, 210). Dying in childbirth recur elsewhere in the novel through the trope of lamentation. While the trope offers recognition of women's sacrifice, it also tightens the knot between fertility, womanhood, and sacrifice that needs to be unraveled to create the change of conditions from which we read *female* experience—the experience of women as tied to and read through their bodies. Origin myths of women's sacrifice and repopulation are mythical configurations of more general notions that women are supposed to play this role due to their bodies' "purpose" of childbearing. In relation to childbirth, the ideological social and religious underpinnings allow lamentation but not change.

RAPE: A LOVE STORY

Reading "The Beast Thingumbob" as rape allegorized as a love story points to mythical re-presentations of love but also, more generally, to the choice of focus in our reading. The story in the chapter explains that "she was fettered to the earth for harvest after which she was to return to the gods" (Barnes 1928/2010, 199), alluding to Proserpina's fate after consuming the pomegranate seeds that would chain her to the Underworld. In the myth, Proserpina was raped by Pluto and brought to the Underworld, but was allowed to walk the earth six months a year, making her continuous return as the goddess of spring growth. The allusion is obfuscated by adding that "the underworld had fathered and mothered her" (ibid., 119), which euphemistically suggests incestual grooming whereby Cheerful appears as "willing" in the story, an alternative framework for family relations. The satire of genealogy that the novel frames in the frontispiece that parodies the image of a family tree suggests that, while branches represent descendants and relationships, its hidden volatile relations cross such "organic" delineated lines.

The Rape of Proserpina in Ovid's *Metamorphoses*[7] emphasizes the multiple accounts of the Rape of Proserpina and the various interpretations that follow, through the two nymphs—Cyane and Arethusa—and Jupiter. The victim is mostly absent and witnesses express their take on what happened, presenting different issues of silence through description and interpretation. When Ceres, the goddess of agriculture and fertility, is looking for her daughter, she meets the nymph Cyane. Cyane's lamentation of Proserpina turned her into a pool of tears—her body merging with the surroundings, transforming her from female form to nature. The disembodiment of Cyane, an annihilation through empathy, also silences her. Cyane cannot recount the story because she is turned into a pool, and all her facial features are erased, leaving her without a mouth and tongue: "But for that change had told her all: but tongue / And voice—all organ of articulate speech—/ Were lost. Yet on her surface, manifest, / What sign she could she gave" (l. 591–94, Book V). She gives a sign to Proserpina's girdle, which becomes the evidence of the abduction. The need for physical evidence reflects the silence and devaluation of voices in rape narratives, and Barnes's drawing and chapter conflate the images of the victim and witness in the myth through Cheerful's erased features. By playing with the multiple meanings of the word "rape" and its continuous displacement, the story of Cheerful inverts the chain of evidence to be the story told *through* others, allegorized in the willing self-sacrifice of the creature-goddess evidential of her love for the Beast and her offspring.

On her journey, Ceres also meets another nymph, Arethusa of Elis, who promises her to smile again when relieved of her anxiety (l. 634–35). Arethusa describes how she came to terms with her own uprooting before admitting that she saw Proserpina in the Underworld looking sad and afraid. Nevertheless, she offers the silver lining that while Proserpina's face still bore witness to terror and sadness, she is now the wife of the ruler of the Underworld (l. 640–45)—an elevation of status from merely a woman, like Wendell Ryder's dying mothers who become saints. The recontextualization of what she has perceived—Proserpina as a tragic figure—underscores rather than criticizes her new status as queen. If viewed in opposition to Cyane's annihilation through empathy, Arethusa as witness articulates and rationalizes the situation, but ultimately dehumanizes Proserpina with the titles of wife and queen. Cyane has seen too much and she metamorphizes into the simultaneous translucent and reflective body of water.[8] While Cyane's metamorphosis is a form of silencing, it also points to the first reaction to rape as a bodily reaction also narratively before Arethusa's articulation of the aftermath.

Arethusa's observation functions as a comment on the event rather than an account of the situation; yet, all these examples point to a trope in rape narratives and visualization, namely to suffer "prettily." As Daniela Caselli has pointed out, Barnes's work ironizes "suffering prettily" (2016, 14)[9] as a cultural and aesthetic trope, and this novel's chapter situates it specifically in the context of rape narratives—a tendency in art history that Wolfthal frames in three interrelated questions: "Do these images depict rape? Is the victim willing? And, is she pretty?" (1999, 28). Iconographic readings that metaphorize facial features and presentation of bodies to reflect gendered virtues mirror the absence of violence in re-presentations of rape. Barnes's re-presentation of the artistically unfinished and narratively absent face in the text and drawing undercuts critical positions of displacing violence. In relation to the myth of the Rape of Lucretia, Mieke Bal argues that sixteenth-century iconography re-presented the figure without violence, thereby leading to interpretations of the figure as "serene" (1994/2006b, 43) highlighting A. Robin Bowers's description of the depictions of a "serene, partly nude figure to show the external beauty which reflected her inner virtue" (quoted in ibid). This is only an example of how descriptions also form(ulate) the content, which Barnes strips down in the image of Cheerful parodying notions of suffering prettily as female virtues coded in the body.

The play with different signs open to interpretation through facial expressions and displacement of voice culminate in one constellation of Cheerful's faceless figure, which underscores the narrative function instrumental in rape accounts. Wolfthal (1999, 4) comments on the distinction of events and their implications in critical exegeses of Poussin's *Rape of the Sabines* and Titian's *Rape of Lucretia*, and argues that by regarding rape as merely abduction, it silences the aftermath and the fact that the women were often abducted to produce children. By reducing it to abduction, the act obscures the event to the point where rape ceases to be a crime. In the *Metamorphoses*, Ceres confronts Jupiter with Pluto's Rape of Proserpina whereby Jupiter demands that "Give we things / Their proper names. 'Twas Love, not brutal force, / That to this deed impelled" (l. 664–66).

The notion of proper names and redefinitions of events are parodied in "The Beast Thingumbob." "Cannot a beastly thing be analogous to a fine thing, if both are apprehensions?" Barnes's novel *Nightwood* (1936/2001, 113) asks. This example exposes the underlying structures that different perspectives appeal to for legitimacy, such as notions of motherly sacrifice, love, and fertility. What is notably absent in these themes is suffering in itself—a hole, a loss; instead it is displaced in ideological perspectives. The redefinition of rape to love appears here through jarring details that upsets a linear reading. While the event can be redefined based on the developments in a narrative, the staging of the textual and visual layout upsets a linear reading through disjunction between text and image. The drawing appears in the beginning of the chapter, and Cheerful's aftermath is already displayed before the romance narrative. The figure of Proserpina reappears fragmented, ironizing the treatment of her and similar embodiments in artistic re-presentations. The point is not so much about the identification of the figure of Proserpina but to unpack the conditions for recognizing and tracing likeness, and consistent tropes that remain even in reimaginings.

THE PASSION OF CHEERFUL: REFRAMING LAYOUTS

The abduction of Proserpina is a popular theme in visual arts, and in Renaissance and Baroque art the emphasis is often on the abduction. A reimagination of the figure is also notably portrayed in Dante Gabriel Rossetti's *Proserpine* (1874), depicted with the elongated neck popular in Pre-Raphaelite paintings. Instead of depicting the abduction, Rossetti shows Proserpina holding the pomegranate that banished her to the underworld for most of the year. The Pre-Raphaelite call for a reintroduction of narrative in painting and illustration also meant reimagining and re-presenting mythical and literary figures, borrowing existing titles, and reinterpreting them.

Critics have noted Barnes's irreverence toward the Pre-Raphaelites, whose portraits of voluptuous women with long, flowing hair and soft gazes had become a visual standard by the end of the nineteenth century. Carolyn Burke argues that for women artists to establish themselves they had to challenge the conventions of portraying women before establishing their own style, either through critique or abandonment. An example of this is the *fin-de-siècle* portrayal of women as muses.[10] In a satirical article from 1922, Barnes writes "I am wearing Burne Jones [*sic*] gowns and stretching my throat till it ached" (Barnes 1922, 60), referring to the elongation and contortion of necks in the Pre-Raphaelite style. Contrasted with Rossetti's version, Cheerful has no visible neck to speak of and it is bent in the opposite direction. The horizontal line of the body breaks at the neck and is hidden by the hair which separates the head and the body. *Ryder*'s aforementioned use of body parts in allegorization is here re-presented through Cheerful's body that creates a fragmented composition of symbolic and idealized readings. As such, Cheerful's neck is closer to the contortions of Proserpina's body, showing resistance during depictions of the abduction. However, in terms of ambiguous visual clues, such as the described serenity in Lucretia, the ambiguous curve obscured by the hair does not bear any more witness to the event beyond the unambiguous result of Cheerful's death. As a contrast to depictions of "beautiful suffering" in narrative moments, Barnes's drawing reimagines the act of choosing a narrative moment to visualize by refusing to participate in the conditions for aestheticizing suffering.

The problem that the story poses is also an aversion to reading rape. Cheerful's name is another factor that is not supported in the text or the drawing. While the drawing complements the text's description of an unfinished face, the impossibility of reading joy, or indeed any emotion in Cheerful's figure, foregrounds appeals to assumed emotions after the event to contextualize rape based on "happy endings" such as marriage and childbearing. Bal argues that "an expository gesture is always also allegorical" (1994/2006b, 61), and that dehistoricizing old material can be useful to separate it from "'pre-texts' that both precede it and sustain the effort to take the critical sting out of it. There is a tendency to dismiss the subject of the rape story on the grounds that it is an allegory" (ibid., 41). The displacement of Barnes's figure Cheerful not only recasts and refigures Proserpina, but it is the figure that changes the allegory, and not the allegory that explains the subject. The lack of a face simultaneously makes Cheerful no single mythological figure but rather several mythological figures. Moreover, it signals a rejection of the projections of a muse's face onto depictions of different mythological figures and idealizations of facial features in artistic conventions. Cheerful is fettered and an object of desire, an enigma of artistic portrayals. The passion of Cheerful mirrors the motif of suffering with her tilted neck in a grotesque *pietà* fashion, but her passion as metaphor is ultimately metonymic, her suffering contingent on her female form.

The composition of the drawing, of a looming winged creature, also appears in William Blake, whose composite works have received considerably more critical attention than those of Barnes. In his revised edition of *For Children: Gates of Paradise* (1793), retitled *For the Sexes: Gates of Paradise* (1818), "To the Accuser" was one of the additional plates. Blake is an intertextual reference in Barnes's *Nightwood* and *Creatures in an Alphabet* (1982).[11] There is also a Blake reference in Barnes's drawing through the looming figure and play with the emblem form. Blake's drawing shows a moment in a traveler's dream, where the text's play with binaries is shown through the identification of Satan with God and Jesus, and the harlot and the virgin, which "shocks the orthodoxy of the ordinary emblematist" (Salemi 1981/1982, 121–22). In Barnes's story, Wendell describes Cheerful as "not virgin as other women are" (1928/2010, 119), and the novel ties notions of virginity both to sexual assault, mythologizations, and the arbitrariness of the word. This form of juxtaposition in Blake that severs the emblem's "one-to-one symbolism" (Salemi

1981/1982, 108) can also be seen in Barnes's sacred heart of Jesus inscribed with "THE BEAST" in the upper left-hand corner. Barnes's composition takes the question of visual ambiguity from the conceptualization of beastly and fine things and concretizes it in challenging readings of a look in a face that is not there, an ambiguous paw on a thigh, and the angle of a contorted neck. The terms for reading Blake's composition are arguably different than the terms that Barnes's drawing works from and stages within the chapter.

BLIND SPOTS AND RENDERING THE INVISIBLE

The chapter's aesthetic of blind spots emphasizes the tropes in allegorizing rape as reflected in aesthetic readings. In terms of the reimagination of women figures in art and literature, "The Beast Thingumbob" centers the question on the complexity of rape allegories as the story-within-the-story creates an intertextual web and appropriation of visual layouts. As the story of the Beast and Cheerful unravels, the elevated mode of allegory is subverted and becomes parody and irony, revealing that rape allegories by and large hinge on relations between notions of sacrifice, desire, fertility, and women's suffering re-presented aesthetically. These themes obfuscate gaps in the story as they are stitched together by emblematic lessons. Barnes's chapter exemplifies the invisibilization and silencing in readings of rape narratives, and makes the reader/the eye into a complicit actor. The work suggests that allegorization obscures women's suffering with a wanton veil that restricts the possibility of its figurations and readings, while the text and the drawing obliterate its pre-texts and refuse to be mediated in preestablished terms.

The question is, however, if rape can be re-presented in any other way. The reason why rape is often displaced, Bal argues, is because it "cannot be visualized . . . the experience is, physically as well as psychologically, *inner*. Rape takes place inside. In this sense, rape is by definition 'imagined'; it can only exist as experience and as memory, as *image* translated into signs, never adequately objectifiable" (1994/2006b, 44–45). Barnes's comment on art's potential to initiate the reader and communicate the unspeakable (quoted in Caselli 2016, 195, n13) suggests that while the re-presentations of rape depend on nonvisualization and displacement, it is not necessarily the work's job to tell, but rather to create an experience. The critical move of talking about *everything but*—faces the problem of filling gaps with familiar contextualizations and terms, and sublimating the abject. Whereas rape cannot be visualized, Barnes reverses the process by visualizing tropes in allegorizations of rape, and makes description into an arresting figure. While invisibility can be a form of silencing, silence in *Ryder* is also an all too familiar noise of the allegorizing, *garrulous eye*.

NOTES

1. The definition and word choices hinge on arguments of its "acceptability" in historical and cultural contexts, where discussions of the criminal aspect—*Was it a crime?*—influence its readings. Diane Wolfthal points out that "Not only artists but also art historians have traditionally sanitized and aestheticized rape" (1999, 28). See also Wolfthal (1999, 4–5; 28–29); Mieke Bal points out that rape can obscure the cultural status of an event. However, as an event it also carries an "internal divisiveness" through narrative duplicity. To adopt an historical definition does not necessarily acknowledge the multiplicity of narrative agents (1994/2006a, 155–57); in relation to the discussion of rape and women's status as wives, marital rape was not criminalized in the United States until 1993, the earlier definition of rape as sexual assault included spousal exemption. Rape legislation developed as extensions of property laws where a wife was considered the husband's property. See also Bergen (2016, 20).

2. Philip Nel also argues that "The Beast Thingumbob" depicts rape and compares the faceless figure in The Beast drawing to René Magritte's "The Rape" (1945) and Meret Oppenheim's "Stone Woman" (1938), and argues points of convergence in representations of violated bodies through erasure of the face. He argues that Barnes juxtaposes "the erotic with the monstrous, voyeuristically offering us the woman who will be the Beast Thingumbob's victim while simultaneously making her undesirable and grotesque" (2002, 26–29). Erin Edwards also points out the discrepancy of textual and visual information, and questions how Cheerful can have a voice and show emotion when she lacks facial features (2018, 154). Edwards reads the chapter as a perpetuation of the myth of the Family Man (ibid., 153–58); Sheryl Stevenson presents it as a feminist twist on Mikhail Bakhtin's carnivalesque and the image of the grotesque body, and points out that Barnes "shows women tied to the earth, part of a process which betrays them at once to pleasure, maternity, physical suffering, and death" (1991, 91). Bonnie Kime Scott also points out that Thingumbob is a version of Wendell, and the connection between his procreation and canonization of mothers dying in childbirth (1995, 108).

3. Bal posits that "an expository gesture is always also allegorical" (1994/2006b, 61) and to approach old material, dehistoricizing can be useful to separate it from "'pre-texts' that both precede it and sustain the effort to take the critical sting out of it. There is a tendency to dismiss the subject of the rape story on the grounds that it is an allegory" (ibid., 41).

4. The quote goes on to say that "the others will let it go, but when its [*sic*] told to a client for cash its [*sic*] mucked up by the sale."

5. Of sixteen drawings intended for *Ryder*, nine were included in the first edition. Two were added for the 1979 reprint, but "The Beast" drawing is one of six remaining drawings that were not included until the Dalkey Archive 1990 edition. The original manuscript is lost and Barnes "declined the opportunity to restore the censored passages for St. Martin's 1979 reprint" (1928/2010, viii).

6. Writing under the pen name Lydia Steptoe, Barnes satirized the idealization of motherhood and notions of what is considered natural: "Now what I want to know is

why babies are considered such justifiers of a woman's existence? To justify yourself more than five or six times in a life is rather insisting on the point, it seems to me; a point that even Nature would drop—and Nature almost never drops a point. Yet some women go right on to the seventh or eighth. I think it would be far more delicate of women, in every way, to stop clinching arguments with children. Womanhood should not be thrust upon the attention" (1922, 60).

7. All line references are from Ovid (1871). This edition is listed in the catalog of Djuna Barnes Library. Special Collections and University Archives at the University of Maryland Libraries. Location UMCP HBK Maryland Room Barnes PA6522.M2 K55 1871.

8. Andrew Zissos argues that Cyane must also be considered a rape victim and is an example of Ovid's implicit descriptions of rape: "There is a conflation of the experience between of the goddess and nymph: since Cyane is both struck and forcefully penetrated by the *raptor* Dis, she must also be considered a victim of rape" (1999, 100).

9. Caselli is referring to Barnes's 1923 article "What is Good Form in Dying: In Which a Dozen Dainty Deaths Are Suggested for Daring Damsels"; *Ryder* reworks the sentimental trope that aligns femininity and suffering as a bodily imperative, "in which erotic suffering is projected onto the bodies of young girls" (Taylor 2012, 102).

10. Burke sees Barnes's poetry collection *The Book of Repulsive Women* (1915) and Mina Loy's *Others* (1915) as dealing with the issue of "looking at women" (1991, 69–70).

11. Caselli (1999, 79). The drawing in the chapter "Midwives' Lament" in *Ryder* has also been referred to as "a Blakean illustrated poem" (Stevenson 1991, 88, n17).

WORKS CITED

Bal, Mieke. 1994/2006a. "Scared to Death." In *A Mieke Bal Reader*, 149–168. Chicago: University of Chicago Press.

———. 1994/2006b. "The Story of W." In *A Mieke Bal Reader*, 40–67.

Barnes, Djuna. [Lydia Steptoe] 1922. "Against Nature: In Which Everything that Is Young, Inadequate and Tiresome Is Included in the Term Natural." *Vanity Fair*, August: 60, 88.

———. [Lydia Steptoe] 1923. "What Is Good Form in Dying: In Which a Dozen Dainty Deaths Are Suggested for Daring Damsels." *Vanity Fair*, June: 73, 102.

———. 1928/2010. *Ryder*. London: Dalkey Archive.

———. 1936/2001. *Nightwood*. London: Faber and Faber.

Bergen, Raquel Kennedy. 2016. "An Overview of Marital Rape Research in the United States: Limitations and Implications for Cross-Cultural Research." In *Marital Rape: Consent, Marriage, and Social Change in Global Context*, edited by Kersti Yllö and M. Gabriela Torres, 19–28. New York: Oxford University Press.

Berger, John. 1953/2001. "Drawing." In *Selected Essays*, edited by Geoff Dyer, 10–15. London: Bloomsbury.

Burke, Carolyn. 1991. "Accidental Aloofness: Barnes, Loy, and Modernism." In *Silence and Power: A Reevaluation of Djuna Barnes*, edited by Mary Lynn Broe, 67–80. Carbondale: Southern Illinois University Press.

Caselli, Daniela. 2009/2016. *Improper Modernism: Djuna Barnes's Bewildering Corpus*. New York: Routledge.

Edwards, Erin E. 2018. *The Modernist Corpse: Posthumanism and the Posthuman*. Minneapolis: University of Minnesota Press.

Levine, Nancy J. 1991. "Bringing Milkshakes to Bulldogs: The Early Journalism of Djuna Barnes." In *Silence and Power: A Reevaluation of Djuna Barnes*, edited by Mary Broe Lynn, 27–36. Carbondale: Southern Illinois University Press.

Martyniuk, Irene. 1998. "Troubling the 'Master's Voice': Djuna Barnes' Pictorial Strategies." *Mosaic: An Interdisciplinary Critical Journal* 31(3): 61–81.

Miller, Tyrus. 2019. "'The Havoc of Nicety': Djuna Barnes's Ryder and the Catastrophe of Epochal Change." In *Shattered Objects: Djuna Barnes's Modernism*, edited by Elizabeth Pender and Cathryn Setz, 163–176. University Park: Pennsylvania State University Press.

Nel, Philip. 2002. *The Avant-Garde and American Postmodernity: Small Incisive Shocks*. Jackson: University Press of Mississippi.

Nochlin, Linda. 1995. *The Body in Pieces: The Fragment as Metaphor of Modernity*. New York: Thames and Hudson Inc.

Ovid. 1871. *The Metamorphoses of Publius Ovidius Naso*. Translated in English blank verse by Henry King. Edinburgh: W. Blackwood. https://hdl.handle.net/2027/loc.ark:/13960/t6zw2pz91.

Russo, Mary. 1995. *The Female Grotesque: Risk, Excess and Modernity*. New York: Routledge.

Salemi, Joseph S. 1981/1982. "Emblematic Tradition in Blake's The Gates of Paradise." *Blake: An Illustrated Quarterly* 15, no. 3 (Winter): 108–124.

Saunders, Corinne J. 2001. *Rape and Ravishment in the Literature of Medieval England*. Cambridge: D.S. Brewer.

Scott, Bonnie Kime. 1995. *Refiguring Modernism: Postmodern Feminist Readings of Woolf, West, and Barnes: Vol. 2*. Indianapolis: Indiana University Press.

Stevenson, Sheryl. 1991. "Writing the Grotesque Body: Djuna Barnes' Carnival Parody." In *Silence and Power: A Reevaluation of Djuna Barnes*, edited by Mary Lynn Broe, 81–91. Carbondale: Southern Illinois University Press.

Taylor, Julie. 2012. *Djuna Barnes and Affective Modernism*. Edinburgh: Edinburgh University Press.

Wolfthal, Diane. 1999. *Images of Rape: The "Heroic" Tradition and Its Alternatives*. New York: Cambridge University Press.

Zissos, Andrew. 1999. "The Rape of Proserpina in Ovid 'Met.' 5.341–661: Internal Audience and Narrative Distortion." *Phoenix* 53(1/2): 97–113. https://doi.org/10.2307/1088125.

Chapter 8

Metonymy and the "Art of Reading the World Slowly"

Genevieve Liveley

This chapter sets out to explore the suspenseful sense-making that drives the art of "reading the world slowly"—characterized here as the art or aesthetic of narrative metonymy. Its aim is to glean new insights into the narrative dynamics that shape aesthetic imaginaries in our readerly encounters with silences and absences in stories of various forms. Narrative and narrative sense-making, it will demonstrate, are both predicated on silence and invisibility—reading to make sense of what is left unsaid, untold, unrepresented, underrepresented. It argues that it is necessary to mind these gaps, to hear what is being spoken in these silences, and to make salient connections between presence and absence, if we are to see the larger whole that is left unexpressed, to see the bigger picture, and recognize the story behind the narration, recognize the *fabula* behind the *syuzhet*. Taking as its central case study a mid-twentieth-century American short story or micro-narrative titled "Expenses for the Month," this chapter sets out to look afresh at the pitfalls and possibilities opened up by the operations of narrative metonymy and to recognize its pivotal role in directing the aesthetic conditions in and through which we imagine silenced and absenced words and worlds in story form. It works with a flexible and heuristic definition of "metonymy" throughout, treating the figure of synecdoche (part for whole, or whole for part) as a subsidiary mode of metonymy and embracing the conventional association of metonymy as a trope of contiguity, that is, as a figure characterized principally by lateral association and connection (in contrast to metaphor, as a trope of analogy, typically characterized by similarity and substitution).[1] And while it takes some conventional literary-aesthetic classifications of metonymy into consideration (particularly "part for whole," "cause for effect," "product for producer," "object for concept," "place for person," "agent for action"), its primary focus is not upon the defamiliarizing effects of these rhetorical or lexical operations of metonymy but is instead centered upon its structural and narrative dynamics.[2]

Narratologists have long recognized a crucial metonymic quality to narrative sense-making, to the telling of stories, and to the art practiced by the reader in processing both the defamiliarizations and false familiarities encountered in narrative texts.[3] The oft-cited source for this connection between narrative and (indeed, as) metonymy is Roman Jakobson, who famously introduced the idea that in poetry "metaphoric constructions predominate," while in narrative prose "the metonymic way is preponderant" (Jakobson 1956, 78). In following the plot and story of a novel, Jakobson suggests, both author and reader follow a "path of contiguous relationships," which "metonymically digresses from the plot to the atmosphere and from the character to the setting in space and time" (ibid.). He offers as illustration of this theory the example of Tolstoy's focus upon Anna Karenina's "little red handbag" (and the English novel contained within it) in that novel, suggesting that such "synecdochic details" are part of a wider storytelling technique, prevalent in—though certainly not restricted to—the realist genre, in which both character and plot development are achieved laterally by drawing the reader's attention to ostensibly insignificant contiguous details which are actually and structurally meaningful (ibid.).

Jakobson does not consider the narrative dynamics of these metonymies, or go beyond what he describes as the "verbal level" to explore the deeper metonymic structures of narrative prose. Yet subsequent generations of narratologists have seen Jakobson's interest in narrative transitions (from plot to atmosphere, from character to spatiotemporal context) as heralding their own understanding of the fundamentally metonymic character of narrative discourse. Following Jakobson's lead, one of Meir Sternberg's core narratological tenets is the idea that plots unfold according to a "metonymic logic of progression"; that "exposition . . . digressively proceeds by purely metonymic transitions—that is, quasi-mimetic transitions based on contiguity in time or space or both" (1978, 208). Michael Riffaterre's work on the poetics of reading in the nineteenth-century novel has also helped to demonstrate that subplots and minor plot strands gain their core narrative coherence and significance principally through their metonymic contiguity to major plot lines (1982, 28). Gerald Prince in his influential *Dictionary of Narratology* describes narrative as "predominantly metonymic" on the grounds that (*pace* Jakobson) its "motifs and functions are integrated into sequences primarily through relations of contiguity (the narrated situations and events constitute logico-temporal chains)" (1987, 52). Monica Fludernik points out in her landmark study of narratology that "entire plot sequences are sometimes built on metonymical relations"—particularly those built on cause–effect dynamics (2009, 45). And Gerard Steen similarly understands "structural metonymy . . . to lie at the basis of almost all narrative," declaring that any—every—narrative can be seen as "so many metonymic moves by the narrator, taking the [reader] from one situation to another, with the situations constituting contiguous parts evoking a larger whole that is left unexpressed" (2005, 307–08).

However, the Russian Formalists, as early as the 1920s, were already interested in the narrative operations of metonymy, and specifically in ways that the *syuzhet* (or plot) metonymically selects and represents salient parts of the *fabula* (or story), that is, in the ways that an emplotted narrative self-consciously presents its readers (and other kinds of audience) with only a partial, fragmented, account of a wider story, and in the ways in which a plot necessarily silences and hides certain details of a wider storyworld. Yury Tynyanov characterized the *fabula* as "the entire semantic (conceptual) basting of the action," a cognitive construct or aesthetic imaginary effected by and in the mind of the reader who cooks it up in the process of "searching for the story" that is only partially revealed by the *syuzhet*, that is, the fragmented structure through which the *fabula* is made accessible to the mind of the reader ([1927] 1981, 95–96).[4] For Tynyanov, all storytelling is inherently metonymic and readers negotiate narrative metonymy—as they negotiate the dynamic interactions at play between *fabula* and *syuzhet*—as a selection and re-presentation of contiguously associated parts. In processing a narrative artifact therefore, Tynyanov suggests that readers must, above all, mind the gaps, that is, they must imagine "the linkages of material (including the story as a linkage of actions)" and all the connecting parts of the story about which the text itself remains silent (ibid.).

For the Russian Formalists, a narrative achieves its aesthetic character precisely through such dynamic, metonymic, operations. Indeed, Viktor Shklovsky's groundbreaking definitions of the interrelationship between *fabula* and *syuzhet* in narrative discourse emerge from his interest in theorizing this narrative aesthetic, the devices and patterns which impact most upon the reader through their "defamiliarization" (*ostranenie*) of ordinary language and discourse—a concept at the forefront of Shklovsky's formalist project.[5] According to this aesthetic-formalist principle, "a work is created 'artistically' so that its perception is impeded and the greatest possible effect is produced through the *slowness of the perception*" (Shklovsky [1921] 1990, 12, emphases added). Further elaborating upon this idea in his own distinctively slow style, Shklovsky insists that

> art exists that one may recover the sensation of life; it exists to make one feel things, to make the stone stony. The purpose of art is to impart the sensation of things as they are perceived and not as they are known. The technique of art is to make objects "unfamiliar," to make forms difficult, to increase the difficulty

and length of perception because *the process of perception is an aesthetic end in itself and must be prolonged.* (ibid., 22, emphases added)

This is, indeed, precisely what happens when raw story material (*fabula*)—or the temporal sequence of narrated events in chronological contiguous order—is transformed into an emplotted narrative (*syuzhet*)—that is the selection and rearrangement of such events according to aesthetic principles involving the silencing of some things and the speaking of others, resulting in the slowing of the reader's perception and experience of both.

Shklovsky's observations upon this aesthetic experience of narrative drew upon similar insights offered by Aristotle some two thousand years previously. Although Aristotle had declared that consideration of an audience's "powers of perception (*aisthesis*)"—their aesthetic experiences—were "not part of this treatise" (*Poetics* 7.1451a 6–7), in his *Poetics* he actually devotes considerable attention to such matters. As Jan Christoph Meister explains, in the definition of narrative plot (*muthos*) as the "arrangement of incidents" (*sunthesin ton pragmaton*: *Poetics* 6.1450a 3–4), Aristotle drew a crucial distinction "between the totality of events taking place in a depicted world and the *de facto* narrated plot or *muthos* . . . a construct presenting a subset of events, chosen and arranged according to aesthetic considerations" (2014, 627).[6] Indeed, Aristotle insisted that, to qualify as narrative, it was not enough in an account of events for incidents simply to follow one after another in temporal (*post hoc*) sequence. Rather, there must be a logical causal (*propter hoc*) connection between them, because (from the audience's perspective) this arrangement is more artistic: "It makes all the difference whether a thing happens because of, or only after, its antecedent" he claims (*Poetics* 10.1452a 18–21).

If we consider the narrative texts upon which Aristotle draws to illustrate his *Poetics*, the grounds for these insights into the art of storytelling and into the audience's aesthetic experience of narrative discourse as involving fundamentally metonymic operations become clear. Aristotle notices, for example, that Homer's *Odyssey* might have opened with and proceeded to focus upon any one of the various familiar adventures in which its eponymous hero traditionally featured. However, Homer excelled in selecting the first link in a causal sequence designed to arouse the desire in his audience to learn of the contiguous consequence (*Poetics* 8.1451a 22–9).[7] So, the *Odyssey* opens with the Homeric narrator invoking the Muse to help him tell the story from a particular point—from "somewhere" (*hamothen*: *Odyssey* 1.10)—selected from the wider well-known *fabula* of Odysseus's action-packed journey home from Troy. Similarly, the *Iliad* opens with an invocation to the Muse to sing of the wrath of Achilles "from the time when" (*ex hou*: *Iliad* 1.6) he quarreled with Agamemnon. The *Odyssey* thus self-consciously sets out to narrate not the whole but only a part of Odysseus's ten-year homecoming. The *Iliad* declares that it too will tell only part of the familiar history of the ten-year-long Trojan war.[8] Both of these ancient epic narratives are not only structurally synecdochic in presenting a part for a whole, then, but narratively metonymic in their emplotment of the selected actions and events that contiguously follow on from that initial "somewhere" and "when." Indeed, these basic metonymic principles are core among those which Shklovsky would later identify as the drivers of "defamiliarization" (*ostranenie*) and thus the "art" of narrative.

It is in this light, moreover, that Gerard Genette—his Structuralist narratology heavily indebted to both Aristotle and the Russian Formalists—argues that individual narratives must necessarily begin with such metonymic moves involving selection and connection. In fact, he suggests that this is how "Narrative" *qua* narrative begins:[9]

> Without metaphor Proust (roughly) says, we have no true memories; we add for him (and for all): without metonymy, there is no chaining of memories, no *story*, no novel. For it is metaphor which retrieves Lost Time, but it is metonymy which reanimates it, and puts it back in play/in movement: which returns it to itself and to its true "essence", which is at once its own escape and its own Search. So here, only here—through metaphor but *in* metonymy—it is here that [the] Narrative begins. (Genette 1972, 63)

> Sans métaphore, dit (à peu près) Proust, pas de véritables souvenirs; nous ajoutons pour lui (et pour tous): sans métonymie, pas d'enchaînement de souvenirs, pas *d'histoire,* pas de roman. Car c'est la métaphore qui retrouve le Temps perdu, mais c'est la métonymie qui le ranime, et le remet en marche: qui le rend à lui-même et à sa véritable « essence », qui est sa propre fuite et sa propre Recherche. Ici donc, ici seulement—par la métaphore, mais *dans* la métonymie—ici commence le Récit.

Among the Post-Structuralist narratologists, Peter Brooks follows Genette (forging another link in the metonymic chain contiguously connecting back to Aristotle and Homer here) in viewing the reader's movement through (a) narrative from beginning through middle to end as a dynamic driven along metonymically and contiguously. Brooks's psychoanalytically inflected narratology suggests that the reader's experience of a narrative is analogous to the tropic effects of metonymy, that is, the linear, sequential linking of articles through their similarity, association, or relation in part or in whole.[10] But what, for Brooks, really drives this progress is the reader's desire for connection, for relation, for recognition, and for the consummation of a satisfying end point. For Brooks,[11] the key figure of narrative must in some sense be not metaphor but metonymy: the figure of contiguity and combination, the figure of syntagmatic [as opposed to paradigmatic] relations. The description of narrative needs metonymy as the figure of movement, of linkage in the signifying chain, of the slippage of the signified under the signifier . . . the very motor of narrative, its dynamic principle. (1977, 280–81)

For both Genette and Brooks then, metonymy is what puts the stuff of story into movement, transforming individual events into emplotted narrative discourse. But if so, metonymy is a motor that drives both reader and narrative forward *slowly* . . . Genette suggests that it is through metonymy that the reader's experience of "Time" (Proustian or otherwise) is reanimated, but neglects to say that it is also through metonymy that the experience of time is slowed. Brooks, meanwhile, infamously likens the unfolding of a narrative to a literary-aesthetic striptease, placing heavy emphasis upon delay and upon the deferral of readerly desire as the essence of storytelling. The desirable point of consummation and closure must be delayed, the gratification of the reader's desire "reached only through the at least minimally complicated detour, the intentional deviance . . . which is the plot of narrative" (Brooks 1984, 104). That is, the reader's aesthetic experience of the narrative is enhanced by devices and dynamics which necessitate a *slow* reading.

To test these principles and explore the slow dynamics of these narrative metonymies in further detail, we turn now to "Expenses for the Month" as our case study. This micro-narrative illustrates the metonymic power of absence and silence in storytelling particularly well. Written in America sometime in the middle of the last century by that prolific author "Anonymous," the story unfolds through a sequence of chronolinear fragments purporting to give a literal and metaphorical "account" of an old-fashioned (and to modern eyes inappropriate) office romance, itemized in terms of dates and of "dates," each occasion and expense figured in terms of US dollars, and of other, hidden, costs[12]:

Oct. 1 Ad for female stenographer 1.00
Oct. 4 Violets for new stenographer 1.50
Oct. 6 Week's salary for new stenographer 45.00
Oct. 9 Roses for stenographer 5.00
Oct. 10 Candy for wife .90
Oct. 13 Lunch for stenographer 7.00
Oct. 15 Week's salary for stenographer 60.00
Oct. 16 Movie tickets for wife and self 1.20
Oct. 18 Theater tickets for steno and self 16.00
Oct. 19 Ice cream sundae for wife .30

Oct. 22 Mary's salary 75.00
Oct. 23 Champagne & dinner for Mary & self 32.00
Oct. 25 Doctor for stupid stenographer 375.00
Oct. 26 Mink stole for wife 1,700.00
Oct. 28 Ad for male stenographer 1.50
Total expenses for month $2,321.90

This is a self-consciously metonymic narrative in which each fictionalized expense-book entry signifies a discrete episode or chapter in a brief but impactful erotic affair. As the Chicago School narratologist Ralph Rader puts it:

> our experience of the story is tacit: we are caught by its illusion and feel its effect without explicit awareness of how [the expenses] are obtained. Questioned about these matters, many readers will point to the "real document" form of the expense diary and the sense it gives of the autonomy of the diarist as accounting for the illusion of the story, whereas . . . [m]ixing as it does business and personal expenses, with no completeness on either score, the diary bears only the most minimal likeness to a business account, a likeness sufficient to serve the mind as a premise for the illusion which, as it were, it actively chooses to entertain. (1974, 251)

The narrativity of this piece, of the fragments that together add up to offer "the illusion of" a story, emerges as the effect of a false familiarity. The form of the story is just enough like a business expense diary so as both to foster the fiction and to expose it as such: a familiar and ancient form of narrative mimesis. The formal metonymic structure of this fictional expense account—in which each item stands for a contiguously dated event—builds into a coherent, unified story of an office romance. Indeed, there is a classical shape to the story here: temporal–causal connections are organized into a unified sequence with a clear beginning, middle, peripeteia, and end. Aristotle would certainly recognize the traditional shape of this story's *muthos*.[13] We read between the lines of the metonymic plot of "Expenses for the Month," constructing a whole from the combination of what is narrated and what is not. What is more, we tacitly accept that the parts we are given here are not the whole story, but that they are the salient elements of this plot. We would be confused and dissatisfied by references to buying typewriter ribbon and paper, or to finding a phone bill or even "lunch for client," among the list of expenses for the month recorded here. Indeed, we recognize that the given narrative *syuzhet* here is only a combination of selected and salient parts from a much wider *fabula*.

Ostensibly, "Expenses for the Month" is represented as a sequence of temporally isolated chronological events figured (metonymically) as financial transactions which, in turn, the reader figures out as standing in (metonymically) for unnarrated actions and events. Thus, although our anonymous author does not explicitly specify any links between these chronologically sequenced incidents, the reader supplies temporal–causal connections to forge a connected series of contiguously related action-to-action (metonymic) links in this narrative chain. The stenographer's weekly salary rises from $45 to $60 to $75 in the course of just a few weeks, and the value of her weekly bonuses—if we may call them that—rise at a similar rate (from a simple and inexpensive bunch of violets to expensive champagne and dinner). Each expense simultaneously charts the rise in her character's "worth" in the eyes of our businessman-diarist-narrator, too; each rise plots the rate of increasing intimacy between the stenographer and her employer, perhaps even a level of services rendered; and each rise leads us and these characters toward those final—telling—expenses.

Reading between the lines in this account, the reader is similarly invited to attribute unspoken motivation for the personal expense on October 10 ("Candy for wife") as arising causally—and guiltily—from the action and expense of the previous day ("Roses for stenographer"). The reader is encouraged to attribute a similar cause–effect relation to the expensive "Theater tickets for steno and self" on October 18, and the cheap "Ice cream sundae for wife" on the nineteenth. As the plot thickens in this slender story, the reader no less readily draws a causal connection between the "Champagne & dinner for Mary & self" on October 23 and the expense on October 25 ("Doctor for stupid stenographer"). Or rather, the reader draws a connection between the need for the "stupid" stenographer to see a doctor and what happened in the unnarrated interval *after* that champagne dinner. Thus, primed in how to read the metonymic chains that connect the sequence of events that this account narrates, the reader readily draws a further causal connection between *these* two events (the champagne dinner and the doctor) and the ensuing compensatory extravagance on October 26 ("Mink stole for wife"). The careful reader can also see a cumulative cause–effect pattern building up across the course of the "account" of this expensive month: that advertisement (the initiating metonymic "Ad") for a specifically "female" stenographer on October 1 appears as the first sign of illicit intent for this businessman-diarist-narrator to initiate an adulterous office liaison (a reading strengthened by the gender shift in the advert placed twenty-eight days later for a "male" replacement). The slow reader will also notice how violets lead to roses which lead to lunch which leads to the theater—which leads to champagne which leads to dinner which leads to . . . a gap in the story and in the timeline, an unnarrated episode which we see only through its financial affect(s). But these metonymic moves—both separately and in sequence—force the reader to read slowly, to pay heed to the gaps and silences in this story, to listen to what is not said.

Such slow reading allows the reader to recognize what happens in these gaps: champagne and dinner lead to bed, which leads to sex, which leads to unwanted pregnancy (hence the "Doctor for stupid stenographer") and unemployment—for the unfortunate stenographer at least. And to remorse and reform on the part of our businessman-diarist-narrator.

The metonymic selection and re-presentation of associated elements and the slow reader's recognition of effect for cause (and vice versa) is what configures the narrativity of "Expenses for the Month." By reading slowly we are able to see that the temporal gaps in the story's chronological framework form just one aspect of its meticulous emplotment. So meticulous, in fact, that we simultaneously mind and don't mind the gaps—the silences and the absences. Nor do we mind the unlikely speed with which stenographer Mary's apparent pregnancy impacts upon the narrator and narrative of this story.[14]

By slow reading, for example, we notice how the metonyms used to identify the character of the secretary in this account shift over time. On October 1 she is simply and generically "female." On October 4 she is "new." By October 9, she is established in her professional office role as "stenographer," but by the eighteenth, the abbreviation of that title to "steno" suggests a more casual intimacy between our businessman-diarist-narrator and his employee, and this prepares us to recognize the "Mary" of the October 22 entry as the same stenographer, enjoying her generous salary increase (and not, as might legitimately be inferred, another more senior office employee named Mary). But after that intimate champagne and dinner on October 23, Mary disappears from view; she is now the "stupid stenographer" who is—we infer—pregnant, and she is consequently written out of the account.

By slow reading we notice, too, how descriptions of a character's external appearance and direct environment stand in metonymic relation to significant character traits, adding texture and depth to this slender narrative. Physical and sartorial details such as hair, clothes, gait, and even names can all metonymically contribute to the representation of character. Indeed, we infer a great deal about the character of our accountant's wife in "Expenses for the Month" simply from what she eats (the candy of October 10; the ice cream sundae of October 19) and what she wears (that expensive mink stole of October 26). But, if physical and sartorial details metonymically configure character, so too do contextual details. As Shlomith Rimmon-Keenan suggests: "A character's physical surrounding (room, house, street, town) as well as his human environment (family, social class) are . . . trait-connoting metonymies" (1983, 66).[15] In "Expenses for the month," allusions to the office, the cinema, and the theater metonymically connote an urban storyworld, with contiguously urbane modes and morals; just the kind of environment for a young stenographer to find herself "in trouble."

According to Monika Fludernik, such descriptive details in literary discourse configure "a possible world when metonymic processes of expansion are triggered during the act of reading . . . [D]etails activate frames . . . [and] schemata in which one part of the frame evokes the whole thing" (2009, 54). The metonymic narrative of "Expenses for the month" builds an expansive storyworld from a few words, and from the cues it gives to the reader to supply additional details, that is, to fill in the gaps, the invisibilities, to read what isn't recorded here, to listen to what isn't being said, and to see a more expansive storyworld and story frame beyond the narrow window of the "document" itself. This is achieved, in part, by appealing to external frame narratives and wider cultural schema which flesh out the slender story skeleton that the account itself delineates.

One such cultural schema (albeit one already partially fossilized for most twentieth- and twenty-first-century readers, whether slow or fast) relates to the symbolic—metonymic—language of flowers: violets, in Anglo-American floriography, stand for modesty and humility, and are (or were) commonly associated with the Virgin Mary.[16] One of the earliest "Expenses for the Month"—violets for the new stenographer—nicely, subtly, foreshadows, then, the reader's later comprehension that the new stenographer's name must be Mary. In contiguous juxtaposition, the roses given a few days later stand for a blossoming romance between Mary and her employer, but readers must be able to recognize these cultural scripts and schema if they are to negotiate these particular metonymies, and some will be more obvious than others. Thus, according to the familiar and still prevalent cultural script in which roses stand for romance, we recognize that the theater tickets, the champagne, and the dinner expenses in this story as also standing for metonymic moves in a classic seduction script. We know what (indeed, who) comes next. We can therefore infer that the "doctor" required to attend the "stupid stenographer" on October 25 is not called in because Mary has dropped a typewriter on her toe. And we can identify that $375 doctor as euphemistic metonym—agent for action—under which to couch the abortion apparently necessitated by the causal action resulting from those roses and that champagne.[17]

But perhaps one of the most important metonyms in this story is the "figure" of the narrator. For Uri Margolin, the narrator designates "the hypothesized producer of the current discourse, the individual agent who serves as the answer to Genette's question who speaks?"; the product of a "process of metonymic transfer and anthropomorphization" (Margolin 2014, 351).[18] Margolin invites us to see the narrator—or narrative "voice"—as a mere metonymy for a narrative function, but that narrative function is at once the "hypothesized producer" of a narrative *and* the hypothesized *product* of a reader's imagination. In "Expenses for the Month" there is no overt narrator as such: it is a nonnarrated or minimally narrated story. Yet the diary-like entries configure a powerful sense of narrative voice. In just over one hundred words and figures, a distinct and distinctive narrating character emerges—a "self." A married man. A wealthy man. Of a certain age. A professional. An urbanite. A generous man. A callous man. A casual misogynist. A romantic. An adulterer. This characterization, this narrating persona, is built up metonymically. The reader constructs a coherent picture of this narrating character or voice in the same way that she constructs his storyworld from the salient metonymic features revealed in what is said—and what is unsaid—in his telling account.

Moreover, this characterization, this narrating persona, is further built up by the narrative point of view it invites the reader to share. The voice of the narrator here corresponds with the narrator's focalization and is similarly configured metonymically—in snapshots. Recall how the adjectives and nouns used to identify the stenographer in this story show us only the narrator's narrow point of view of this key character—who does not see, who does speak in this narrative, who remains a silent and absent presence. On October 1 she is merely "female." On October 4, "new." On the eighteenth, "steno." On the twenty-second she is "Mary." On the twenty-fifth, "stupid." Thereafter, presumably "damaged goods," she disappears from view entirely. However, the "Ad for male stenographer" which appears as the story's conclusion, a metonymic echo of the opening "Ad for female stenographer" at the start of the month and the start of the story, works both to erase her character and to bring it to mind: a poignantly metonymic speaking silence. Indeed, as Seb Matzner observes of metonymy's aesthetic and affective powers, "Prominent among the more general literary-aesthetic effects of metonymy's lateral shifts are the creation of a poignantly condensed impression of what is at issue" (2019). And what is at issue here, especially for the twentieth-century slow reader attuned to the historically silenced voices of the "Me Too" movement, is precisely this silencing of the female characters in this story—not only Mary but the narrator's "wife" too. However, we only recognize this impression by reading (and rereading) each word—and thus the condensed world represented in this story—*slowly*.

To look back to the start of this chapter as we reach our own conclusion here, let us return to Shklovsky and his account of the metonymic operations of defamiliarization, where he asked:

> Why is it that, in fashioning an *Art of Love* out of love, Ovid counsels us not to rush into the arms of pleasure? A crooked road, a road in which the foot feels acutely the stones beneath it, a road that turns back on itself—this is the road of art. ([1921] 1990, 15)

Rather, this is the art of reading the world and the word slowly—the art of narrative metonymy.[19]

NOTES

1. On the history of flawed attempts to define metonymy and its operations, see Matzner (2019).

2. The scholarship on metonymy is extensive, but see in particular Allan (2008), Bredin (1984), Jakobson (1956), Lodge (1977), Matzner (2016, 2019), and Panther and Radden (1999).

3. Gerald Prince in his *Dictionary of Narratology* defines metonymy as: "A figure of speech whereby a term designating a notion, A, is used for another term designation another notion, B, related to A as cause and effect, container and thing contained, or part and whole" (1987, 52).

4. All translations in this chapter are my own unless otherwise indicated.

5. See Sher in Shklovsky ([1921] 1990, xviii–xix) on the range of meaning and suitable translations for Shklovsky's neologism *ostranenie*.

6. On Shklovsky's indebtedness to Aristotle, see Liveley (2019, 112–19).

7. See also Booth (1961, 126): "When we see a causal chain started, we demand . . . to see the result. Emma meddles, Tess is seduced, Huck runs away—and we demand certain consequences."

8. See Barchiesi (2001, 15): "Any telling of a story is partial, made up of stories and diverse, autonomous parts thereof . . . This is how one narrates."

9. On Genette's debts to Aristotle and Formalism, see Liveley (2019, 189–93).

10. Cf. Cobley (2014, 13). Brooks bases his own model of narrative metonymy here on Lacan's. Lacan views metonymy as a sequential movement of meaning "from word to word" ("mot à mot") along the linear signifying chain of language, meaning produced and linked through contiguity and combination. For Lacan, metonymy therefore has the same (parallel) structure as desire—a desire for something else ([1966] 2002).

11. Brooks reiterates these ideas in his 1979 paper on "Freud and Narrative Understanding": "metonymy itself speaks of desire, as Jacques Lacan has argued. Desire is the motor of narrative, and metonymy is its master trope" (78). He argues further: "As well as form, plots must have force: the force that makes the connection of incident powerful, that shapes the confused material of a life into an intentional structure which in turn generates new insights about how life can be told" (80).

12. The story is quoted and discussed by Rader in his essay "Fact, Theory, and Literary Explanation" (1974). He notes: "I came across the story as a giveaway item on a shop counter; so far as I know it is anonymous" (252 n7). Phelan (2017, 37–41) also discusses this story.

13. Cf. *Poetics* 7.1450b, 25–34.

14. See Phelan (2017, 37–41).

15. As Riffaterre suggests, "[Metonymies] . . . cause the reader to infer all sorts of moral judgments about a character from his behavior or some minor feature of physical or sartorial appearance" (1982, 273).

16. See Seaton (2012) on the history of the language of flowers.

17. As Riffatterre states, "[M]etonymies generate textual amplification" (1982, 274, 291) and thereby open up the possible-world-building potential—the narrativity—of the most slender of stories.

18. The concept of the narrator (a strictly textual, narratological, category) also metonymically substitutes for that of the author—the extra-textual person or persona—whose narrating role is thereby also revealed to be merely a part in and of a narrative whole.

19. I'm immensely grateful to audiences at Bristol, Cambridge, and Bergen for their feedback on earlier drafts of this paper, and to Jim Phelan for first introducing me to "Expenses for the Month." I would also like to thank Jena Habegger-Conti, Lene M. Johannessen, Ruben Moi, and the most metaphorical Tim Saunders for their generosity and general loveliness.

WORKS CITED

Allan, Kathryn. 2008. *Metaphor and Metonymy: A Diachronic Approach*. Chichester: Wiley-Blackwell.

Barchiesi, Alessandro. 2001. *Speaking Volumes: Narrative and Intertext in Ovid and Other Latin Poets*. London: Duckworth.

Booth, Wayne C. 1961. *Rhetoric of Fiction*. Chicago/London: University of Chicago Press.

Bredin, Hugh. 1984. "Metonymy." *Poetics* 5(1): 45–58.

Brooks, Peter. 1977. "Freud's Masterplot." *Yale French Studies* 55/56: 280–300.

Brooks, Peter. 1979. "Fictions of the Wolfman: Freud and Narrative Understanding." *Diacritics* 9(1): 72–81.

Brooks, Peter. 1984. *Reading for the Plot: Design and Intention in Narrative*. Cambridge, MA: Harvard University Press.

Cobley, Paul. 2014. *Narrative*. Abingdon: Routledge.

Fludernik, Monica. 2009. *An Introduction to Narratology*. London/New York: Routledge.

Genette, Gérard. 1972. *Figures III*. Paris: Editions du Seuil.

Jakobson, Roman. [1956] 2002. *Fundamentals of Language*. Translated by Morris Halle. The Hague: Mouton.

Lacan, Jacques. [1966] 2002. "The Instance of the Letter in the Unconscious, or Reason Since Freud." In *Écrits: A Selection*, translated by B. Fink, 412–444. New York and London: W. W. Norton.

Lively, Genevieve. 2019. *Narratology*. Oxford: Oxford University Press.

Lodge, David. 1977. *Modes of Modern Writing: Metaphor, Metonymy, and the Typology of Modern Literature*. London: Edward Arnold.

Margolin, Uri. 2014. "Narrator." In *Handbook of Narratology*, edited by Peter Hühn, et al., 646–666. Berlin/New York: Walter de Gruyter.

Matzner, Sebastian. 2016. *Rethinking Metonymy: Literary Theory and Poetic Practice from Pindar to Jakobson*. Oxford: Oxford University Press.

Matzner, Sebastian. 2019. "Metonymy." *Oxford Classical Dictionary*, January 25, 2019. Oxford University Press. https://oxfordre.com/classics/view/10.1093/acrefor e/9780199381135.001.0001/acrefore-9780199381135-e-8229.

Meister, Christoph. 2014. "Narratology." In *Handbook of Narratology*, edited by Peter Hühn, et al., 623–645. Berlin: De Gruyter.

Panther, Klaus-Uwe, and Günter Radden, eds. 1999. *Metonymy in Language and Thought*. Amsterdam: John Benjamins.

Phelan, James. 2017. *Somebody Telling Somebody Else: A Rhetorical Poetics of Narrative*. Columbus: Ohio State University Press.

Prince, Gerald. 1987. *A Dictionary of Narratology*. Lincoln: University of Nebraska Press.

Rader, Ralph. 1974. "Fact, Theory, and Literary Explanation." *Critical Inquiry* 1(2): 245–272.

Riffaterre, Michael. 1982. "Trollope's Metonymies." *Nineteenth-Century Fiction* 37(3): 272–292.

Rimmon-Keenan, Shlomith. 1983. *Narrative Fiction: Contemporary Poetics*. London/ New York: Routledge.

Seaton, Beverly. 2012. *The Language of Flowers: A History*. Charlottesville: University of Virginia Press.

Shklovsky, Viktor. [1921] 1990. *Theory of Prose* [*O teorii prozy*]. Translated by Ben Sher. Elmwood Park: Dalkey Archive Press.

Steen, Gerard. 2005. "Metonymy." In *Routledge Encyclopaedia of Narrative Theory*, edited by D. Herman, M. Jahn, and M.-L. Ryan, 307–308. London/New York: Routledge.

Sternberg, Meir. 1978. *Expositional Modes and Temporal Ordering in Fiction*. Baltimore: Johns Hopkins University Press.

Tynyanov, Yury. [1927] 1981. "On the Foundations of Cinema [Ob osnovakh kino]." In *Russian Formalist Film Theory*, edited by Herbert Eagle, 81–100. Ann Arbor: University of Michigan Press.

Chapter 9

Aesthetic Apprehension, Hauntology, and Just Literature

Ruben Moi

How do you distinguish between false familiarities and the heterotopically aesthetic? In other words, how do you discern the mind-breaking qualities of new artistic works, and the resuscitation of old ones, from the works of art that appear new but merely reinforce stale ideas and congealed concepts? And who decides upon this heterotopical quality according to what criteria? Such hermeneutic possibilities of imaginative creativity belong to Jean-Luc Nancy and Jacques Rancière's inquiry into the present human condition. "Where does art stand today? What is happening with art today?" asks Nancy in "Art Today" (2010, 92). "Why speak of an aesthetic heterotopia?" asks Rancière in "The Aesthetic Heterotopia" (2010, 15). These two articles offer a condensed view of Rancière and Nancy's comprehensive philosophical engagement with arts and aesthetic discourses in the humanities.[1] The two French philosophers place the questions on contemporary art within their own context in these articles. Kant's philosophy, logically in these debates of aesthetics, remains central to both Nancy and Rancière's meditations. Kant's ideality and reason also remain important to Nancy and Rancière in their search for an aesthetic judgment that balances Kant's principles of aesthetic autonomy with current contexts of intellectual debate and social immediacy.

With Kant's aesthetics as an imperative, both Nancy and Rancière attend to arts and hermeneutic discourses for the qualities that intimate imaginative novelty and aesthetic reorientation. Nancy points to "gesture" as a contemporary means to escape the "repetition of forms" (2010, 92). Rancière examines "the heterotopic" as a possibility to avoid "the hierarchy of levels of discourse" (2010, 24). Nancy observes mainly historical -*isms* and current contours of a number of art works. Rancière locates his argumentation for aesthetic heterotopia in the philosophical and theoretical discourses. Both of them attend mainly to visual arts in these articles. Rancière keeps *Boys Eating*

Grapes and Melon from 1646 by the Spanish Baroque painter Bartolomé Esteban Murillo as a touchstone for his philosophical reorientations of aesthetics.[2] Nancy constellates *Été 93*, Sylvie Blocher's art instillation from 1993 on the violation of women, with one of Claudio Parmiggiani's smashed glass labyrinths, *Sea of Glass*, at le Collège de Bernardins from 2008.[3] Both articles intimate that false familiarities and heterotopic aesthetics appear more often as entangled strands in the singular artwork than they operate as categories for distinguishing the many new artists and works from each other. Furthermore, both articles incorporate the dimension of ethics; Rancière's explicitly and Nancy's more implicitly. However, Rancière and Nancy, for all their common ground and sodality of aesthetic hermeneutics, tend to think differently on the set of philosophical traditions and ethical configurations that govern the current discourses on aesthetics. They also argue differently on what the gesture and the heterotopic might indicate for the present state and future possibilities of arts and aesthetics—the importance of familiarity and defamiliarization in a world where the encounters of the known with the unknown occur in increasingly more places, and in a very rapid tempo. Furthermore, the questions and dimensions of Rancière and Nancy's articles are both very relevant for just literature, a type of literature that places written arts on the cusp of aesthetic heterotopia and predefining ideologies, -*isms* and schema. Why, where, and how the silent medium of literature reinvents itself forms one cluster of relevant questions in just literature. Why, where, and how just literature balances its own creative force in relation to contentious discourses of justice articulates another incumbent inquiry. These aesthetic and judicial discourses intensify in several border zones, in the intense encounters between the old and the new, the known and the unknown, the familiar and the heterotopic. Northern Ireland and Guantánamo Bay present two such border zones in which the national constitution, state authority, and legal practice are caught up in the concerns of international legislation, human rights, and philosophy of justice. Just literature, from Northern Ireland and Guantánamo, as so many other places, tends to articulate the many judicial concerns that are frequently ignored, silenced, and familiarized into falsity.

In their engagement with Kant's aesthetics and in their many mutual concerns, Nancy and Rancière tend to argue similar and divergent ideas of art today. They both engage profoundly with ideas and formations of the new. Nancy declares: "The question of art is obviously posed as the question of a formation of forms for which no preliminary form is given" (2010, 94). Nancy acknowledges the position of Kant in the philosophy of aesthetics "down to our day, including Hegel, Nietzsche, Kierkegaard, Adorno, Heidegger and our contemporaries, Derrida for instance": "I think that the whole history of art and of reflection about art, especially since the time when there was a reflection about art, as such, because you are well aware that art is a very late, modern concept, no older than the eighteenth century, which received its first philosophical analyses essentially from Kant" (2010, 97). He also has recourse to Kant for articulating his own mind:

> I would say it with the words and concepts of Kant that are useful here: I would say that it is a question of forms for which there are no preliminary schemas (you know that Kant calls "schema," as he says, a non-sensible image that precedes the possibility of sensible images). Perhaps the task of art today is that of having to proceed without any schema, without any schematism. There is nothing that contains a pre-donation, a pre-disposition of possibilities of forms—but I say "forms" in a very, very general sense, not just visual forms, but also sonorous forms, verbal forms. (2010, 94)

With a view to Kant's, and his own "forms for which there are no preliminary schemas," Nancy declares that he is often "embarrassed" and "very offended by works of contemporary art," which he often finds "greatly disapproving" (2010, 95). He acknowledges the diversity of contemporary arts, but articulates strict reservations concerning large parts of current activity: "Yes, there is form in these works, but a message precedes it and dominates it" (2010, 95). He enumerates some of these messages: "The idea of art for art's sake is the falsest idea of art, just as the idea of art for a signification is, whether religious, political or ethical: that's the other extreme of two wrong ideas about art" (2010, 98). On these grounds Nancy denunciates Sylvie Bloucher's art installation, *Été 93*, which Nancy terms *Rape in Bosnia*, as a paradigmatic example of the embarrassing art today, and, presumably, a work of art where the message precedes the form and where the art installation engages with the religious, political, and ethical. In contrast, Nancy "pays homage to Italy and to a friend," that is, to Parmiggiani's smashed labyrinths as an installation that is not "social, political or ethical" (2010, 98; 99).

Nancy's considerations of art today contain a number of disputable points. First of all, the elevation of Kant and the reduction to name-dropping of succeeding philosophical expositions of aesthetics locate the imperative in the heydays of Enlightenment and cut short the past two centuries of aesthetic debate. Second, Nancy takes for granted that art for which no preliminary form is given actually exists, and that such art distinguishes itself entirely from previous forms and concerns. Such novelty remains an ideal, but ignores the importance of past form, if only to distinguish the new from the old one—if that could be so easily done. The search for contemporary art is always predicated upon the temporary of the past. Third, art today tends in Nancy's aesthetics always to be separated from any type of religious, political, and ethical association, as much as "art for art's sake." Imagination, arts, and aesthetics are frequently based upon freedom from constraints and principles of autonomy, whereas Nancy imposes reductive strictures. Four of these impositions—the religious, the political, the ethical, and the artistic— exclude large swathes of art today. The imposition of reductive imperatives and the enumeration of concrete examples oppose many tendencies in art and aesthetics today. Finally, art that tends to offend refined sensibility appears to be excommunicated from the cathedral of aesthetics. Sylvie Boucher's *Été 93* turns out to be the paradigmatic example of a type of offensive art installation that engages with the religious, the political, and the ethical in a form where "a message precedes it and dominates it" (2010, 95). Consequently, a work of art by a French woman that concerns itself with war and violence at a time of civilizatory crisis in Europe is denigrated by a French male professor of philosophy for being "offensive." The silent assumptions for the aesthetic judgment on *Été 93* appear far from new. On the contrary, these positions are very familiar. They silently confirm the established position of gender, class, erudition, morals, and fixity of a traditional type of aesthetics that continuously elevates aesthetics for aesthetics' sake. Nancy finds the abstract and deconstructive smashed glass labyrinths in the cathedral of his Italian friend Parmiggiani much more approving. Consequently, to turn Nancy's critique of Boucher and wide swathes of art today against himself: "a message precedes" and "dominates" Nancy's preferred art works. This is the message of canon, autonomy, and orthodoxy. It is the message of abstract and complex art that always intrigues the intellectual mind before, above, and beyond any type of discourse beyond that of aesthetics itself.

Nancy and Rancière cover common ground, they agree and disagree. For Rancière, as for Nancy and most debates on aesthetics, Kant's philosophy provides the inescapable point of departure. Rancière writes:

> This withdrawal is at the heart of the very definition of the aesthetic judgment in Kant's "Analytic of the Beautiful." It takes the form of a twofold negation. The object of the aesthetic judgment is neither an object of knowledge nor an object of desire. The "excellence" of the aesthetic form has to be judged apart from epistemic or ethical criteria. . . . This is what the "disinterestedness" of aesthetic judgment means. (2010, 18)

Rancière, however, as opposed to parts of Nancy's engagement with Kant, articulates reservations of the Kantian legacy. He raises doubt about the idea of absolute autonomy: "It thus appears that the aesthetic difference cannot be equated with the distance between empirical reality and artistic appearance" (2010, 16). Rancière also discloses in his argumentation how Kant, Schiller, and Hegel imbricate their ethical stance in their aesthetic position: "What they determine as the aesthetic affect is a supplement to the ethical distribution" (2010, 19). Furthermore, Rancière uncovers the seminal flaw of a type of aesthetics that always absolves itself entirely from thematic concerns: "It has become commonplace to call 'aesthetic' this capacity to abstract the form of a representation from its content" (2010, 16). He also indicates how hermeneutics "has always been intertwined with the distribution of social occupations" (2010, 16). Rancière's post-Kantian aesthetics include the later meditations of Bourdieu and Derrida and engage with complex and less absolutist considerations of art: "a form of aesthetic discourse which is not a specialization within philosophy, but, on the contrary, crosses the frontiers of the disciplines and ignores the hierarchy of levels of discourse" (2010, 24). He concludes his article on the aesthetic heterotopia in the following words:

A topography of the thinkable is always the topography of a theater of opera-tions. We have to hear the rumble of the battle, said Foucault in a famous text. In order to make the rumble audible, one has to reinscribe descriptions and arguments in a war of discourse where no definite border separates the territo-ries, where no definite border separates the logos of philosophy or science from the voices that are their objects. One has to re-inscribe them in the equality of a common language and the common capacity to invent objects, stories and arguments. The thinking of the aesthetic heterotopia requires the practice of indisciplinary discourse. (2010, 24)

The antiestablishment *animus* of art, its heterotopic, unfamiliar, and disrup-tive power, needs to assume vociferous and cross-generic form in order to combat the concentration of the familiar, the congealed, and the confirmed that always reproduces itself silently and peacefully. Aesthetics cannot avoid this indisciplinary quality in a world where the wars and border zones expand far beyond the rumble of discursive battles. A kind of aesthetics that always defines its heterotopia in relations to its own specific form and its own intro-spective tradition of autonomy, in lieu of Kant, Hegel, Schiller, and recent avatars, always comes with an element of culpable evasion and cognitive comfort, however different and unfamiliar the new work of art might appear. An indisciplinary art is called for in which the aesthetic creates itself at the controversial conjunctions of its own discipline, the many discourses of our time, and the complex world from which such discourses stem.

Rancière's conclusion places heterotopic aesthetics on the border zones of intellectual disagreement, "in a war of discourses where no definite border separates the territories" (2010, 24). Rancière's analysis and conclusion also open the becoming of heterotopic literature today from canonization and other familiar processes of exegesis to indisciplinary judgment and radical democracy. Acts of literature have always intervened in ethical orthodoxy, epistemological competence, and aesthetic hegemonies, but to sever radi-cal writing entirely from these humanist disciplines by reduction of critical interest to form only impairs literature as much as ethics, epistemology, and aesthetics. When, how, and why do what types of literature challenge as well as change our world? The questions are large, and the answers many.

Two positions over the recent decades on writing today and heterotopic literature manifest themselves in Harold Bloom's *The Western Canon* (1994) and Melvyn Bragg's *Twelve Books That Changed the World* (2006). "'Aesthetic value' is sometimes regarded as a suggestion of Immanuel Kant's rather than an actuality, but that has not been my experience during a lifetime of reading," Bloom (1994, 1) states and indicates how the aesthetic autonomy of literature precedes the philosophy of Kant. Still, he limits his book studies to twenty-six writers only and admits to "a certain nostalgia, since I seek to isolate the qualities that made these authors canonical, that is, authoritative in our culture" (1994, 1). Bloom, in the New Criticism tradition of F. R. Leavis, William Empson, T. S. Eliot, and Cleanth Brooks, elevates literature as a law unto itself, driven in its own sphere by literary principles. Bloom argues vehemently against "the fashion in our schools and colleges, where all aesthetic and most intellectual standards are being abandoned in the name of social harmony and the remedying of historical injustice" (1994, 7). These fashionable modes he terms sarcastically "the rabblement of lemmings" and "the School of Resentment" (1994, 4). The school of resentment includes feminist, postcolonial, New Historicist, and postmodernist approaches to literature—anything French you might say. Bloom's condemnation echoes Nancy's denunciation of Sylvie Bloucher's art installation *Été 93*. Furthermore, his aesthetic autonomy is predicated upon nostalgia, upon an extremely censorious number of authors and upon the cooption of literature into the existent ethical order, aesthetic hegemony, and social occupation that remain unstated, familiar, and silent.

Bloom and Nancy have a clear tendency to define their enemies. In their preference for disciplinary works of art and literature that always reproduce silently their own aesthetic etiology, both Bloom and Nancy contribute to familiarities. These familiarities may not be entirely false in the sense of truth and aesthetic value, but they are custodians of comfort and status quo. Their view of literature and artworks endorses the aesthetic conviction of art as a hermetically sealed sphere that never opens up to any other discourse. Bloom and Nancy's view of art subscribes to the idea that art is always only answerable to its own aesthetic criteria. Such a subscription is certainly disputable, possibly also untenable.

Melvyn Bragg's *Twelve Books That Changed the World*, as opposed to Bloom's *The Western Canon*, incorporates the sociopolitical, gender-conscious, religious, and historical contexts of his selected books—Bloom's "School of Resentment" and Nancy's "message that precedes" the art work. Bragg has selected books according to their historical importance, religious significance, democratic reform, industrial success, gender equality, political impact, and popular consequences. In his wide sense of literature and contextual awareness, Bragg's chosen twelve side with Rancière's disclosure of literature's relationality, and with Rancière's admonition that "the aesthetic difference cannot be equated with distance between empirical reality and artistic appearance" (2010, 16). Nevertheless, Bragg's predominant focus on the consequences of his twelve selected books, his astute awareness of context, and his wide definition of books tend to overshadow his distinct insensitivity to any understanding of aesthetics—the very forceful element in Bloom, Nancy, and Rancière's discussion of arts.

In its selection of imaginative literature and in its stringent focus on established aesthetics, Bloom's *The Western Canon* provides a tradition of literary arts and hermeneutics that appeared radical, new, and heterotopic during the dominantly theory-driven final decades of the last millennium. Bloom's blast from the past appeared as a breath of fresh air. It still does. Bragg's criteria and pragmatics revealed the relationality of literature to the complex society from which it stems. Bloom's canon preserves a familiarity of aesthetics that opposes Rancière's admonition that aesthetics is not always best judged by its distance and difference to the society, ideas, and values with which the specific artwork interacts. Bloom's hermetically sealed sphere of aesthetics is extremely familiar, if not entirely false. This type of introspective aesthetics reproduces automatically its own status as an institution of self-proclaimed heterotopic power, while it simultaneously eclipses totally how and why this institution came into being. Contrarily, Bragg's diverse framework for important literature depends more explicitly upon sociohistorical conditions and ideological positions that precede and dominate the chosen text. This pragmatic view of literature is extremely familiar to any type of social formation or cognitive structure that reproduces itself without rupture. Nevertheless, Bragg's approach to literature allows for a type of protean aesthetics that creates itself anew in complex relations with the society from which it stems.

"We have to hear the rumble of the battle, said Foucault in a famous text." Rancière's (2010, 24) reference to Foucault's *Discipline and Punish: The Birth of the Prison* is very pertinent. First of all, justice and literature, together with the university, the freedom of speech, and the liberal arts, serve as institutions of autonomous critical and creative corrective to state authority, executive government, religious imposition, ideological hegemony, ruthless capitalism, and institutional power abuse in any healthy democracy. As democratic institutions, literature and justice can be regarded as the creators and custodians of radical democracy. Justice, like literature, appears as both its own discipline and its own philosophical discourse. The concerns of both justice and literature cross the many other clamorous discourses today, such as those of war, climate change, global inequality, mass migration, gender issues, and animal rights. In a world where vociferous agitation almost eclipses the human tragedy from which it is stems, the humanist concern for art and aesthetics appears as important as ever. Many of Nancy and Rancière's concerns overlap with the issues of just literature. Does the silent, frequently ignored and sometimes strictly censored medium of imaginative writing concede to preceding discourses or provide heterotopia? Does just literature present false familiarities or indisciplinary artworks that unsettle our discourses and our ideas of justice? Does just literature relate to our contemporary human condition?

Undoubtedly, just literature has always contributed to the etiology, philosophy, and practice of justice. Sophocles's *Antigone* (fifth century BCE), in its multiple moral dimensions of divine law, state order, and individual responsibility by a woman caught in the family feuds and civil war of a male-dominated society, offers the paragon of just literature from classical antiquity. In the early modern period, most of Shakespeare's plays are saturated with dimensions of justice. Justice runs as a prominent theme in his plays from the wars and power play of his histories, via the capitalist, religious, cultural, and gender contextualizations of justice in *The Merchant of Venice* to the disastrous quest for an ideal state beyond moral corruption, royal fratricide, and misgovernment in *Hamlet*. The struggle for justice between moral compassion and strict legislation marks *Measure for Measure*. *The Tempest* remains remarkable for its distinct emphasis on forgiveness and redemption. In more recent history, just literature has gradually assumed radical roles of critique, subversion, and transformation of the existing law and order, in contents, themes, language, and form. Franz Kafka, Paul Célan, Salman Rushdie, and Nobel Peace and Literature laureates such as Elie Wiesel (1986), Wole Soyinka (1986), Toni Morrison (1993), Seamus Heaney (1995), John Maxwell Coetzee (2003), Svetalana Aleksijevitj (2015), and Bob Dylan (2016) exemplify some of the many writers who have explored the ideas of justice against prevailing moral paradigms and authorities of law and order in their fiction, poetry, drama, and documentary accounts. Many of these writers and works are already included in Bloom's *Western Canon*. Shakespeare also figures in Bragg's list. Justice—the ideals of right and wrong and fair, of retribution and redemption and altruism, of individual responsibility, social organization, world order, and a settled past and a common future—runs as a perennial theme in literature. The aesthetic heterotopia of just literature has contributed to define and defend the democratic idea of liberty and justice.

Texts from at least Sophocles to Shakespeare could easily be argued to precede one of the most defining periods of both aesthetics and justice in the Western world: the era of Kant. Kant's three major works on moral philosophy, *Groundwork of the Metaphysics of Morals* (1785), *Critique of Practical Reason* (1788), and *The Metaphysics of Morals* (1788), constitute a pivotal point in the philosophical meditations upon individual responsibility in concerns of justice. With his groundbreaking *The Critique of Judgement* (1790) Kant can also be regarded as the founding father of modern aesthetics. It is, of course, worth noting that Kant's work on ethics and justice largely preceded his work on aesthetics.

In the field of literature, basically all of Derrida's *Acts of Literature* (1992) engages with the institutions of literature and justice. The French philosopher also attends explicitly to unruly literature in "Force of Law: The Mystical Foundation of Authority," "Before the Law," and "The Law of Genre." Derrida illuminates literature's unique position and its imaginative, formal, and linguistic powers as a formidable and flexible medium for radically engaging with the moral and hermeneutic discourses of justice. Even in retrospect, Derrida's engagement with the literature of such canonical writers as James Joyce, William Shakespeare, Franz Kafka, Stéphane Mallarmé, and Paul Célan, offers few, if any, familiarities, in lieu of the heterotopic qualities of these writers' imaginative writing. Derrida's philosophical critique of Western metaphysics, language, and literature acts as a countervailing analytical practice to any grand ideas of literature and arts as an institution fixed in its own realm of aesthetics. Derrida's involvement with the phenomena of literature carries the hallmarks of an indisciplinary spirit, to which Rancière rallies in his aesthetic heterotopia. Similarly, Derrida also intervenes in many discourses of justice with his theme *hauntology* in *Spectres of Marx*. *Hauntology* is Derrida's term for "*responsibility*, beyond all living present, within that which disjoins the living present, before the ghost of those who are not yet born or who are already dead, be they victims of wars, political or other kinds of violence, nationalist, racist, colonialist, sexist or other kinds of exterminations, victims of oppressions of capitalist imperialism or any form of totalitarianism" (1994, xix). Such a responsibility entails a quest for unfound justice irreducible to laws and legal documents, requires "respect for justice concerning those who *are not there*" and continuously unsettles an unknown future: "This question *arrives*, if it arrives, it questions with regard to what will come in the future-to-come" (1994, xix). Such a justice, according to Derrida, assumes the qualities of the specter, it defies the finality of life and death, but is dependent upon both dimensions. Justice is not immediate consensus—if that were ever a possibility—nor arbitrary legal decision; nor is it an ontological solidity of Kantian proportions. Justice is "neither substance, nor essence, nor existence, *is never present as such*" (1994, xviii). As the specter appears as the manifestation of the spirit, the spirit of justice disappears whenever the ghost shows itself. Justice appears as spectral possibilities: untimely, uncertain, and unsettling moments of responsibility that haunt the living present with a commitment to the dead of the past and the living of the future. Spectral moments arrive again and again to raise the problems of justice for the dead and the undead. "To learn to live finally," for the individual human being under the onerous obligation of responsibility, becomes a question of empathy and death: "To live, by definition, is not something one learns. Not from one self, it is not learned from life, taught by life. Only from the other and by death" (1994, xviii). Derrida's engagement with justice, like his acts of literature, subverts several familiarities, and reveals the silencing and possible falsity of hegemonic discourses of justice. Whereas any metaphysical underpinning of justice *in lieu* of Kant transports the concept beyond its empirical and ontological actuality, justice based upon the life of the living present enters the problems of relativity. The former, the recourse to universal, abstract, and preconceived ideals of justice, offers a familiarity that frequently outweighs and silences the complexities of individual cases. Contrarily, individual cases, especially from literature and the arts, can challenge and change abstract ideals of justice.

Derrida's analysis of judicial axiomatics and human responsibility in *Spectres of Marx* proposes an indisciplinary, heterotopic aesthetics. His book is dedicated to Chris Hani, the leader of the South African Communist Party and a fierce opponent of Apartheid who was assassinated on April 10, 1993, as an instance of naming the numerous unknown victims of unjust history. Chris Hani's suffering of injustice results from the brutal violation of Kant's deontological moral theory and categorical imperative. Nevertheless, Hani's tragedy also undermines the abstract, idealist, universal, and disinterested philosophical detachment of the eighteenth-century German philosopher. Furthermore, *Spectres of Marx* constitutes a double examination of the spirits of Shakespeare's *Hamlet* and of Marx's radical theories. Derrida's act of justice also proposes a stern response to Fukuyama's triumphalist celebration of free market economics in the crisis of communism in post-Berlin Wall Europe, *The End of History and the Last Man* (1992). In Derrida's hauntology, the spirits of responsibility, radical critique, and emancipatory promise in Marx's areligious, internationalist communism eclipse the specters of historical materialism, class struggle, and revolution. Consequently, Derrida's deconstructive reading of responsibility, justice, victims of violence, and the spectral legacies of Marxist philosophy and Shakespearian tragedy appears pertinent to any place divided against itself at a disjointed time that has caused the questions of responsibility and justice to be raised repetitiously and indisciplinarily in a catalog of aesthetic representations. As such, Derrida's acts of literature and hauntology are of great relevance to the literature where literature, in its silent medium, articulates a type of indisciplinary aesthetics predicated upon conflictual discourses of justice in the border zones of civilizatory crisis. Just literature acts with all the creative and corrective power of Derrida's and Rancière's multidiscursive heterotopic aesthetics.

Over the last recent decades, Foucault and Rancière's "rumble of the battle" has been noticed in just literature from Northern Ireland to Guantánamo Bay, despite forceful structures of familiarization, silencing, and suppression. Jail journals run in Irish and Northern Irish literature from John Mitchel's *Jail Journal, or, Five Years in British Prisons* (1854) and Oscar Wilde's *The Ballad of Reading Gaol* (1898) to Brendan Behan's *Borstal Boy* (1958), Bobby Sands's *One Day in My Life* (1983), and Gerry Adams's *Cage Eleven* (1990). A couple of statements in *Voices from the Grave*, the documentary statements of paramilitary IRA and UVF prisoners Brendan Hughes and David Ervine edited by Ed Moloney in 2010, capture the critique of justice so widespread across the divide in a Northern Ireland on the brink of civil war in the latter three decades of the previous millennium: "There weren't too many people who were walking out of the courts, and under the Diplock regime it was democracy defending itself by undemocratic means. . . . There's no such thing as justice. I think that there's loads of law, but I don't believe I ever saw justice, I don't believe justice is done in courtrooms" (2010, 356–57). Writers at the time appeared less categorical about the possibilities of justice. The poetry, drama, and critical essays of 1995 Nobel Laureate Seamus Heaney, whom Harold Bloom includes in his appendix of authors who aspire to permanence in the Western Canon, offers a very specific case in question. The Nobel Prize Organization awarded Heaney the Prize for Literature in 1995 for his "lyrical beauty and ethical depth," and Professor of Law Yxta Maya testifies to the persistent power of Heaney's poetry in "Punishment and the Costs of Knowledge." Heaney's writing is one that questions, in a Derridean sense, "respect for justice" (1994, xix) and, in Rancière's view, "requires the practice of indisciplinary discourse" (2010, 24) in far more nuanced and imaginative ways than the documents of paramilitary prisoners. Such a poem as Heaney's "Punishment" lays bare the problems of defining justice in the border zones of Kantian philosophy, national jurisdictions, social suppression, and individual responsibility. The controversy on his "Punishment" and *North* (1975), the volume in which the poem appears, reflects lucidly the concerns of justice that also run prominently in the poetry of Thomas Kinsella, Eavan Boland, Michael Longley, and Paul Muldoon, in the drama of Brian Friel, Field Day, and the Tricycle Theatre, and in the popular culture of films and music at the time.[4] The plethora of artistic engagement with the concerns and challenges of justice in Northern Ireland constitutes one particular example of Rancière's heterotopic discourse.

Indisciplinary writing from the US military detention center Guantánamo Bay on Cuba provides another example of just literature, a variety of documentary and imaginative writing that exists upon the margins of many discourses and numerous border zones. Guantánamo Bay literature, for example, *Poems from Guantánamo* (2010) edited by Mark Falcoff and Mohamedou

Ould Slahi's *Guantánamo Diary* (2017), bears resemblance with literature from Northern Ireland over the last fifty years, not least in its complex relations to justice, and in its prison poems and jail journals. Many of the Muslim detainees in Guantánamo Bay were extradited from their home countries and interred without charge, trial, and conviction. The Guantánamo detention center was silenced and ignored for a long time. It was, in the words of Mark Falcoff, "a 'black hole' from which no information—and certainly not the voices of the detainees—could escape" (2007, ix). When the information did escape, in the forms of poems and diaries from the detainees, the texts were censored and redacted. The detainees and the judicial principles at stake were familiarized into falsity, invisibility, and oblivion.

Mohamedou Ould Slahi's detainment and his *Guantánamo Diary* were subjected to silencing, censoring, and familiarizing. Slahi was detained in Mauritania on November 20, 2001, extradited to Guantánamo Bay detention camp via intelligence centers in Jordan and Afghanistan, and kept incarcerated on suspicion of terrorism until October 16, 2016. In these fifteen years, his case was never tried in court. Slahi's story accounts for daily life, human relations, interrogation methods, and principles of justice in the prison camp. His jail journal strikes to the core of judicial and moral morass in our conflicted world today, such as the dilemmas of individual human rights and state security, the constancy of the constitution in times of crisis, the balance between national jurisdiction and international law, the nexus of ethical concern with regards to illegal confinement and forced confession, and the censoring of freedom of speech. The censored edition of *Guantánamo Bay* was published in 2015, the restored version in 2017. The first edition was only published due to the dedication and assiduity of lawyers and volunteers. The manuscript was controlled and censored by the governmental authorities, and the book contains several multipage erasures. The most conspicuous state-sanctioned redaction might be the censoring of Slahi's poem in the journal.

Slahi's case and diary confront the core principles of humanity, justice, and literature. His fifteen years of incarceration without any trial or any conviction criticize severely the abuse of the human rights and Kantian ethics upon which most Western democracies are constituted: "In 2004, three years after Guantánamo opened, the US Supreme Court finally decided a question whose answer should have been obvious from the start: that GTMO prisoners must have some way to challenge the government's claims that they are dangerous terrorists" (2017, xxxiv). His extradition from Mauritania to the United States upbraids the violation of Mauritanian national jurisdiction: "But kidnapping me from my house in my country and giving me to the U.S., breaking the constitution of Mauritania and the customary International Laws and treaties, is not OK" (2017, 126). The authoritarian suppression and the extensive censoring of Slahi's *Guantánamo Diary* corrupt the fundamental principle of freedom of speech. "Writing became my way of fighting the U.S. government's narrative. I considered humanity my jury," Slahi states and asks appropriately: "I wonder what would America's founders think of this censorship?" (2017, xxxix and xlvii). The redaction of his poem in the book demonstrates censorship and animosity toward artistic creativity. "I cannot follow the logic of many of the redactions," Slahi declares, and counters: "Why on earth would the U.S. government censor a poem I wrote for my interrogator as a parody of a well-known literary classic?" (2017, xlvi). In addition to his perspicacious disclosure of fundamental principles of justice, Slahi's diary distinguishes itself in his almost unbelievable capacity to act and think humanely in his tormented situation, in his ability to treat his interrogators as individuals and not stereotypes, and in his magisterial references to Western history and classical and popular culture, for example, America's founders, Shakespeare and *Star Wars*, as much as to Eastern history and classical and popular culture. With the full force of Montaigne's humanist meditation, Swift's sardonic satire, and Kafka's alienation, Slahi battles for fundamental principles of justice in his indisciplinary jail journal.

The silencing and censoring of Slahi's intertextual and indisciplinary diary contributed to the domestication of the outlandish condition of Guantánamo Bay. The placing of the military interrogation center on Cuba ensured an effective distancing of this secret intelligence operation from the vigilant eye and perceptive ear of the public. The incarceration, silencing, and hiding away of *habeas corpus* detainees, such as Slahi, suited the national familiarization of suspects as vile terrorists. This concealment and silencing made sure the inter/national, familiar, and prevailing stereotyping of detainees as terrorists was not disturbed by the individual cases or the questioning of American convention and opinion. The lead editorial in the *New York Daily News* on March 23, 2010, at the time of Slahi's appeal and included in the editor Larry Siems's introduction to Slahi's diary, epitomizes such processes of familiarization: "It is shocking and true: a federal judge has ordered the release of Mohamedou Ould Slahi, one of the top recruiters for the 9/11 attacks—a man once deemed the highest-value detainee in Guantanamo" (2017, 386). The Guantánamo detainees are obviously guilty until proven innocent—and afterward. Detainees possess no *habeas corpus* rights. The trial in court of a detainee amounts to an abomination of justice. The silencing of Guantánamo detainees is mainly broken for condemnation. It takes just literature and rumble and battle to break the silencing and to liberate controversial cases of detention from the logics of familiarization.

In their indisciplinary qualities on the cusp of Kant's philosophy and artistic discourses of justice from *Hamlet* to Derrida's *hauntology*, Heaney's *North* and Slahi's *Guantánamo Diary* offer aesthetic heterotopias in which the rumble of the battle roars against the silencing, the censoring, and the familiarizing of inviolate principles of humanity, imperatives of justice, and conventional ideas of literature. Rancière recognizes and acknowledges the heterotopic aesthetics of such literature. Just literature, such as Heaney and Slahi's, engages profoundly with the ethics of the human condition and the justice of individual human rights in the contexts of law enforcement.

NOTES

1. For Nancy's books on arts and aesthetics, see for example: *The Literary Absolute*, trans. Philip Barnard and Cheryl Lester (Albany: SUNY Press, 1988); *The Muses*, trans. Peggy Kamuf (Stanford: Stanford University Press, 1997); *The Ground of the Image*, trans. Jeff Fort (New York: Fordham University Press, 2005). For Rancière's books, see for example: *The Politics of Aesthetics*, trans. Gabriel Rockhill (London: Continuum, 2004); *The Aesthetic Unconscious*, trans. Debra Keates and James Swenson (Cambridge: Polity Press, 2009); *Dissensus: On Politics and Aesthetics*, trans. Steven Corcoran (London: Continuum, 2010).

2. For Murillo's: *Boys Eating Grapes and Melon*, see *Wikiart*, accessed May 15, 2020: https://www.wikiart.org/en/bartolome-esteban-murillo/two-children-eating-a-melon-and-grapes-1646.

3. For Bocher's *Été 93*, see Institut D'Art Contemporain, accessed May 15, 2020: http://i-ac.eu/fr/collection/443_ete-93-SYLVIE-BLOCHER-1993. For an impression of Parmiggiani's broken glass installations, such as *Sea of Glass* at le Collège de Bernardins in 2008, see Richard Nahem 'Claudio Parmiggiani at Le College des Bernardins' in *Eye Prefer Paris*, accessed May 15, 2020, https://www.ipreferparis.net /2009/01/-claudio-parmiggiani-at-le-college-des-bernardins.html.

4. See Ruben Moi, "'In a ghostly pool of blood/a crumbled phantom hugged the mud': Spectropoetic Presentations of Bloody Sunday and the Crisis of Northern Ireland," in *Crisis and Contemporary Poetry*, eds. Anne Karhio, Seán Crosson and Charles I. Armstrong (Basingstoke and New York: Palgrave Macmillan, 2011), 61–82.

WORKS CITED

Adams, Gerry. 1990. *Cage Eleven*. Dingle: Brandon Book Publishers.

Behan, Brendan. 1958. *Borstal Boy*. London: Hutchinson.

Bloom, Harold. 1994. *The Western Canon*. New York: Harcourt Brace.

Bocher, Sylvie. 1993. *Été 93*. Mixed materials, 210 × 70 × 15 cm. Institut D'Art Contemporain, Villeurbanne. Accessed May 15, 2020. http://i-ac.eu/fr/collection/4 43_ete-93-SYLVIE-BLOCHER-1993.

Bragg, Melvyn. 2006. *Twelve Books That Changed the World*. London: Hodder and Stoughton.

Derrida, Jacques. 1992a. "Before the Law." In *Acts of Literature*, edited by Derek Attridge, 181–221. London and New York: Routledge.

————. 1992b. "Force of Law: 'The Mystical Foundation of Authority.'" In *Deconstruction and the Possibility of Justice*, edited by Drucilla Cornell, et al., 3–68. London and New York: Routledge.

————. 1992c. "The Law of Genre." In *Acts of Literature*, edited by Derek Attridge, 221–253. London and New York: Routledge.

————. 1994. *Spectres of Marx*. Translated by Peggy Kamuf. London and New York: Routledge.

Falkoff, Marc, ed. 2007. *Poems from Guantánamo*. Iowa City: University of Iowa Press.

Fukuyama, Francis. 1992. *The End of History and the Last Man*. Harmondsworth: Penguin.

Heaney, Seamus. 1975. *North*. London: Faber and Faber.

Mitchel, John. 1913 [1854]. *Jail Journal, or, Five Years in British Prisons*. Dublin: M.H. Gill.

Moi, Ruben. 2011. "'In a Ghostly Pool of Blood/A Crumbled Phantom Hugged the Mud:' Spectropoetic Presentations of Bloody Sunday and the Crisis of Northern Ireland." In *Crisis and Contemporary Poetry*, edited by Anne Karhio, Seán Crosson, and Charles I. Armstrong, 61–82. Basingstoke and New York: Palgrave Macmillan.

Moloney, Ed, ed. 2010. *Voices from the Grave*. London: Faber and Faber.

Murillo, Bartolomé Estaban. 1646. *Boys Eating Grapes and Melon*. Oil on canvas, 146 × 104 cm. Alte Pinakothek, Munich. In *Wikiart*. Accessed May 15, 2020. https://www.wikiart.org/en/bartolome-esteban-murillo/two-children-eating-a-melon-and-grapes-1646.

Murray, Yxta Maya. 2015. "Punishment and the Costs of Knowledge." In *Hearing Heaney*, edited by Eugene McNulty and Ciaran Mac Murchaidh, 131–139. Dublin: Four Courts Press.

Nahem, Richard. 2009. "Claudio Parmiggiani at Le College des Bernardins." In *Eye Prefer Paris*. Accessed May 15, 2020. https://www.ipreferparis.net/2009/01/-cl audio-parmiggiani-at-le-college-des-bernardins.html.

Nancy, Jean-Luc. 1988. *The Literary Absolute*. Translated by Philip Barnard and Cheryl Lester. Albany: SUNY Press.

————. 1997. *The Muses*. Translated by Peggy Kamuf. Stanford: Stanford University Press.

————. 2005. *The Ground of the Image*. Translated by Jeff Fort. New York: Fordham University Press.

————. 2010. "Art Today." Translated by Charlotte Mandell. *Journal of Visual Culture* 9(1): 91–99.

Parmiggiani, Claudio. 2008. *Sea of Broken Glass*. Installation for le Collège des Bernardins. Accessed May 15, 2020. https://delicatematter.tumblr.com/post/1 6526097150/claudio-parmiggiani-sea-of-broken-glass-2008.

Rancière, Jacques. 2004. *The Politics of Aesthetics*. Translated by Gabriel Rockhill. London: Continuum.

————. 2009. *The Aesthetic Unconscious*. Translated by Debra Keates and James Swenson. Cambridge: Polity Press.

————. 2010a. *Dissensus: On Politics and Aesthetics*. Translated by Steven Corcoran. London: Continuum.

————. 2010b. "The Aesthetic Heterotopia." *Philosophy Today* 54(Supplement Issue): 15.

Sands, Bobby. 1983. *One Day in My Life*. Cork: Mercier Press.

Slahi, Mohamedou Ould. 2017. *Guantánamo Diary*. Edinburgh: Canongate Books.

The Nobel Prize Organisation. 1995. "The Nobel Prize in Literature in 1995: Seamus Heaney." Accessed May 15, 2020. https://www.nobelprize.org/prizes/literature/1995/summary/.

Wilde, Oscar. 1997 [1898]. *The Ballad of Reading Gaol*. London: Duckworth Publishing.

Chapter 10

Close Reading and Critical Immersion

Timothy Saunders

Over the course of the past one hundred years, close reading has cemented its position as the dominant critical method for analyzing the aesthetic dimension of works of literature in English and for seeking to explain how their formal properties contribute to their capacity to convey valuable cognitive and emotional experiences.[1] Yet throughout its tenure this familiar feature of literary studies has remained anything but familiar, accommodating or meaningful for many school pupils and undergraduate students. The reasons for this are multiple and encompass a variety of social, cultural, educational, technological, and other factors. My focus here, however, will be on the potentially alienating effects that can derive from close reading's basic assumptions about literature as an aesthetic phenomenon: about the role and scope the sense perceptions (*aesthesis*) should play in reading and interpretation, about the aesthetic structure and nature of a literary work, and about how an aesthetic understanding of literature is to be related to an aesthetic experience of literature.

The assumptions any reading style makes about these issues define its aesthetic imaginary. An aesthetic imaginary is a system for organizing the phenomena of the world and rendering them perceptible to interpretation and evaluation; as such, it validates and privileges some ways of being, perceiving, acting, and knowing over others. Any aesthetic imaginary which is brought into being through the process of reading, moreover, is amenable to a re-presentation in topographical terms, as an environment with both a spatial and a temporal dimension. The idea that a work of literature can be imagined as an environment and that reading therefore consists of some kind of interaction with that environment has, after all, enjoyed a long history in Western literature and criticism. It has been argued, too, that we humans may have learned how to read texts in the first place by adapting neurological networks in our brains which our distant ancestors had in their turn evolved to read their physical surroundings.[2]

This projection of reading as an interaction with a spatiotemporal environment is also sustained by the etymologies of verbs of reading in many languages. These notably fluctuate between defining it as either the process or the product of this engagement. The lineage of the English verb "to read," for example, associates it both with the clearing of ground and with the giving of advice, while the Norwegian *å lese* imagines the reader either setting sail or gathering food.[3] It is because of this dual capacity of reading to be characterized as a movement through time and space on the one hand and the acquisition of something concrete on the other that I have adopted the otherwise cumbersome label "a work of literature" to denote the phenomenon to which reading addresses itself throughout. The verb sheltering within this noun allows the "work" of literature to be understood as itself an activity—a real-time producer of perceptions, experiences, and knowledge—as well as their object; it thereby prevents an aesthetic understanding of literature from consisting solely of the comprehension of a previously fixed and fashioned phenomenon and permits it to give shape to that phenomenon in turn.

The two principal modes of understanding I will consider, *comprehending* and *apprehending*, reflect these two alternatives. Both have their etymological roots in the act of "grasping," but they conduct their business with a contrasting sense of the environment in which they operate.[4] In Latin, the verb *compr(eh)endere* also connotes the traveling over, covering, surrounding, and enclosing of a tract of land, or the finding and seizing of property; it therefore suggests that to comprehend a work of literature is to have surveyed it in its entirety, placed a boundary around it, and grasped and understood it as a discrete entity. To apprehend a work, by contrast, is more open-ended. Lacking an orientation toward a specific endpoint in time or space, to apprehend a work of literature is also to grasp it perceptually, but without an expectation of ever coming to perceive its scope or outer boundary in their totality, or to grasp and own them fully. Those reading practices which aim for comprehension duly establish a teleology which in turn awards the two processes of comprehending and apprehending an antithetical character and value. The former is defined and dignified as a progression toward this desirable outcome; the latter is at best relegated to a preliminary stage of the process, one that is necessary for but separable from the achievement of a genuine aesthetic understanding. At worst, it leads to a persistent state of apprehension: a sense that one is continuing to fail to grasp a work's boundaries, possess its enclosure, or enter its comprehensible environment.

This, I would suggest, is how some pupils and students experience close reading. To bring out what is distinctive, and potentially problematic, about close reading, I will compare its aesthetic imaginary with that of immersive reading. Immersive reading is a popular reading style and one with which close reading sometimes seeks to align itself, but it awards the sense perceptions a greater role and scope than close reading, it perceives the nature and structure of the literary work quite differently, and it intertwines understanding more intimately with experience. One of the consequences of this is that whereas close reading delivers its aesthetic understanding of literature through its analysis *of* the aesthetic properties of a work of literature, immersive reading produces its form of aesthetic understanding *by way of* those properties. Whether these two modes of understanding are compatible and whether immersive reading allows for as "critical" a response to literature as close reading, and is thus an appropriate method for literary study, are questions I will address as we continue.

Even though close reading of one kind or another has been practiced for as long as reading itself, the version that prevails today was introduced as a deliberately pedagogical method in the 1920s.[5] Its early proponents, who included the "practical critics" in Britain and the "new critics" in the United States, hoped their techniques would introduce more rigor to what was then the still relatively youthful discipline of English Literature. They believed that scholarship in the subject had hitherto been hamstrung by an unfortunate tendency to look away from the artistry of a text and to indulge in an evasive blend of philology, biography, literary history, and vague emotional impressionism instead.[6] For them, it was the "literary" nature of a work of literature, the manner in which it shapes and presents its material through a range of artistic techniques, and in this way awards its reader a compelling aesthetic experience that makes literature such a worthy subject of study and an enduring human good. Their hope was that close reading would bring a more scientific precision to the analysis of this phenomenon.

A minimal definition of close reading would be that it involves explaining *what* a work of literature says or does through a careful consideration of *how* it says or does those things.[7] The simplicity of its aims and methods was supposed to make close reading an especially accessible and democratic technique (one did not, for instance, need to be widely read or already possess a deep familiarity with literary history). Nonetheless, it was also introduced to protect the reading and study of literature from the allegedly enervating effects of other cultural practices of a "lower" and more "popular" nature; its reputation for promoting a somewhat exclusive conception of literature is therefore not unfounded either.[8] Advocates of close reading have in any case been particularly vexed by the threat they believe new media has posed to the public's ability to read literature more generally, in the form of cheap paperback fiction, advertising, television, and cinema in the early twentieth century, and of digital technology more recently.[9] This in itself suggests that close reading's aesthetic imaginary, along with the nature of the phenomena

it is able (and willing) to perceive and subject to analysis, may be delimited
by its medium.

With this in mind, it is worth pausing to reflect on why digital technology
especially is taken to be so inimical to the conventions of literary analysis. Far
more people today spend far more time reading a screen than a printed page
and this has received much of the blame for the current decline in the reading of imaginative literature.[10] The reason for this is that the screen and the
page have come to be associated with different modes and patterns of sense
perception (*aesthesis*), with differently structured reading environments, and
with making possible different ways of experiencing and understanding that
environment. As far as their modes of aesthesis are concerned, book reading
and digital reading are commonly distinguished by the levels of attention they
command. Close reading requires intense concentration and the stillness of
the printed page provides a receptive environment; the digital screen, with its
backlighting, movement, sounds, interactivity, and capacity to allow many
different pages and programs to remain open and available at once, tends to
induce a state of cognitive overload and distraction instead.

The structure and nature of the reading environment these two media provide differ in important ways too. Words on a page stay fixed in place and
are therefore conventionally read in linear order and understood through their
spatial (as well as syntactic) relations; words on a screen can often be scrolled
up and down, which inhibits the sense their meaning derives from their location in an interconnected but fixed abode. Combined with the distractedness
encouraged by the medium, this has helped acculturate the eye to travel along
different pathways through a digital text than those it pursues through a printed
page. Digital technology acculturates us, too, to extract and grasp individual
words and phrases independently of their immediate and overarching context,
especially when it offers a search function. Sometimes labeled "reading on the
prowl," this reading style is more akin to what scholars have called an "efferent" approach to literature and contrasted with more "aesthetic" modes.[11] In
these and other regards, the comprehensibility of a text is inflected by its medial
and material form. Some of these inflections are cultural, such as our greater
propensity to believe we own a text we have read in a book we have purchased
than a text we have "accessed" on a screen. Yet some are aesthetic. We are
more likely to believe we can comprehend a work we can hold in our hands,
see as a whole, and sense where we are "in" it at any moment, for instance, than
we are likely to believe we can comprehend a work that appears before us in a
succession of segments on the flat and impersonal space of a screen.[12]

Medium, then, is an important shaping influence in close reading's
aesthetic imaginary. Yet close reading is not the only reading style that
has evolved in response to the perceived amenities of the printed page;
immersive reading—that swifter, less self-conscious style in which we are

"gripped," "wrapped up," and "absorbed" in a work—does too. Both styles require the intense attention the printed page affords and both involve the sensation that every word one reads is a part of a greater whole that the sense of looking at a single page or holding a complete book allows. How these two styles perceive and process these affordances, however, differs markedly. In close reading, for instance, one's attention is directed toward the work of literature as a written text; in immersive reading, the aesthetic qualities of that text enhance this attention but project it into the imaginative world around. This in turn reorganizes one's sense of what constitutes the parts of a work and what constitutes its whole. Close reading concerns itself with elucidating how the work's individual formal elements contribute to its effects and meaning overall; in immersive reading, the moment of reading is itself a partial (and passing) moment in the unfolding of a larger universe.

These two alternative perceptions of the nature of the work (written text or imagined world) and its holistic structure (page/book or cosmos) orient the reader differently toward the work as well. Close reading, with its eyes set on a comprehensive and therefore synoptic perception, nudges us toward its outside; immersive reading embraces our more spatially and temporally contingent location inside. The close reader moves cautiously toward their destination, tracking back, circling, and heading off down hidden byways; the immersive reader is faster and hastens ever onward. From all these informing influences emerge close reading's and immersive reading's distinctive aesthetic imaginaries. Treated as conceptual prisms, these imaginaries offer multidimensional models through which we might contrast the role and scope each reading style allows the sense perceptions, the aesthetic form they recognize in the literary work, the positionality they attribute to the reader, the structure and pattern of the pathways the reader follows through and around the work, and the experiential and the epistemological nature of the ground they cover and mark out.

Some advocates of close reading contend that, for all the departures it makes from the immersive style of reading, the two ultimately complement rather than contravene one another. In the preface to their influential textbook, *Understanding Poetry*, for instance, Cleanth Brooks and Robert Penn Warren contend that "the most natural and fruitful way to approach any poem" is

> to begin with as full and innocent an immersion in the poem as possible; to continue by raising inductive questions that lead students to examine the material, the method, and their relations in the poem—that is, to make an appeal to students' "understanding" of the poetic process; then to return students as far as possible to the innocent immersion—but now with a somewhat instructed innocence to make deeper appreciation possible. (1976, ix)

It is telling that the transition from the "full and innocent immersion" a student might have enjoyed prior to conducting an analysis to the "instructed innocence" they are to bring to it afterward registers a change in what an immersive reading will feel like from that point on. This is something to keep in mind. More telling still is the absence of a precise terminology for describing and defining the hybrid reading style that is to transpire: what is "instructed innocence" after all? Behind Brooks and Warren's and several other attempts to discuss the relationship between "analytical" and "non-analytical" styles of reading, there tends to reside a set of assumptions that are highly questionable: that immersive reading provides an aesthetic experience, but one that lacks any real epistemological substance (hence its "innocence"); and that it therein contains a deficiency which close reading is able to fill, like rain permeating and nourishing parched ground. Immersive reading in turn endows the experience of reading literature with the sensation of pleasure, a sensation with which close reading ought to begin and which it ought to sustain.

My own contention would be that aesthetic experience and aesthetic understanding cannot be disentangled and assigned to separate reading practices so neatly in this way. Close reading and immersive reading both bundle up experience and understanding into their own internally coherent ecosystems, but ones that are distinct and may only appear to overlap. This is why those who find immersive reading "natural and fruitful"—like those who seldom read literature at all—can find close reading barren, artificial, and alienating in comparison. To trace the forces that push the two tectonic plates of close reading and immersive reading apart is to tell once more the story of how, for some pupils and students, close reading seems (despite its name) to create a distance between them and the work. It does this by recasting the work as a self-sufficient and potentially mechanized object with only limited scope for movement and by detaching it from the reader's own lived environment and experience. This story has been told several times before, so I will only rehearse its principal details.[13]

The fondness of the practical and new critics for characterizing works of literature as objects is well attested. It is also a logical consequence of their custom of regarding the aesthetic properties of a work as the *object of* (rather than, say, the *vehicle for*) their analysis. This in itself instills a propensity to objectify the work in the process of reading it. But the particular attention close reading pays to that work's formal elements concretizes it still further, since to conceive of literature's aesthetic dimension as both a consequence and a composite of its individual formal elements is to assume, in effect, that a work's literary form consists of an assemblage of individual devices into which it can be broken down and later reassembled. It is to treat rhyme, rhythm, plot, and so on more in the manner of the physical components of a "thing" like a clock than, say, as participants in a living system or force which animates the literary work but cannot be reduced to its parts. It has been argued that aesthetic analysis of any kind tends to concretize its object in this way because of its disciplinary origins in the visual and spatial arts,[14] and one can at any rate see this pull at work particularly in the analysis of the literary form the practical and new critics privileged: poetry. In an article from 1950, for instance, W. K. Wimsatt declared that

> Poetry approximates the intuitive sensuous condition of paint and music not by being less verbal, less characteristic of verbal expression, but actually by being more than usually verbal, by being hyperverbal. Poetry achieves concreteness, particularity, and something like sensuous shape not by irrelevance of local texture, in its meter or in its images . . . but by extra relevance or hyper-relevance, the interrelational density of words taken in their fullest, most inclusive and symbolic character. A verbal composition, through being supercharged with significance, takes on something like the character of a stone statue or a porcelain vase. Through its meaning or meanings the poem *is*. It has an iconic solidity. (1950, 220)

Despite his initial gesture toward music as well as painting, Wimsatt here overlooks the opportunity provided by this analogy to consider literature's temporal as well as its spatial dimension. The solidification of "verbal compositions" into self-sufficient, timeless, and densely compacted objects that results acts, as if by the laws of nature, to push the reader away from literature's borders. Close reading's favored projection of how aesthetic phenomena participate in nature then gives further energy and momentum to this propulsion.[15] For the attribution of "organic unity" to a fully realized and valuable artistic achievement does not, as might be supposed, assign to a work of literature a degree of "organic life"—a capacity to adapt and change in response to evolving local circumstances, like a tree—but the end-state of an already-achieved "organic form," the product of a natural process rather than the process itself, as if it were an abandoned seashell or fallen leaf. This removes the work from the immersion in time that informs the reader's own existence and projects it into a less contingent, more mechanistic universe. It inscribes the work with a teleological structure, too, and casts it as the "necessary" product of a rationalist natural process, since there is no room for anything superfluous in an organic entity.

In all these regards, the charge sheet concludes, close reading separates the work of literature from its reader. Unable to influence necessity or teleology, and instructed by close reading's intellectual method (analysis) and goal (comprehension) to step back far enough so as to achieve a synoptic perception of the work as a whole, the reader can feel coerced into inhabiting a reading environment which is neither that of the work nor one's own. It is a small wonder, then, if close reading has at times been experienced as a mechanical, bodiless, and meaningless activity: a production line of silent texts passing slowly before the serried ranks of intellectually detached and emotionally absent student laborers.

Advocates of close reading have frequently sought to rebuff these charges. They insist they do not perceive a work of literature as a univocal or one-dimensional monolith; rather, their founding belief that *what* a work says or does cannot be extricated from *how* it says or does those things ensures it can never be reduced to a single message or replaced by a paraphrase.[16] Furthermore, the aesthetic properties that make the saying and doing of the work possible, and are the pivots of their aesthetic analysis, are themselves characterized by semantic instability and motion, especially when they include elements such as meter, plot, and repetition, or irony, paradox, and ambiguity.[17] Any work of literature, Brooks and Warren contend, should thus be thought of as a drama, regardless of its actual genre.[18] This is why no two close readings are, can, or should ever aspire to be entirely the same.[19] It is also why, in their projection of the experience of close reading, they emphasize its immersive qualities: it involves our souls and bodies,[20] our fingers and eyes.[21] Literary analysis, Brooks and Warren attest, should give access to "a full-bodied imaginative experience that provides adequate motivation for the responses for which it asks" (1976, 128). It does not expect us to assent to a propositional truth, but to experience that truth and sense it as a "lived" truth (1976, 10).

Even as these same critics prepare to pitch their imagined reader into the experiential environment of immersive reading, however, they often reintroduce some version of organic unity into that environment and thereby extract the reader again from their full-bodied absorption. "The human being is a unity," Brooks and Warren declare (1976, 268), which is questionable in itself, but has in any case been experienced as a somewhat conformist and homogenous kind of unity. In a later article, Brooks dismissed the notion of an "ideal reader" as "a platonic idea, an ideal terminus never actually attainable" (1979, 600). "Nevertheless," he continued, "common sense and an appeal to the dictionary and the text in question would indicate that some of us read more sensitively and intelligently than others," which rather suggests that some kind of ideal destination is still in place, at least as an aspiration or seat of judgment.

This expectation that the close reader should adhere to a shared goal—or, indeed, to any goal at all—distinguishes close reading from the radically and constitutively open-ended nature of immersive reading. It is inscribed, for instance, in the propensity of some of the practical and new critics to perceive in the organic unity of an aesthetically successful literary work both a memory of and a way of recovering an organic community of judgments and values to which they wished their students to subscribe.[22] The scope and extent of this propensity has perhaps been overblown,[23] but it is certainly well attested and points to some of the reasons that close reading has felt instrumental, alienating and unwelcoming to those pupils and students who cannot or will not adopt what they experience to be its mechanistic, teleological, nostalgic, and comfortable worldview.

This goal-oriented conception of the process of experiencing and understanding literature is at any rate difficult to integrate with an immersive style of reading and any attempt to effect such an integration is likely to be either nonsensical or disruptive. In the passage I cited from their preface, for instance, Brooks and Warren indicated that close reading was a means to a more immersive end, but it is not obvious how something as open-ended as immersive reading can serve as an analytical goal in any meaningful way. Were one to switch these terms around and make "understanding" literature the goal of "experiencing" literature—as many critics in practice seem to do—one would bind immersive reading to a teleological logic of experiencing and understanding to which it is alien, and thus at best transform and at worst destroy it in the process. Immersive reading's constitutive practice of apprehending, for one, would be utterly metamorphosed when it is incorporated into the epistemological and evaluative environment of close reading. Having previously been valued in and of itself as a means worth pursuing regardless of any specific ends it might bring about, under the critical jurisdiction of close reading it would now become either "on track," in which case it no longer apprehends but comprehends, or "off track" and thus emblematic of failure. David Greenham's mapping of what happens to the quality of pleasure which immersive reading is commonly assumed to bring to the experience of literature illustrates this clearly. The "spontaneous and intuitive" pleasures one acquires from immersive reading are, he acknowledges, "rich and of significant value" (Greenham 2019, 2). "But what's really valuable for a student of literature," he continues, "is 'analytical pleasure.'" This is both because it helps us appreciate the sources of our intuitive pleasure and because it adds more of its own. Yet in doing all this it destroys the very character of the pleasures of immersive reading—their freedoms, openness, sense of risk, joys of getting lost and finding one's way again, and so on—in pursuit of an all-conquering analysis and comprehension of the work. "One of the most pleasurable parts of re-reading," Greenham states, is that "it leads to a mastery of the text" (Greenham 2019, 91).

The hope that a literary analysis might be able to return us to the conditions of an immersive reading, but with the quality of our experiences and understanding enhanced, ignores the distinctive experiential and epistemological composition of these two reading environments. Brooks and Warren's "instructed innocence" sheds its mists over the fissures between them, but elsewhere they are more open about this divide. In their appendix on metrics, for instance, they acknowledge that their "scansion is not intended to compete with a tape recording. It is necessarily arbitrary in the same sense as an abstract scheme like a map, which does not pretend to be a photograph of the area to which it applies, but which can be very useful—for certain purposes, more useful than a photograph" (1976, 501). These analogs of the map and the tape recording capture effectively the differences between close reading's and immersive reading's perceptions of literary ground: to experience and understand a work of literature in the context of the former is to perceive its *workings* in spatial terms; to experience and understand a work of literature in the context of the latter is to perceive it *working* (i.e., at work)—in the production of a world—in both space and time.

In recognition of this distinction, some scholars have suggested that the study of literature as an aesthetic phenomenon should consist not of an integration of these two styles of reading but an interlocking "double reading or dividing of attention" (Bennett and Royle 2015, 24).[24] This tends to continue to presuppose, however, that whereas immersive reading offers the best form of "aesthetic experience," close reading alone provides "aesthetic understanding." But does this convention really hold? In the remainder of this chapter I would like to explore the possibility that there might be a form of "critical immersion" that is every bit as valuable and even scholarly as the "critical distance" with which close reading is at home: one that can speak where the latter is silent and open up pathways into literary study which the other keeps closed.

To do this requires a return to that single defining feature of close reading which all its manifestations share—even those which refuse to associate it with any kind of aesthetic unity—and which distinguishes it more than anything else from immersive reading: its directing of its attention toward the words on the page rather than any imagined world beyond. For Jane Gallop, for instance, who openly celebrates close reading's capacity to resist totalizing interpretations of complete works, close reading "means looking at what is actually on the page, reading the text itself, rather than some idea 'behind the text.' It means noticing things *in the writing*, things in the writing that stand out" (2010, 12).[25] This, in effect, is what makes close reading critical, in the sense of being rigorous and precise;[26] but since being critical also involves at its root being sensitive to alternative pathways one might follow and alternative perspectives one might adopt, it is worth considering how many of these alternatives close reading shuts down.

I have already outlined how close reading has a tendency to regard a work of literature as concrete rather than fluid and how immersive reading is better attuned (like the tape recording of Brooks and Warren's analogy) to register the temporal as well as the spatial dimension of reading literature. Yet close reading's attentiveness to the words on the page also restricts the role and scope it awards to the sense perceptions. More than anything else, it encourages the reader to comprehend literature as a written (as opposed to, say, a spoken) phenomenon and in this way shrivels both the literary work and the process of reading it to largely silent activities. This deployment of the stillness of the page in a sonic as well as a static sense corresponds with another significant restriction in close reading's aesthetic approach: its assumption that literary reading proceeds almost solely by way of the sense of sight. "Words are not . . . transparent," Greenham asserts, "but are part of what is interesting about a book, a poem or a play. For the close reader, language needs to become opaque in important ways such that visibility is returned to it" (2019, 32). This emphasis on visibility is typical of aesthetic thinking in general and of the terminology it employs in pursuit of its goals; it has also characterized many of the early discussions of the aesthetic imaginary.[27] Whatever the reasons for this might be, one of its results in the case of close reading has been to encourage a more cerebral and disembodied enactment of reading as a knowledge-gathering process.

There is no natural reason why an emphasis on sight should result in an aesthetic outlook that privileges distance over immersion or rational cognition over more experiential or emotional forms of understanding.[28] This, however, has long been the convention in Western culture, in which sight has traditionally been regarded as the most rational of our senses. Aristotle's *Poetics* offers one of the more illustrious examples of the possible consequences of this when, in opting to look at a number of Greek tragedies on the page rather than the stage, Aristotle comes up with the astonishing assertion that drama does not require movement to achieve its goals, since its essence lies elsewhere (1462a11). This perhaps explains why close reading's claim to treat every work of literature as if it were a living drama is not always felt to be exemplified in practice. Their anchorage on the page and frequent subjection to a synoptic gaze circumscribes the sphere of action to which close reading allows its principal aesthetic actors—its ironies and paradoxes, rhymes, rhythms, and plots—and often forces them to interlock like the mechanical parts of a clock.

Many of these philosophical traditions which conceive of aesthetic activity primarily in visual terms and treat works of literature principally as texts,[29] actually take the medium of paper (or papyrus) and the mode of sight so much "as read" that they allow them to fade almost entirely from view. This permits literature's material environment to dissolve into a largely abstract and metaphysical realm instead (of the kind indicated by Brooks and Warren's "map"), while the physical sense of sight becomes at best a stepping-stone toward, or metonym for, insight and acts as a conduit into this abstract literary domain for a disembodied visual vocabulary of "theory" and "speculation." In this aesthetic imaginary, in short, the sense perceptions and process of *aesthesis* are reduced in scope and role alike: to the single sense of sight and a preliminary stage of analysis, in which once the objects of analysis have been apprehended or "grasped" through the eyes, the rational mind takes over and organizes them into a coherent, comprehensible whole.

In immersive reading, by contrast, the sense perceptions are neither single nor univocal, and neither are they restricted to specific stages of the understanding process. They are instead the vehicles by way of which understanding is kept in motion and developed, not so much directed toward but propelled further onward by the aesthetic properties of the literary work into the multidimensional world it projects. Research suggests that the more attentively we read a work of literature in this manner, the more our bodies replicate the physical sensations, emotions, and motor functions we would expect to experience if we were to be propelled into that same situation in real life.[30] There is no reason to assume that this sensorial experience is empty of epistemological content or that the real-time experience of apprehending, thinking, and responding it provides is negated by its lack of a concrete teleological goal. Immersive reading's greater sensitivity toward the temporal and contingent experience of reading literature may well unfold different modes of understanding from those valued by close reading—such as incomprehension, hesitation, boredom, knowing when to embrace being lost or when to withhold evaluation—but these are not deficient forms of knowledge or in any way uncritical by nature.[31]

Immersive reading derives this greater sensitivity to time and contingency from its practice of allowing a greater range of sense perceptions to contribute to the experience of reading literature. Sight is not the only intellectual sense, but touch, taste, smell, and hearing convey their distinctive modes of understanding too, with the result that their combination is likely to produce a multimodal and multifaceted response to a literary work. It is true that close reading also frequently emphasizes the pivotal role sound plays in shaping a work's effect and meaning (in poetry at any rate)[32] and it is notable that whenever Brooks and Warren encourage their readers to "soak" themselves in a work this invariably involves attending to its aural qualities.[33] Nonetheless, the understanding that is to be derived from this attention is seldom permitted to leave its berth in the understanding that resides in the words on the page. "The most important thing to recognize and to work with in your close reading," Greenham asserts, "is that sound, on its own, doesn't mean anything: it is too open" (2019, 102).[34] Yet as Charles Bernstein points out in his introduction to the collection *Close Listening*, to impose this restriction is to lose so much of what a work's aural qualities have to offer. Sound and its semantic orientations *are* open and they cannot be harmonized so readily with what is taken to be the overall meaning of the written words without either greatly reducing their range and resonance or silencing them completely. "When textual elements that are conventionally framed out as nonsemantic are acknowledged as significant," Bernstein continues, "the result is a proliferation of possible frames of interpretation" (1998, 5). This is a proliferation that allows the work to become multimedial, multimodal, and multivalent, especially in performance. "To speak of the poem in performance," Bernstein states in summary,

> is, then, to overthrow the idea of the poem as a fixed, stable, finite linguistic object; it is to deny the poem its self-presence and its unity. Thus, while performance emphasizes the material presence of the poem, and of the performer, it at the same time denies the unitary presence of the poem, which is to say its metaphysical unity. (1998, 9)

Bernstein's emphasis on performance offers a useful counter to the overarching false familiarity that continues to govern literary studies today: the working assumption that literature consists of—and should therefore be read and interpreted as—the words on the page. "Literature" as a category and "English literature" as an academic discipline have enjoyed a much shorter history than the poems, plays, novels, and so on they purport to contain and their emergence at a time when the printed book was dominant and aesthetic philosophy was sectioning off both artistic objects themselves and scholarly ways of knowing and evaluating them from the objects and understandings of everyday experience has tended only to reinforce the limits of that container.[35] To "read" literary works immersively as a multimodal and multidimensional "lived experience" of the kind a private reading as well as a public performance can deliver is thus to liberate them from this enclosure. It is to cease to apprehend them primarily as "verbal icons" that are likely to be experienced in practice as inadequate participants in our current, visually saturated culture and to set in motion the many multifaceted and pleasurable forms of critical thinking and feeling they afford.

Billy Collins's poem "Introduction to Poetry" ([1988] 2006, 58) outlines what such an immersive pedagogy might look like. It invites the student to encounter literary works through the senses of sight, sound, and touch and to bring an inquisitive and explorative attitude to the diverse formations the work might acquire as a result. It seems as good a place as any with which to end, as well as to start.[36]

"Introduction to Poetry"
I ask them to take a poem
and hold it up to the light
like a color slide

or press an ear against its hive.

I say drop a mouse into a poem
and watch him probe his way out,

or walk inside the poem's room
and feel the walls for a light switch.

I want them to waterski
across the surface of a poem
waving at the author's name on the shore.

But all they want to do
is tie the poem to a chair with rope
and torture a confession out of it.

They begin beating it with a hose
to find out what it really means.

NOTES

1. Bennett and Royle (2015, 24), Goring et al. (2010, 19), and Greenham (2019, i) offer three recent restatements of the continuing importance of close reading for literary study. Schaeffer (2013, 271) notes that even radical theoretical approaches to literature tend to retain close reading's analytical methods.

2. Hayles (2010, 69) reviews this hypothesis. Wolf (2016, 147) also alludes to this belief. Her book explores how human literacy evolves and changes in response to alterations in our "environment" more generally.

3. These etymologies are discussed in the *Oxford English Dictionary Online* (www.oed.com) and The Language Council of Norway's *Bokmålsordboka* (http://ordbok.uib.no), respectively. The latter traces *å lese* to the Latin verb *legere* (to gather, collect, or read), but this in turn draws upon the Greek *legein* (to gather, read, sail).

4. See the entries on *apprehendo* and *compre(he)ndo* in the *Oxford Latin Dictionary*.

5. Culler (2010) discusses the range of practices that have been loosely grouped together as "close reading." For histories of close reading in the sense understood by the practical and new critics and their successors, see Davis (2011), Gallop (2000), Greenham (2019, vi–vii), Guillory (2010), Hilliard (2012), and Wellek (1978), among many others.

6. See, among others, Brooks (1979, 593), Davis (2011), Dubois (2003, 4), Hilliard (2012, 9–10), and Wellek (1978, 212–13).

7. For similar definitions, see Bennett and Royle (2015, 24) and Federico (2016, 31).

8. Widdowson (1999, 51–52) contrasts practical criticism's democratic instincts with its elitist aesthetic. See also his consideration of new criticism (56–7).

9. Guillory (2010, 13) discusses I. A. Richards's negative views of new media. Guillory himself suggests in this article that digital technology may be responsible for bringing the era of close reading to a close.

10. The discussion that follows is based primarily upon Baron (2015), Guillory (2010), Hayles (2010), and Wolf (2016). These works also present the evidence for the rise in digital reading and the—possibly corresponding—decline in the reading of imaginative literature.

11. For "reading on the prowl," see Hayles (2010). For "efferent" versus "aesthetic" approaches, see Rosenblatt ([1978] 1994).

12. See Baron (2010, 240 and 19) for these two points, respectively.

13. For this story see, among others, De Man (1983, 20–35), Federico (2016, 31–44), North (2017, 21–55), and Widdowson (1999, 56–59).

14. I. A. Richards made this very point in *Principles of Criticism* ([1926] 2001, 16–17, 149–50).

15. I owe the summary that follows to Fairer (2009, 21–26).

16. See, for example, Brooks and Warren (1976, 270, 311), Dubois (2003), Federico (2016, 39–40, 59, 166–67), and Richards ([1926] 2001, 215).

17. Dubois (2003), Widdowson (1999, 58–59).

18. Brooks and Warren (1976, 69, 93, 112–15).

19. Greenham (2019, 46).

20. Brooks and Warren state that "Poetry, in this as in other ways, insists on the unity of experience: mind and body, idea and emotion" (1976, 542). See also pp. 2, 9, and 49.

21. Bennett and Royle (2015, 24), citing Nietzsche.

22. Richards, for instance, opens *Principles of Literary Criticism* with the statement that "[a] book is a machine to think with, but it need not, therefore, usurp the functions either of the bellows or the locomotive. This book might better be compared to a loom on which it is supposed to re-weave some ravelled parts of our civilization" ([1926] 2001, vii). For the new critics, see Marx (1999).

23. Hilliard (2012, 46–71) argues that F. R. Leavis and the *Scrutiny* movement was less invested in the idea of an organic community than has often been suggested.

24. See also Federico (2016, 9–10) and Rødnes (2014, 12–15).

25. See also Guillory (2010, 11).

26. It is in something like this sense that Goring et al. (2010, 19) define literary "criticism."

27. The approach taken by the majority of the contributors to Johannessen and Ledbetter (2019) provides ample evidence of this.

28. Richards ([1926] 2001, 137) speculates it is because the eye is peculiar among our sense organs in that its receptor, the retina, is a part of the brain and not solely connected to it.

29. This tradition begins at least as early as Plato, Aristotle, and the Neoplatonists and continues through the practical and new critics into the present day.

30. See, for instance, Baron (2015, 160–61) and Wolf (2016, 96–97).

31. See Schaeffer (2013) for a discussion of the value of these forms of under-standing for learning.

32. Brooks (1979, 595) chides another critic for remaining "oblivious to the fact that . . . poems are meant to be intoned rather than merely perceived as characters on a printed page."

33. See, for instance, Brooks and Warren (1976, 36, 88).

34. See also Winters (1951, 436) who insists that even the tone in which one reads a poem should be formal and uniform because "without such a formal tone to unify the poem, the poem becomes merely a loose assortment of details."

35. See Widdowson (1999) for this history.

36. I would like to thank Stephen Dougherty, Juan Christian Pellicer, the Literature Research Group at Volda University College (especially Marit Brekke and Kjetil Myskja) and the other members of this research project for invaluable help with this essay.

WORKS CITED

Baron, Naomi S. 2015. *Words Onscreen: The Fate of Reading in a Digital World.* Oxford: Oxford University Press.

Bennett, Andrew, and Nicholas Royle. 2015. *This Thing Called Literature: Reading, Thinking, Writing.* London: Routledge.

Bernstein, Charles. 1998. "Introduction." In *Close Listening*, edited by Charles Bernstein, 3–28. New York: Oxford University Press.

Brooks, Cleanth. 1979. "The New Criticism." *The Sewanee Review* 87(4): 592–607.

Brooks, Cleanth, and Robert Penn Warren. 1976. *Understanding Poetry.* 4th ed. Fort Worth: Harcourt Brace College Publishers.

Collins, Billy. [1988] 2006. *The Apple That Astonished Paris.* Fayetteville: The University of Arkansas Press.

Culler, Jonathan. 2010. "The Closeness of Close Reading." *ADE Bulletin* 149: 20–25.

Davis, Garrick. 2011. "The Well-Wrought Textbook: The Making of the Mid-Century English Department Classic, *Understanding Poetry.*" *Humanities* 32(4). https://www.neh.gov/humanities/2011/julyaugust/feature/the-well-wrought-textbook.

De Man, Paul. 1983. *Blindness and Insight.* 2nd ed. Minneapolis: University of Minnesota Press.

Dubois, Andrew. 2003. "Close Reading: An Introduction." In *Close Reading: The Reader*, edited by Frank Lentricchia and Andrew Dubois, 1–42. Durham: Duke University Press.

Fairer, David. 2009. *Organising Poetry: The Coleridge Circle, 1790–1798.* Oxford: Oxford University Press.

Federico, Annette. 2016. *Engagements with Close Reading.* London: Routledge.

Gallop, Jane. 2000. "The Ethics of Reading: Close Encounters." *Journal of Curriculum Theorizing* 16(3): 7–17.

Goring, Paul, Jeremy Hawthorn, and Domhnall Mitchell. 2010. *Studying Literature: The Essential Companion.* 2nd ed. London: Bloomsbury Academic.

Greenham, David. 2019. *Close Reading: The Basics.* London: Routledge.

Guillory, John. 2010. "Close Reading: Prologue and Epilogue." *ADE Bulletin* 149: 8–14.

Hayles, N. Katherine. 2010. "How We Read: Close, Hyper, Machine." *ADE Bulletin* 150: 62–79.

Hilliard, Christopher. 2012. *English as a Vocation: The Scrutiny Movement.* Oxford: Oxford University Press.

Johannessen, Lene, and Mark Ledbetter, eds. 2019. *Emerging Aesthetic Imaginaries.* Lanham: Lexington Books.

Marx, Leo. 1999. "Reflections on American Studies, Minnesota, and the 1950s." *American Studies* 40(2): 39–51.

North, Joseph. 2017. *Literary Criticism: A Concise Political History.* Cambridge, MA: Harvard University Press.

Richards, I. A. [1926] 2001. *Principles of Literary Criticism.* 2nd ed. London: Routledge.

Richards, I. A. [1929] 2017. *Practical Criticism: A Study of Literary Judgment.* London: Routledge.

Rødnes, Kari Anne. 2014. "Skjønnlitteratur i klasserommet: Skandinavisk forskning og didaktiske implikasjoner." *Acta Didactica Norge* 8(1): 1–17. https://doi.org/10.5617/adno.1097.

Rosenblatt, Louise M. [1978] 1994. *The Reader, The Text, The Poem: The Transactional Theory of the Literary Work.* Carbondale and Edwardsville: Southern Illinois University Press.

Schaeffer, Jean-Marie. 2013. "Literary Studies and Literary Experience." *New Literary History* 44(2): 267–283. Translated by Kathleen Antonioli.

Wellek, René. 1978. "The New Criticism: Pro and Contra." *Critical Inquiry* 4(4): 611–624.

Widdowson, Peter. 1999. *Literature.* London: Routledge.

Wimsatt, W. K. 1950. "The Domain of Criticism." *The Journal of Aesthetics and Art Criticism* 8(4): 213–220.

Winters, Yvor. 1951. "The Audible Reading of Poetry." *The Hudson Review* 4(3): 433–447.

Wolf, Maryanne. 2016. *Tales of Literacy for the 21st Century.* Oxford: Oxford University Press.

Chapter 11

Indians, Aliens, and Superheroes

Countering Silence and the Invisual in David Mack's Echo: Vision Quest

Sara L. Spurgeon

Silence isn't always quiet, sometimes it's deafening. The invisible isn't always absent, sometimes it's simply disguised, covered over. *Whitewashed.* And sometimes it's hidden in plain sight. Consider this (falsely) familiar-to-the-point-of-cliched plot that has launched a thousand mainstream science fiction narratives. The story begins on an otherwise ordinary day in a small, idyllic community where life is violently disrupted by the landing of alien crafts piloted by murderous beings who view the people they encounter as inferior forms of life, to be killed or enslaved at will. The aliens use a combination of advanced weapons technology and epidemic diseases to carry out a brutal war of extermination in order to gain control of planetary resources. The slaughter is unimaginable. Vast cities and entire nations are wiped from existence. The dead number in the tens of millions. Although local populations fight bravely against hopeless odds, after years of unrelenting warfare and resource extraction, the alien invaders control most of the territory on multiple continents. Desperate survivors now wage a daily battle to keep themselves and their culture alive on a devastated Earth teetering on the brink of environmental collapse.

When we locate that small community in the Caribbean, and note that the three alien ships arrived on October 12, 1492, fiction is revealed as history. But how is it possible that what appears to be wildly speculative sci-fi is actually mundane historical facts obediently memorized by every American six-year-old? How is it possible that obviously imaginary genocide and ecocide are not imaginary at all, but part of our unremarkable, everyday world, literally in front of our faces and yet somehow unseen? And how do the survivors of this nonimaginary apocalypse counter the thundering silence and cloak of invisibility this ubiquitous story throws over the all-too-real?

Ranjan Ghosh argues that "[t]he aesthetic imaginary is built inside the borders of a nation, a culture, a society, a tradition, or an inheritance; but, it disaggregates and reconstructs itself when exposed to the callings and constraints of cross-border epistemic and cultural circulations" (Ghosh 2017, 450). The familiar sci-fi plot above is an example of an aesthetic imaginary built inside the contested borders of settler colonialism that renders silent and invisible both history and the present by engaging in what Anne McClintock calls victor–victim reversal, obsessively retelling a thinly disguised version of settler colonialism's history of alien invasion and genocide so loudly it drowns out all other voices (McClintock 2014, 189). This flipped story of Indians[1] and aliens effectively disappears contemporary native peoples, as it must in order to maintain itself. Patrick Wolfe points out that the role of the native in settler colonialism is to disappear so that the colonizers may inhabit, guilt-free, the lands their ancestors seized, without being forced to see or hear unpleasant reminders of their own status as alien invaders (Wolfe 2006). Hence the weird invisibility, the strange absence and echoing silence of native people in mainstream American literature and culture, even, perhaps *especially*, when that culture is compulsively retelling stories of alien invasion, genocide, and the theft of someone's land. This long tradition of insisting on the disappearance of the natives—*They all died out back in the 1800s, didn't they?*—means contemporary Indigenous authors and artists must constantly reify their very existence, reinserting their lives and identities back into the blank, Indian-shaped absence settler colonialism has carved out for them in the white aesthetic imaginary.

This essay examines the ways Cherokee comics artist and author David Mack dismantles and rebuilds an aesthetic imaginary that has attempted to disappear nations, cultures, societies, and traditions, working from within one of the most mainstream of pop-culture genres—the world of Marvel Comics.[2] He does so, ironically, through a character who exists within both invisibility and silence. Performance artist Maya Lopez, secretly the superhero known as Echo, is one of the few Native American superheroes in mainstream comics, and one of a tiny handful of deaf superheroes. She is even rarer, however, because unlike Marvel's Red Wolf, for example, her creator is also Indigenous.[3] Mack introduced Maya/Echo as a secondary character in his first story for Marvel's Daredevil series in a storyline centering absence in its very title, "Parts of a Hole" (Mack 1998, issue 9). He later gave Maya her own storyline and history, released as a collection of comics in trade paperback in 2004, then reissued in 2010 with additional artwork and materials in hardcover as *Echo: Vision Quest* (Mack 2010). Although this graphic novella is purportedly a superhero's backstory, punching and kicking play a surprisingly small role. Rather, the text is a native-centric memoir about an Indigenous artist's attempts to decolonize the silences and absences settler colonialism has imposed by subversively imagining the Indigenous refusal to disappear as a kind of superhero origin story on the level of the personal, the cultural, and the historical.

In her essay on the importance of what is left unsaid in the 1849 letters of David Wilson, an otherwise anonymous American gold-seeker hoping to strike it rich in California, Lene M. Johannessen utilizes the term "invisual," borrowed from Chiara Brambilla and Holger Potzsch who, she writes, define it as "a cultural frame that hides certain subjectivities and/or lives" (Johannessen 2019, 211). Johannessen points out, for example, the effect of invisuality in Wilson's hand-drawn map of a California creek in which he hopes to find gold. The oddly truncated map, she explains, "takes no notice of features other than those that serve business and profit; what we see is what this one perspective wants us to see" (Johannessen 2019, 210). Wilson's map makes invisual all landscape features not directly connected to the hoped-for presence of gold dust, but also acts, according to Johannessen, as "an eerie analogy for all that is rendered invisible by this history of the West—Native Americans first and foremost. . ." (Johannessen 2019, 210). I argue the map is also an uncanny forerunner of the silencing and disappearing of history made evident in the sci-fi plot sketched out at the beginning of this essay. The result of this long-standing tradition is that Indigenous creators must constantly labor within and around invisuality and silence, working to tell their stories in the spaces in between. As Maya, a trained dancer who feels music as vibrations in her body rather than noises in her ears explains, some stories "don't happen in the sound of the notes but in the silence in between them" (Mack 2010, 6).

Even so, we can see how the act of making natives invisual works as well today as it did in 1849 by looking briefly at its iteration in the 2011 Hollywood blockbuster *Cowboys & Aliens* (Favreau 2011). The provocative title might suggest the film will make visible connections between settler colonial fantasies of innocent white people victimized by alien invaders and the actual historical European invasions of Indigenous nations, but in fact it winds up imagining nothing more than a community of white ranchers and townspeople in 1870's Arizona who are the innocent victims of an invasion by gold-hungry creatures from another world. Once again (we are told loudly and insistently) violent, greedy aliens have arrived in search of gold, but they aren't *us*. Like Wilson's map, the film and the generic plot it appropriates build an aesthetic imaginary structured as a gaping hole, history emptied of history, and the people we might logically expect to find there. In the ringing silence this story creates, there are no Indians, there are only the cowboys (and miners) who have replaced them. Far from being an anomaly, however,

Cowboys & Aliens joins a long line of American texts designed to make us look at Indians while imagining they aren't actually there, training us to see them instead as always/already the "Vanishing Americans," from *The Last of the Mohicans* (Cooper 1826) to James Earl Fraser's often-reproduced sculpture, "The End of the Trail," depicting a limp Dakota warrior slumped hopelessly over the neck of his exhausted horse, caught in a moment of eternal disappearance under the onslaught of modernity and whiteness (Fraser 1915).

READING ABSENCE/VISUALIZING SILENCE

Especially in works like *Vision Quest* in which Mack is both artist and writer, Mack's style of visual storytelling is unusual in mainstream comics. In this text in particular, the arrangement of elements (written words and images) in the space of the page, known as page layout, is relatively loosely bound to each other. In other words, instead of the images functioning mainly to illustrate or support the action or exposition on a given page, the art itself is an equally important driver of the narrative, sometimes moving in obvious conjunction with the story told in the written text, sometimes carrying narrative and illustrative elements the written text does not directly engage. This creates a comic that constructs meaning layer by layer, in which the written word provides only one layer of meaning among many as it builds a narrative defined by its first-person narrator's negotiations of the experience of silence and absence. One accomplishment of this unusual blurring of text and image is to teach readers how to read between, around, and within the mainstream-white-hearing culture's false familiarities with indigeneity *and* deafness as things supposedly defined by lack, loss, or absence.

Jacques Rancière argues that our aesthetic apprehension is shaped by politics, that what we see or apprehend—the visible and the invisible, the audible and the inaudible, the thinkable and the unthinkable—are delimited for us by a combination of politics and aesthetics we inhabit as a kind of "topography of the thinkable" (Rancière 2009, 19). Johannessen posits that texts encountered within such a topography can be excavated by readers in a process "not entirely unlike archaeology . . . from underneath the sedimentations of time" (Johannessen 2019, 211). She argues for employing "'what Pearson and Shanks call 'archeological poetics,' a condition of an archeological method of assemblage, a rigorous attention to things, to the empirical in making connections, following the traces'" (Johannessen 2019, 211). Mack's layered, multimodal comics with their complicated collages of paint, ink, and pencil, photographs, found objects, handwritten notes, and historical documents invite such a reading, one that burrows into a page or image, or conversely bursts forth from it.

While some readers may be disconcerted by the notion of comics as an appropriate medium for Indigenous storytelling, Dean Rader suggest that in fact the form of the graphic narrative or comic is especially well suited for Indigenous narratives which are often complex, multilayered stories about storytelling, about whose voices get heard and whose get silenced, and about how something like indigeneity (or deafness) can problematize or enrich our assumptions. Comics, with their fluid integration of words and images, resonate in multiple ways with both traditional and contemporary forms of Indigenous expression. Rader explains that,

> paying attention to how image and text enter into conversation with each other within the realm of Indian cultural production can serve as a particularly useful lens for looking at the sophisticated manner in which Native art and literature *speaks* to us. . . . One might argue that Native artists and writers see the distinction between *writing* and *image* as a false distinction, that merging image and text is a symbolic act—a unified field of expression [emphasis in original]. (Rader 2014, 300)

Mack's page layouts in *Vision Quest* guide readers through the experiences of silence in an audible world and of indigeneity in settler colonialism in part by inviting readers to question how they experience the page itself, what they see first, the order in which they read/excavate written and visual texts. Unlike more standard comics where we would expect to see rows of panels stacked in tiers that would most commonly be read from left to right and top to bottom (in what is called sequential style), Mack frequently experiments with page layouts that deliberately disrupt expected reading practices. In *Vision Quest*, each page is a coherent, stand-alone work of art, generally without any sense of standard panels or tiers. For example, on the page where readers learn how Maya first begins to understand the ways hearing culture perceives her as Deaf, and the ways white culture perceives her as Native, the background is a wash of deep blue-violet in which figures from Maya's childhood float behind an image of her at the age of perhaps four or five (figure 11.1).

Her face is broken up by what might be called panels, seemingly random boxes formed of rigid white lines, suggesting she is not yet able to generate a coherent or meaningful understanding of her life. Overlaid on that layer are a series of small squares that appear to be cut from a Big Chief writing tablet decorated with the young Maya's childish crayon illustrations. They include an image of Maya's hand holding a pencil and a square that says, "Dad's gun. It's a secret. He takes it to work," and "Mr. Fisk. My dad works with him" (Mack 2010, 9).[4]

One square on this page is empty, and it tumbles down the right side, inviting us into a spiral reading path that circles around the image of the face

Figure 11.1   David Mack, *Echo: Vision Quest*. NY: Marvel Comics (2010, 9).

of Maya's father in the center of the page. His face is also broken and inter-
rupted by the angular white borders of several panels or tiers held by Maya.
Directly below the empty square of Big Chief tablet paper is a washed-out
blue text box that reads: "It was a long time before anyone realized that I was
deaf," and below that, "Very early on in my life I was diagnosed and labeled

by a certain word I had come to recognize on people's lips" (Mack 2010, 9). Six wooden children's alphabet blocks below this statement actually spell out *two* words. One is "RETARD." The other word is contained within the first in what is known as a kangaroo or marsupial word, that is a word that contains within itself another word, often one that can be considered its synonym. The second word within the first is spelled out using the only three blocks with painted letters. This second word defines Maya's racial identity from the point of view of whitestream culture—RED—visually tangling together the threads of Maya's identity in a way that colonizes both her deafness and her indigeneity.

Following a clockwise, spiral reading path, readers next encounter a yellow text box in which words appear upside down at the bottom of the page: "I was sent to a special school where I quickly learned to read the lip movements for: 'No Maya, no!'" (Mack 2010, 9). Being able to mimic the ability to hear spoken speech by reading lips appears to offer Maya a genuine benefit, even if the first words she learns are a negation, but in fact that benefit, like the kangaroo word REtarD, carries within it a second meaning that uncomfortably echoes or colonizes Maya's abilities as a mimic. As Homi Bhabha explains, the purpose of the British system of mission education in India conducted entirely in English was to produce "colonial subjects who would thereby become Anglicized but nonetheless never be English" (Bhabha 1994, 86). Lip reading for Maya (and many in the Deaf community) functions as a potentially troubling form of colonial mimesis, allowing/compelling her to imperfectly mimic a means of communication structured around a sense of personal identity and subject formation anchored in white hearing culture, thus guaranteeing a constant sense of absence, lack, and difference kangarooing along with the ostensible goals of education and assimilation.

Mark Sherry points out that many scholars, such as Harlan Lane, have examined the ways "that hearing people have acted as colonialists because their behaviors have been marked by paternalism, ethnocentrism, negative stereotypes, the artificial creation of dependence, and economic exploitation," creating an aesthetic imaginary of deafness constructed by and for hearing people (Sherry 2007, 26). While being able to understand the spoken speech of hearing people via lip reading is seen as generally advantageous by many, though not all, in the Deaf community, it is also seen by some as patronizing and oppressive, a way of diminishing and colonizing Deaf culture and languages. As Bhabha reminds us, the architect of the British education project in India openly proclaimed its ultimate aim was to produce "an empty form of 'the imitation of English manners which will induce [the colonial subjects] to remain under our protection'" (Bhabha 1994, 86). Similarly, Jennifer Nelson and Bradley Berens argue that the mainstream assumption in hearing culture, that spoken language is inherently superior to sign language and that deaf people should be discouraged from signing and compelled to communicate only via oral speech and lip reading, can function as "linguistic colonialism," a kind of enforced colonial mimesis that defines Deafness as nothing more than a tragic lack that should be "fixed" through mimicry of aurality and orality (Nelson and Berens 2013, 68). The choice to communicate instead using American Sign Language (ASL) is presented in many corners of the Deaf community as a decolonizing form of linguistic sovereignty for Deaf people.

For an Indigenous person in the United States, ASL can itself represent yet another layer of linguistic colonization and enforced mimicry, rendering invisible American Indian Sign Languages (AISL) that for millennia were a commonly understood lingua franca employed by Indigenous nations from the Subarctic to Meso-America, allowing users from different tribal groups to communicate regardless of different spoken languages. Although still used in some parts of Native North America today, specifically in the Northern United States and Canada among communities of Crow, Northern Cheyenne, Lakota, and Blackfoot, Jeffrey Davis explains that "AISL has undergone a dramatic decline since the nineteenth century, due in part to its replacement by English and, in some cases, ASL" (Davis 2017, 1). Mack visually reframes this colonial silencing in the pages in which Maya is first introduced to sign language at a mysterious location known as the Reservation. (The metaphysics of the Reservation are never fully explained, but in a sly reversal of the typical meaning of invisuality, it seems to be a kind of safe-house or hidden Indian nation invisible to white people that can only be found by natives.)

The scene depicts both ASL and AISL, using visual representations of the signs to build layers of meaning on the page from background to middleground to foreground, from the inside out so to speak, with no clearly defined reading path (figure 11.2). If read visually from the background to the foreground, we see a line drawing of the face of a man people on the Reservation call "chief" but who identifies himself as a shaman and storyteller. Many years later he will talk with the adult Maya while wearing jeans and a buttonup shirt, sitting on a chair on the front porch of an ordinary-looking house, but when she first encounters him as a child, he appears as an elderly man with long braids, clad only in a loincloth, in the center of a page washed in shades of sepia, sandstone, and sage-green.[5]

This image of the shaman, evoking a stereotypical nineteenth-century vision of indigeneity, appears to be the furthest back (both on the page and in historical time), but the leaf-shaped speech bubbles proceeding from his mouth and his upraised hands actually lay on top of the middleground, a wide border extending over the left, right, and top of the page, which frames the central images. The intrusion or irruption of these speech bubbles disrupts a sense of strictly separated background, middleground, and foreground, and also begins to disrupt the colonialist fantasy that natives have all been

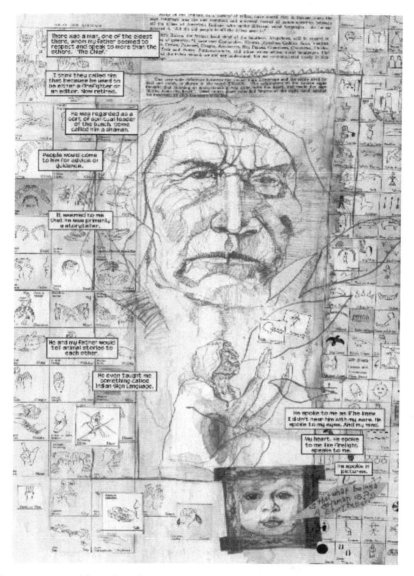

Figure 11.2   David Mack, *Echo: Vision Quest*. NY: Marvel Comics (2010, 12).

successfully confined to the historical past and are absent from modernity. The storyteller's presence at the heart of the page, along with his non-oral forms of speech pushing forcefully out from the past, performs a visual decolonization of the silencing colonial fantasy of the vanished native.

The wide middleground borders framing this page are constructed of visual representations of three forms of non-oral communication. First are the two sign languages, ASL and AISL (in this case, the variation known as Plains Indian Sign Language), depicted in a series of small, stacked boxes running along the left side of the page and straying partly across the bottom. The second form consists of pictographs from various tribal traditions, similarly shown in a series of boxes framing the right side of the page. Scott McCloud points out that pictographs, which represent perhaps the most ancient forms of non-oral storytelling in the Americas, along with Aztec screenfold picture manuscripts and Mayan codices, can all be classified as comics, "juxtaposed pictorial and other images in deliberate sequence, intended to convey information and/or to produce an aesthetic response in the viewer" (McCloud 1994, 9). And finally, three cramped paragraphs of typed text in English are wedged into a narrow box at the top of this page. These paragraphs are excerpts from US Army officer and Indian fighter William P. Clark's 1885 tome, *The Indian Sign Language with Brief Explanatory Notes of the Gestures Taught Deaf-Mutes in our Institutions for their Instruction and a Description of Some of the Peculiar Laws, Customs, Myths, Superstitions, Ways of Living, Code of Peace, and War Signals of our Aborigines*, one of many similar texts purporting to preserve for posterity a record of American Indians before their supposedly inevitable vanishing (Clark 1885).

Scattered among the boxed signs and pictographs on the left and right borders are several boxes picked out in white, contrasting with the muted earth tones of much of the rest of the page. These boxes contain the Plains Indian Sign Language signs for "chief," "deaf," "medicine," and "talk," next to a box with the ASL sign for "hear" (visually negated by a red X slashed through the center), and the pictographs for "medicine man" and "prayer" (Mack 2010, 12). A pencil-drawn line that also frames the shaman storyteller crosses over and through the third paragraph from Clark, partly obscuring the typed words and visually countering that text. The leaf-shaped speech bubbles proceeding from the shaman storyteller's mouth and upraised hands contain the pictographs for "talk (intense)," "inspired," and "prayer" (Mack 2010, 12). In addition to indicating a connection between storytelling and the sacred, these speech bubbles cross over the boundaries formed by the excerpted text from Clark's book, suggesting that despite the sepia-toned air of antiquity on much of this page, Indigenous visual languages leap out from the past and into the present, where they connect directly with Maya.

HISTORY AND THE SUPERHEROIC

Within Rancière's topography of the thinkable, contemporary Native Americans are, for white Americans, an empty, unthinkable gap in modernity. As Johannessen suggests, using a kind of archaeological poetics to follow traces or excavate meaning in what might otherwise be rendered invisual can help us to begin the process of filling in "the gradual accumulation of absences, pauses, gaps and the withheld," allowing us to see the shape of that thing silenced or unseen which, Johannessen continues, "denotes precisely the deferment of its own being: nested in the sedimentary systems of an 'invisual' history" (Johannessen 2019, 207). While Johannessen is not addressing the ways in which settler culture imposes invisuality upon contemporary Native Americans, her ideas offer a useful lens for reading how Mack's narrative shapes itself around the invisual, silenced presence of native peoples, inviting us to follow the traces left behind, underneath, or within the whitewashing story told by settler colonialism.

For Mack, whose maternal uncle was a traditional Cherokee storyteller who encouraged his nephew to try to draw the stories he was hearing, telling native stories that connect history and the present is precisely what allowed native peoples to survive centuries of ethnic cleansing and attempted genocide—imagined here as a superheroic history of what Gerald Vizenor (Anishinaabe) terms survivance, that is, something greater than the mere survival of victimhood, indicating instead a creative, ongoing process of change and transformation rooted in native worldviews (Vizenor 2008, 17). Mack illustrates this in the section of *Vision Quest* narrating Maya's family's experience of the Trail of Tears, presented as an historical reality with very real effects on the lives of his contemporary characters.

Before he dies, Maya's father passes on to her a detailed oral history of her ancestors' journey on the Trail of Tears, the term commonly used to refer to the forced displacement of the majority of the citizens of the Creek, Cherokee, Choctaw, Chickasaw, and Seminole nations from their homes in what is now called the US Southeast. This mass ethnic cleansing was initiated by the Indian Removal Act of 1830 which allowed for the seizure of native-owned farms and houses by white planters, and the forced marches of an estimated 60,000–80,000 people across nine states (Alabama, Arkansas, Georgia, Illinois, Kentucky, Missouri, North Carolina, Oklahoma, and Tennessee) over a distance of nearly 5,000 miles, resulting in tens of thousands of deaths. Maya's father continues his stories well beyond their family's arrival in what is now called Oklahoma, narrating marriages, births, and deaths across multiple tribal nations in the years that follow. Similar to the spiral reading path employed on page 9, the story of the Trail of Tears and Maya's ancestors loops continuously, moving from the present to the past and back again. The pages containing this history are washed in shades of amber and pale gold, highlighted with areas of the deep lavender that is Maya's signature color, connecting her directly to this historical telling. On the first of these pages, three wide panels are stacked atop each other (Mack 2010, 37). The top panel encloses the face of Maya's father. A line drawing of a different, much older man, his long hair in braids, sits below the first panel, while in the bottom panel the face of Maya's father is repeated, creating a sort of visual echo or repeating loop of faces.

In the top panel, a text box from Maya's father reads, "He said much of the story was told to him by his father," indicating he is about to tell her a story he heard from his grandfather, who heard it from his father. He tells Maya, "My grandfather's tribe and many other tribes, the Chickasaws, Choctaws, Cherokee, Muskogee, they were called the Creek Indians but that is only because they lived by the creek and people called them that." "They are really the Muskogee Nation. So them and many more nations . . . they were all rounded up. . ." (Mack 2010, 37). Her father goes on to explain the origins of his and his grandfather's shared name, its roots in Lakota history, the violent mixing of formerly separate Indigenous nations and languages the Euro-American invasion initiates, and the stubborn refusal of Maya's ancestors to quietly vanish into history. This living linkage of generations and stories is suggested visually in the series of layered, line-drawn images cascading down the second page of this section, showing a column of figures on horseback traversing a rough map of the nineteenth-century United States with dashed red lines leading from various parts of the US Southeast to Oklahoma (figure 11.3).

The somber red also outlines the map itself, bleeding over the image of a woman holding a baby in a cradleboard at the bottom of the page, while at the top looms an image of a twenty dollar bill bearing the likeness of President Andrew Jackson, the slave-owning Southerner who authored the Indian Removal Act in order to free Indian farms and towns across the South to be seized by white farmers and plantation owners. Text boxes explain, "It was then that my grandfather's tribe and many other tribes . . . were all rounded up and made to walk all the way to what the government called '*Indian Territory*' [emphasis in original]. Later they called this territory Oklahoma. That's a Choctaw word that means 'red man's land'" (Mack 2010, 38). In Maya's father's careful explanation to his young daughter, readers come to understand that this is a story not just of Maya's family and their personal journey, but of a continuous native refusal to disappear into American history or to forget the lives and stories of those who survived the slow violence of what many Indigenous people refer to as a 500-year apocalypse.

In this section, Mack literally remaps a topography of the thinkable, reifying the powerful cords connecting contemporary New Yorker Maya Lopez, with the voices and faces of supposedly vanished natives. The attempted genocide of native nations meant the tragic loss of many languages and cultural traditions, horrifyingly deliberate attempts to make silent and invisible millions of people, but in this narrative, Indigenous characters resist that loss by remembering and repeating their histories. On the final page of the story of the Trail of Tears the line of stories and ancestors is connected directly to

Figure 11.3   David Mack, *Echo: Vision Quest*. NY: Marvel Comics (2010, 38).

Maya. A series of panels alternating between the face of Maya's father and
Maya's face tumble unevenly down the center. Speech bubbles from Maya's
father explain the devastating effects of ethnic cleansing and the response
of tribal people to the attempted genocide of their families and cultures by
the alien invaders. This is framed rhetorically as the white theft of native

children, languages, and stories, which must be resisted in each generation. In a series of text boxes, Maya's father explains,

> "The children were taken from their parents and forced to go to boarding schools. They were not allowed to speak their native tongues. They were not allowed to tell their own stories. So my grandfather had to remember all of the stories." "My grandfather lost all of his family from his own tribe. But he married someone from another tribe that he met in the new territory and they had my mother. He told all of his stories to my mother." "But soon my mother lost all of her family. So she married someone from another tribe and they had me. And they told all of their stories to me." "And then I came all the way here to the city and I met someone not in any of those tribes." "And now I have you. And I tell all of my stories to you." "All of that traveling and joining parents and grandparents has made you." "You are the future of all their stories." (Mack 2010, 39)

Indigenous survivance is spoken into being, performed repeatedly across generations and languages, remembered and retold in defiant resistance to the settler colonial imperative to disappear and be silent. At this point readers begin to suspect that Maya's vision quest will have little to do with her becoming better at martial arts. Rather, in order to complete her vision quest, Maya must succeed at a truly superheroic task—she must literally embody the future, to ensure that the stories passed on to her are never silenced but are continually reimagined in new iterations of indigeneity. The visual echoes of the faces of Maya's father and grandfathers, all of whom are depicted in the act of storytelling, imply that stories, like faces, are passed down through generations, blurring and changing as they move through time, yet still persisting, their survivance a direct contradiction to the whitestream fantasy of the "Vanishing American" trapped in nineteenth-century stasis at "The End of the Trail."

As an adult, Maya will take up her father's challenge to oppose the silencing of native stories and the attempts to make invisual their superheroic history in *both* her identities: the masked superhero Echo who battles evil alongside the Avengers, and ordinary performance artist Maya Lopez who stages one-woman shows in her gritty New York neighborhood, performing her own plays combining paintings, dance, and sign languages to tell her story and the stories of those who came before her. These performances, which have no spoken words, are aimed at children, but are designed to be understood by any audience, including those in the Deaf community, a group that crosses every tribe and nation. Mack's use of sign languages subverts the mainstream meaning of nonoral communication forms, flipping them from signifiers of *dis*-ability and markers of absence or lack, instead claiming sign languages as markers of communicative *super*-ability and cultural richness, particularly for Native Americans. Deaf culture in the United States refers to this as Deaf-gain, suggesting that when we consider Deaf communities and languages "within the framework of biocultural diversity . . . deafness is not so much defined by a fundamental lack, as in *hearing loss*, but as its opposite, as a means to understand the plenitude of human being, as *Deaf-gain* [emphasis in original]" (Bauman and Murray 2010, 217).

To return us to the opening science fiction plot from the beginning of this essay, what Mack attempts in *Vision Quest* is to reinsert natives into both history and the present by disrupting the white noise of settler colonialism's aesthetic imaginary in which aliens are never Europeans, the people invaded are never Indians, and none of us are allowed to see the historical realities of genocide and ecocide right before our eyes. Rather Maya's indigeneity, like her deafness, offers a ringing retort to the false familiarities of settler colonialism's aesthetic imaginaries that can think nothing but silence and invisuality for native and Deaf communities.

NOTES

1. This essay will alternate between the terms "Indigenous," "native," "Native American," and "Indian." There is at present no universally accepted nomenclature to refer to the Indigenous nations of what is now called the United States, and while Gerald Vizenor, among others, has argued convincingly that the term "Indian" is a colonialist attempt at erasing the history of the Indigenous peoples of the Americas, when I use the term here I intend to deliberately invoke precisely that history of attempted erasure.

2. Mack is best-known within the world of comics for his creator-owned series *Kabuki*, his collaborative work for Marvel Comics on the character Daredevil, and elsewhere for his Emmy-nominated artwork in the opening credits of the Netflix series *Jessica Jones* and his collaborative work on the opening credit art for the 2014 Marvel film *Captain America: The Winter Soldier*.

3. Other Indigenous superheroes, like Arigon Starr's (Kickapoo) eponymous *Super Indian*, published by Native Realities Press, do not enjoy the mainstream visibility of a Marvel offering.

4. Maya's father is killed when she is nine years old and Wilson Fisk, secretly the villain known as Kingpin, becomes her legal guardian. When she is older and Kingpin realizes she has a rare ability to perfectly mimic any action she sees, thus allowing her to study and reproduce ninja-like fighting skills, he will trick Maya into battling his enemies, telling her, for example, that the hero Daredevil was responsible for her father's death, although later she will discover Fisk murdered her father.

5. Like the metaphysics of the Reservation, the fact that the shaman does not seem to age even as he casually shifts other aspects of his appearance is never explained.

WORKS CITED

Bauman, H-Dirsken L., and Joseph J Murray. 2010. "Deaf Studies in the 21st century: 'Deaf-Gain' and the Future of Human Diversity." In *The Oxford Handbook of Deaf Studies, Language, and Education*, Vol. 2, edited by Mark Marshark and Patricia Elizabeth Spencer, 210–225. Oxford: Oxford University Press.

Bhabha, Homi K. 1994. *The Location of Culture*. London: Routledge.

Clark, William P. 1885. *The Indian Sign Language with Brief Explanatory Notes of the Gestures Taught Deaf-Mutes in our Institutions for their Instruction and a Description of Some of the Peculiar Laws, Customs, Myths, Superstitions, Ways of Living, Code of Peace, and War Signals of our Aborigines*. Philadelphia, PA: Hamersly & Co.

Cooper, James Fenimore. 1826. *The Last of the Mohicans: A Narrative of 1757*. Philadelphia: Carey & Lea.

Davis, Jeffrey. 2017. "Native American Signed Languages." *Oxford Handbooks Online*. Oxford: Oxford University Press. doi: 10.1093/oxfordhb/9780199935345.013.42.

Favreau, Jon. 2011. *Cowboys & Aliens*. Los Angeles: Universal Pictures.

Fraser, James Earl. 1915. *The End of the Trail*. Waupun, Wisconsin.

Ghosh, Ranjan. 2017. "Aesthetic Imaginary: Rethinking the 'Comparative.'" *Canadian Review of Comparative Literature* 44(3): 449–467.

Johannessen, Lene. 2019. "Materiality of the Invisible in David Wilson's 'California Letters.'" In *Invisibility in Visual and Material Culture*, edited by Asbjørn Grønstad and Øyvind Vågnes, 201–225. London: Palgrave Macmillan.

Mack, David. 1998. *Daredevil: Parts of a Hole*, # 9–15. New York: Marvel Comics.

———. 2010. *Echo: Vision Quest*. New York: Marvel Comics.

McClintock, Anne. 2014. "Imperial Ghosting and National Tragedy: Revenants from Hiroshima and Indian Country in the War on Terror." *PMLA* 129(4): 819–829.

McCloud, Scott. 1994. *Understanding Comics: The Invisible Art*. New York: Harper Perennial.

Nelson, Jennifer, and Bradley Berens. 1997. "Spoken Daggers, Deaf Ears, and Silent Mouths: Fantasies of Deafness in Early Modern England." In *The Disability Studies Reader*, edited by Lennard J. Davis, 52–74. New York: Routledge.

Rader, Dean. 2014. "Reading the Visual, Seeing the Verbal: Text and Image in Recent American Indian Literature and Art." In *Oxford Handbook of Indigenous American Literature*, edited by James Cox and Daniel Heath Justice, 299–317. Oxford: Oxford University Press.

Rancière, Jacques. 2009. "The Aesthetic Dimension: Aesthetics, Politics, Knowledge." *Critical Inquiry* 36(1): 1–19.

Sherry, Mark. 2007. "(Post)colonising Disability." *Wagadu* 4(3): 23–34.

Vizenor, Gerald. 2008. *Survivance: Narratives of Native Presence*. Lincoln: University of Nebraska Press.

Wolfe, Patrick. 2006. "Settler Colonialism and the Elimination of the Native." *Journal of Genocide Research* 8(4): 387–409.

Chapter 12

Listening to Ourselves

The Musician as Listener in Rafi Zabor's The Bear Comes Home

Zoltan Varga

In the beginning of his *Listening*, Jean-Luc Nancy raises the question, "Is listening something of which philosophy is capable" (2007, 1)? Contrasting the two French verbs, *entendre* (to hear, to understand) and *écouter* (to listen), he differentiates between two types of listening: one that aims at making sense and one that senses resonance. Dehierarchizing the intelligible and the sensible, or *logos* and *aesthesis*, Nancy proposes that through listening, the subject makes sense of itself not as an objectified *presence* to be understood, something that "is always already given," (21) but as tension, a resonance, a possibility.

If we ask in turn: "Is listening something of which novels are capable?" further questions emerge about listening, reading, and meaning-making. Much of the research attempting to answer such questions has focused on novels from the turn of the nineteenth and twentieth centuries, a period that is especially rich in experimentation with applying musical ideas and techniques to narrative fiction. While modernist *musical fiction* is often highly experimental in terms of narrative technique, it tends to retain the aesthetic conceptions of music established by Romanticism. Due to this, the intermedial musical experience often remains somewhat limited: music may engender new forms, structures, or textures, yet not necessarily explore new ways of listening.

However, musical production and reception changed significantly throughout the twentieth century, and novels rooted in new traditions might have learned to *listen* in a more Nancean sense. This essay attempts to unfold how music is used to develop characters and their narrative trajectories in a novel that draws on a nonclassical musical form, Rafi Zabor's jazz novel *The Bear Comes Home*.

Why exactly jazz? To answer this question, let us step back and have a look at musical meaning-making first. Meaning in music is created by the interplay of the centrifugal and centripetal forces in musical signification. The reason for this, as Kofi Agawu points out, is that "there cannot be a single definition for 'sign' in music, for each work's dimensions display a unique mode of signification" (2009, 16). Each work, then, becomes a specific semiotic field with its specific logic of meaning-making, while at the same time also being interconnected with other such fields, the works in the musical repertoire. Lawrence Kramer addresses these centripetal and centrifugal forces in relation to autonomy and contingency. In his *Musical Meaning* he draws a parallel between this twofold nature of musical meaning-making and the constitution of human subjectivity: music, via its concurrent introversive and extroversive semiosis, enacts both our "absolute self-presence" and our "contingent" social constructedness (2002, 4). Further, he writes,

> [M]usic may act as a *cultural trope for the self*, the subject as self-moved agency that remains when all of its attributes and experiences have been subtracted. Musical affect, expression, and association become pure forms of self-apprehension; music is known by and valued for its "transcendence" of any specific meanings ascribed to it; identity seeks to become substance in music, even though music, *being more event than substance*, continually eludes this desire in the act of granting it. (ibid., emphasis added)

Music thus dramatizes the division of the subject, and music in fiction arguably introduces the nonrepresentational and the *a*rational aspects of the self into the textual. However, it also reveals that there is no substance, no preexisting self. I will focus here on the bodily embeddedness of music as event, and jazz offers good grounds for that with its heightened focus on negating boundaries.

While it would be futile to attempt to define jazz within the limits of these pages (or at all for that matter), one of its main characteristics from the 1960s on has been defying formal, artistic, and technical limitations. This opening up to limitless expression also meant that the limits were set by the limitations of the body. The human body had been the source and the measure of music until the technological developments of the twentieth century. As Vijay Iyer observes, "Music and humanity have arisen in tandem, the former out of the bodily activity of the latter, and so music necessarily bears rhythmic traces of our embodiment: pulse, phrase, gesture, ornament" (2008, 287). Pushing the musical limits to the bounds of the possibilities of the human body is what jazz explores in some of its forms, such as free jazz.

The embodiment of music probably represents one of the reasons for imagining a consciousness, a voice in instrumental music (an example of this is that the lead instrument is often referred to as the *voice* in an instrumental piece). Also, the bodily involvement in music is clearly a reason for music's affinity with sensuality and sexuality, which remains in place even with the technological disembodiment of music in the twentieth century. To return to Iyer:

> Pulse-heavy electronic dance music often makes sonic references to the stomping of feet and to sexually suggestive slapping of skin. It is indeed rather telling that today, the most widespread uses of electronic music are in contexts meant for dance; the least humanly embodied music is ironically that which is *most* dependent on our physical engagement with it. (ibid. 287)

While with techno, or EDM, music goes beyond human possibilities due to its source, jazz presents an in-between phase, where the limits are reached and the embodiment of music culminates in the self-reflection of the performer: a self-sensing, a listening. The following reading of *The Bear Comes Home* investigates musical embodiment in an intermedial perspective, and further complicates the notion of music as a cultural trope of the self.

THE BEAR COMES HOME

Zabor's novel is about a budding alto-saxophonist, his struggles to make it in the music world, and develop his own style (inspired by Coltrane and Coleman). Fictional and real places, made-up figures and real musicians merge in this work, adding to its atmosphere characterized by a real immersion into the jazz universe. As a former jazz critic and drummer, Zabor not only provides an inside look into the New York jazz scene and the underworld of rural music club life, but also gives a knowledgeable account of the development of jazz—juxtaposed with the development of a personal musical style that the Bear works on throughout the story. An important thing to mention: the protagonist is a bear, a talking bear, to be more precise. And he meets and plays with real life musicians like Lester Bowie, Steve McCall, Arthur Blythe, Roscoe Mitchell, and Ornette Coleman, among others.

The Bear is witty, sensitive, original, and empathic, yet somewhat eccentric, which is quite understandable considering his circumstances. He decides to give up his life as a street entertainer with his friend/owner, Jones, and enter the jazz arena. An impromptu appearance at the Tin Palace brings him recognition among some jazz musicians, but also draws the attention of the authorities, who take the Bear away at his second appearance (and first real concert) at the jazz joint. The concert, however, is recorded, and an album is released while the Bear is being locked up in prison. The success of the record enables him to sign with a major label and earns him a contract for a studio album and a promotional tour. Once out of jail, the Bear falls in love with Iris, a medical researcher, and the reader is provided with more technical details of ursine-human sex than probably ever thought possible. Neither the music nor the sex scenes prove off-key and of course neither of those are simply present for their own sake.

Music and sexuality are equally important to the Bear's bearness in the novel. In his existential quest, the Bear sees these two as paths to explore his spirituality, and he has immense capacities in both. While the bear factor cannot be fully nailed down (a common feature shared by a branch of animal characters in fiction, whether they are giant insects or humpback whales), three aspects seem relevant to its significance: Although the Bear is an existential (anti)hero, and he makes explicit allusions to his Gregor Samsa-esque circumstances (which are not due to his being a bear, but rather being an individual embedded in this world), his being a bear is actually quite anti-Samsa-esque: despite the overabundance of references to Kafka's *Metamorphosis* in the story, the Bear was born as a bear. He has always been a talking bear.

The second aspect is that this individual is an artist, and his bearness illustrates the outsider position of the artist in society. Especially, being a jazz musician guarantees his monstrosity as an inhabitant of a nightlife-underworld governed by the seemingly ruleless rules of spontaneity, improvisation, and syncopation. This ursine saxophone player carries the traditional connotation of the jazz/blues musician's *dealing with the devil*.[1] The Bear of course does not deal with either devil or god, only with Beauty. He is strictly a Platonist—"an ideal society would be ruled by saxophone-playing bear kings," he claims—and his metaphysical, musical quest gets clearly expressed: "Right down to it we're in love with beauty," the Bear proclaims at the end of an interview (Zabor 1998, 180). Plato's *Symposium* and the path to absolute beauty provides the program for the Bear's musical endeavors, yet the Platonic quest for beauty will turn out to be more complicated than at first sight.

The third aspect of bearness is related to metaphysics as well. Depicting the male and the female as different species takes their supposed polarity to the extreme. This polarization is related to the Platonic disposition that provides the ground for Zabor's dialectics, and sex and music both get probed as possible bridges between the sensuous and the spiritual throughout the novel. This is where music at first seems to overcome sex: while both are sensuous, music is perceived also as spiritual. The Bear manages to break through the metaphysical ceiling toward the end of the novel in a tour-de-force Coltranian solo—suggestively played at the opening of the Bridge, a jazz joint inside the body of the Brooklyn Bridge. However, what happens at the Bridge is not the reconciliation of the physical and the transcendent, but the recognition that the quest for beauty itself presupposes a static, preexisting self. I will return to this scene in detail after retracing the Bear's steps getting there.

Early on in his life, the Bear realizes that "if you do anything the least bit unusual or interesting in this world, people will figure out a way to catch and kill you for it" (ibid. 110). Yet the "portrait of the artist as a hunted animal" (68) turns out to be more of a self-hunt, due to the Bear's self-disgust related to his monstrosity. Peculiarly though, this monstrosity lies not as much in being a talking bear, but in his musicality: "this powerful equipage that he had always prized above all his other contents: that fine instrumentality that played itself into intelligible shapes of sound and knew what lay ahead uncharted into the sea of time, and could fashion forms that lived their way into the obscurities of that future and thereby lit them: it seemed hideous to him now" (114).

The Bear starts to turn inward in the light of this realization with self-disgust, "dropping like a stone down a well of himself in the dark: not a sound: hadn't reached water yet . . . all his previous solitudes had been masks that this deeper one had worn" (ibid.). So, his real imprisonment derives from himself, or the lack of finding himself, not from the authorities. And it is his music that catalyzes this crisis, imprisoning him into his own emptiness. "His beautiful talent was an ugly thing at heart, and if it came across authentic beauty in its march, it soiled whatever trace was resident there with its own smudge, trod the music into the mud and marched on hungry and destructive as before" (115). What actually happens to him is that as a sensitive artist, he feels that he is not ready. He feels he has given all of himself in his very first concert already and cannot but keep on repeating himself, to "imitate himself" (116), as he realizes that musically he is not where he wants to be; he knows what he should sound like, but there is no essence in his playing, no authenticity, he feels he is faking it.

Billy Hart, a more experienced musician, tells him: "The *music's* like that, B. Whatever level you get to, there's always something further to reach for, something you haven't seen and didn't know was there. Once you stop feeling that, you're finished, basically" (50). And the Bear sets out to learn and learn, trying to establish an originality, creating his musical self. As Hart later adds, "It was only by this kind of inner substance that you could endure decades of unbelievable bullshit and still have something left to play" (355). For the Bear, the battle is that of form versus content. He needs more practice and experience to reconcile the two, and practically turns into a practiceoholic, but also, and perhaps more importantly, he goes on a tour with a band, learning to listen to others first, to be able to hear himself.

So, are we stuck then with the old question of an inherent essence or self? Not exactly. The Bear sets out to create a self *through* his music. What he wants is to establish a voice that makes him feel authentic. He wants to get away from the splitting experience of *self-expression*, through which he relates to himself as re-presentation, and find *self-sameness* in music instead. His problem as he expresses it is "not the intensity, but self-division. If I can't play like a whole spirit again, I'll give up. I didn't come to music in order to find some new way of being all fucked up. I don't think you should have to cripple yourself into beauty" (194).

The last sentence shows that the Bear's Platonist credo, *Right down to it we're in love with beauty*, has become highly complicated by this point yet it may still serve as a guide, as it distils the Bear's struggles to its key elements: we (I), love, and beauty. Having to cripple oneself into beauty presupposes that both self and beauty are fixed, rigid forms. The Bear needs to move away from this static interpretation, and love, that is, the *eros* of Plato's *Symposium* (more specifically the *eros* of Diotima's teaching) is probably the best companion to achieve this. Diotima's *eros* starts with the physical and aims toward a wider sense of love. Progress of any kind is rooted in *eros* and leads through it. As Luce Irigaray points out, *eros* is "both the guide and the way, above all a mediator" (1994, 182). *Eros* leads one to knowledge both in the practical and the metaphysical sense. But it does even more: this already existing bridge, or the intermediary, that comes between the two concepts keeps them in the state of constant renewal. As Irigaray further explains, "[t]he mediator is never abolished in an infallible knowledge. Everything is always in movement, in becoming. And the mediator of everything is, among other things, or exemplarily, love. Never completed, always evolving" (ibid.). It is his *erotic* desire that drives the Bear forward in his musicality.

And eventually he does find the right voice—giving himself up in music creates a new sense of wholeness. He begins to feel that "he and not the saxophone was the instrument, and that all the work he put in was no more than making sure the keys worked smoothly, the pads didn't stick and the reed wasn't thick with slobber. . . .when the right moment came, it was time to step aside and be played upon" (358). The Bear is becoming the *forma formans*—that is the forming form—in the music the moment he becomes a vehicle for that music, to use violin soloist and semiotician Naomi Cumming's terminology, his *sonic self* is reached, he has become a real soloist, who brings music to "life" (2000, 27).

The Bear's finding his voice is described in very practical terms, listing the keys, the pads, and the reed, while also calling attention to the fact that musical sounds are generated by the performer's bodily activity (slobber). The beauty the Bear is after is dependent on the embodiment of music. As Cumming formulates it, "[c]reating a 'beautiful tone,' through a well-balanced physical adjustment to the instrument, is central to creating the impression of musical personality" (ibid. 23). This personality, the *sonic self* is not a static, preexisting self; rather it is produced by the physical actions of the performer. It is "a creation that comes into being with sound" (ibid.).

The soloist, however, is caught in a double bind of risk-taking in the attempt to bring the musical work "alive": on one side, there is the "fear of losing credibility by taking risks" during the performance and, on the other side, the performance "does not have 'life' if the performer fails to risk herself for it" (ibid. 41). The questions Cumming raises at this point in her argument are acutely relevant for the Bear's dilemma as a performer: "*Where is the work, except in the performance? What is it really that you are losing when you take the risk of an [performative] act whose outcome is uncertain?* and *Can you really be losing your "self" if your selfhood is formed in activity?*" (41–2, italics original).

The Bear's issues with monstrosity, authenticity, and self-division point in the direction that via his extensive practice, he may not only acquire mastery on his instrument, but also unlearn his (static) self, or rather his conception of the self as static. It is not a bridge that he needs to reconcile contrasting aspects of his subjectivity, but a radical move from *logos* to *aesthesis*. To return to Nancy, the Bear needs to listen, to become a listening subject, which is "always yet to come, spaced, traversed, and called by itself, sounded by itself." (2007, 21). As the sonorous event is *contemporaneous* with listening, the listener "enter[s] that spatiality" which "opens up in me as well as around me, and from me as well as toward me: it opens me inside me as well as outside," and these multiple openings allow for the *self* to occur, which senses itself "at the same time outside and inside" (ibid. 14). As the musician is both the initiator of the sonorous event and its listener, outside and inside carry extra layers of complexity. As the sonic self emerges through the musical event, the musician as listener simultaneously realizes and senses itself during the performance.

The Bear's characterization in the novel through his musical journey creates a correspondence between the developments in his artistic and personal life. His musical dilemmas and choices affect those around him and the risks and losses described by Cumming become especially tangible for those who are closest to him, Iris and Jones. The Bear has to sort his life out through music; however, his musical steps spark transformations in these two other characters, which are then realized in different degrees. Both characters embark on a quest for their self, which is triggered by their relationship with the Bear: "I want a self," says Iris, and not long after her Jones claims to "need more of a self" (Zabor 1998, 269; 303).

The Bear's relationship with Jones, his best and oldest friend, fades in the wake of his musical career. Taking care of the Bear does not serve as an escape route any longer: with the Bear's professional success he realizes that instead of solving someone else's problems, eventually he has to think about

and act for himself. Their friendship, seemingly lost at first, transforms and
after the initial break reshapes itself on more equal terms. Similarly, the Bear
is losing Iris, who quit her job and gave up her New York apartment to move
in with him upstate New York. After taking back her daughters from her ex-
husband, she becomes overly protective of them and excludes the Bear from
their life. Of course, it does not help that the daughters, not as accepting as
the couple's jazz musician friends, are not too happy about a bear sleeping
with their mother either. It seems clear though that it is the Bear himself who
wakes those around him to their situations; he acts as an agent to induce their
change. Their lives are a mess already before meeting him, but through their
contact with the Bear they realize that they want a change and they also begin
to see what that change entails.

As the relationship between Iris and the Bear evolves, at one point, he feels
that their sexual encounters carry an almost divine element. His attempts,
however, to share the metaphysical as their joint experience fail. Instead of
bringing them closer, the improvement of sex actually distances them in their
communication. "[H]ow could they be so intimate and he still feel that she
was drifting away from him," (262) wonders the Bear. Then, a little later, he
thinks about it in more musical terms: "the moves were better, the sequences
more finely worked, the transitions smoother, the view more gratifying . . .
and yet . . . what bothered him?" (267). When their relationship gets overtly
strained, Iris, in her desperation, also tries to communicate with him through
their bodily contact, but to no avail. At certain points of their relationship they
each think that carnal communication would take them further than linguistic,
yet it is music that eventually opens the way for a new possibility between
them, not because it carries a superior knowledge, but as it enables the Bear
to move away from a teleological *eros* toward an *eros* that resonates, that is,
an *eros* that listens.

The recognition for the Bear arrives in a solo that lasts more than 30 minutes, and which Zabor describes in as many as fifteen pages (!). To bring
all the *ero*tic threads together, the solo is of course "the B-flat-minor-blues
that formed the third part of John Coltrane's *A Love Supreme*" (445). Zabor
reconfirms his musical proficiency in this *ekphrastic* marathon, yet the musical terms give more and more space to the Bear's visions, as he does become
the instrument he wanted to be: music starts flowing *through* him. The origin
of his musical transubstantiation is his actual love, Iris, or rather her lack (the
definition of *eros*), and the ladder toward beauty is music. Finally, the pains-
taking toils of the saxophone-playing bear king come to fruition: the Bear
dissolves in the Dionysiac:

> . . . not just outside time and space but blown clean out of individuation too. . . .
> Notes were nothing. Each note was itself infinite. It made perfect sense.

> Had the Bear still existed he would have laughed beyond being drunk on beauty and drowned in light. Had the Bear ever existed he would have plunged into these seas and tried out his stroke in them. Were he not himself these seas, and these seas him. It was so simple it was inconceivable not to have seen it all those blinkered bearshaped years. (454–5)

Even the ruleless rules are broken; something that only jazz allows for. That is how the Bear knows he has come home. At the climax of his spiritual path, *time and space* collapses for the Bear as he steps out of the realm of *individuation.* Up to that moment, he has never been where he wanted to be either in his music or in his own body. His self-realization occurs through losing himself and becoming an instrument—instead of a self. The moment comes when he dissolves as an *individuum* and creates his *sonic self.* And we could stop here, but then, stepping back from the microphone the Bear starts listening to his band:

> It took him longer than the audience to recognize what he was doing, took a long minute for him to realize, as one of Hatwell's choruses rose to a hint of climax in its middle but then fell back into its own smooth stride, that he was doing something he would have sworn he would never do in front of an audience again on this side of the sky or any other: a shuttle of hips, a dip of shoulder, the feel of boards beneath his feet, the happiness of the wood. It was hard to believe it but he liked the way it went down. He was compelled to admit how pleasant and inevitable and unconflicted it seemed. There were an odd few hundred reasons for him to object, but he submitted his essential substance to none of them. The rules were blown.
> The Bear did what he felt like doing.
> You know what he did. He danced. (456)

And here is where something really interesting happens: The Bear's sonic self not only performs the twofold meaning-making of his subjectivity via his masterful solo, but he also reaches a bodily self-awareness, self-sameness, or self-presence through music. Music entering his body creates a sensuous experience, he is able to feel, sense, and touch himself.

The problem with the Platonic ascent to absolute beauty remains—whether one ascribes the teaching to the philosopher or to Diotima—what is left behind: the body. Nancy's essay "On the Soul" offers a possible way to address this issue and to read this scene. While talking of the soul, Nancy is concerned with the body and recasts the soul as "the experience of the body" (2008, 134). He points at how the body only exists as self-sensing, self-touching: "[t]he soul is the presence of the body," and the body in turn is "the inside, which senses it is outside" (ibid. 128, 131). The body's existence, *ex-* as "out" + *sistence* as "a stance," happens as the "body accedes to itself as outside" (ibid. 128).

The *self-same* and the *contingent* aspects of human subjectivity, and music as a cultural trope for the self, as explained in the beginning, need to be rethought through the body. Following Nancy, we cannot talk about the self without talking about the body. This has repercussions on the *subject* and also on *music* if we turn the analogy around. Both come into being through an opening to the outside, and through the body sensing itself *at the same time outside and inside*. We cannot talk about music without talking about the body.

The Bear's recognition of his involuntary dance returns him into his body, his *extension* and *exposition*, and therefore his self. "The rules are being blown" on several levels: the rules of music as played by the band in their free jazz performance, the Bear's own rule about not dancing in public, and the rules of the Platonic ascent to absolute beauty, as the bodily is *not* left behind. On the contrary, the full scope of beauty is reached when *the body accedes to itself as outside*. Nancy reminds us that music, and the musicalization of fiction, cannot leave the body behind. It starts and ends with the body *in relation to itself*. As in the moment of the Bear's self-realization, "the music moved him. That is to say, he moved" (Zabor 1998, 456).

It is important to state again that it is a return. The Bear's rule not to dance in public is a result of his previous role as a street performer, a dancing bear. Returning into his body through self-sensing, self-touching marks the Bear's recognition of the body as the very *access to self*. As Kodvo Eshun observes, "Sonically speaking, the posthuman era is not one of disembodiment but the exact reverse: it's a hyperembodiment" (2012, 452). Changes in the production and reception of music also have certain ramifications in music as used in narrative fiction. But reaching the limits of the body in music and moving beyond them does not leave the body behind, rather, it refocuses the attention on the body and reverberates music as a cultural trope for the self.

NOTE

1. The virtuoso's Faustian pact with the devil has been the topic of several legends including those of the nineteenth-century violinist Niccolò Paganini and the Delta blues guitarist and singer Robert Johnson. While it was the violin that was traditionally associated with the devil for centuries, the saxophone also maintained a diabolic reputation throughout the twentieth century. (See: Michael Segell's *The Devil's Horn: The Story of the Saxophone, from Noisy Novelty to King of Cool* (New York: Farrar, Straus and Giroux, 2005).)

WORKS CITED

Agawu, Kofi. 2009. *Music as Discourse: Semiotic Adventures in Romantic Music.* New York: Oxford University Press.

Cumming, Naomi. 2000. *The Sonic Self.* Bloomington: Indiana University Press.

Eshun, Kodwo. 2012. "Operating System for the Redesign of Sonic Reality." In *The Sound Studies Reader*, edited by Jonathan Sterne, 449–453. New York: Routledge.

Irigaray, Luce. 1994. "Sorcerer Love: A Reading of Plato's Symposium, Diotima's Speech." Translated by Eleanor H. Kuykendall. In *Re-Reading the Canon: Feminist Interpretations of Plato*, edited by Nancy Tuana, 181–195. University Park, PA: The Pennsylvania State University Press.

Iyer, Vijay. 2008. "On Improvisation, Temporality, and Embodied Experience." In *Sound Unbound: Sampling Digital Music and Culture*, edited by Paul D. Miller, 273–292. Cambridge, MA: MIT Press.

Kramer, Lawrence. 2002. *Musical Meaning: Toward a Critical History.* Berkley and Los Angeles: University of California Press.

Nancy, Jean-Luc. 2007. *Listening.* New York: Fordham University Press.

Nancy, Jean-Luc. 2008. "On the Soul." In *Corpus*, 122–136. New York: Fordham University Press.

Zabor, Rafi. 1998. *The Bear Comes Home.* New York: W. W. Norton.

Chapter 13

Harlem to World and World to Harlem

Revisiting the Transnational Negotiations of Harlem Renaissance Narratives

Nahum Welang

After World War I (1914–1918), the United States underwent a series of profound transformations such as the awakening of an emerging African American consciousness. Black troops, who had fought abroad "to keep the world safe for democracy" (Library of Congress, n.d.), returned home and were confronted by their status as second-class citizens. Emboldened by the agency they had access to during the war, some of them began to demand for civil rights and active participation in the American democratic project (Greene 2019, 2). Around the same time, a great exodus was happening: thousands of African Americans were migrating from the rural South to the industrialized North with lofty hopes of economic prosperity and upward social mobility (Martin 2019, 25). There was also a remarkable rise in the number of black graduates "from black colleges in the South and North" (Stewart and Anderson 2007, 302) and set against this backdrop was the ideological tension between Booker T. Washington and W. E. B. Du Bois. Prior to World War I, Washington was arguably the most famous black person in the United States (Healey 2011, 190). As an influential orator, educator, and writer, he was at the forefront of black political rhetoric and founded "Tuskegee Institute, a college in Alabama dedicated to educating African Americans" (Healey 2011, 190). Born into slavery and raised in the Jim Crow South, he had an acute awareness of the systemic nature of racism and thus adopted what he believed was a more pragmatic approach to civil rights activism. Demanding immediate economic and political equality for African Americans, Washington speculated, would trigger an immense backlash from Southern whites, a backlash with the potential to sabotage the progress he had already made. Hence, "his public advice to African Americans in the South was to be patient, to accommodate the Jim Crow system for the time being, to raise their levels of education and job skills, and to take full advantage of whatever opportunities became available" (Healy 2011, 190). Although he touted this "accommodationist" policy in public, he worked with policy makers and politicians in private to "end discrimination and implement full racial integration and equality" (Healey 2011, 190).

Washington's rhetorical authority was challenged and later subverted by a W. E. B. Du Bois, a young African American intellectual from the North who had studied in some of the world's most elite universities like Harvard (Morrison and Shade 2010, 255). In 1910, the National Association for the Advancement of Colored People hired Du Bois, now an already accomplished writer and sociologist, and he used *The Crisis*, the organization's periodical, to attack Washington's accommodationist policies and the Jim Crow South (Morrison and Shade 2010, 255). Du Bois argued that economic and social caste systems like Jim Crow cannot be "accommodated" because they lay the groundwork for racial oppression and inequality and hinder the United States from moving forward (Morrison and Shade 2010, 255).

This ideological debate between Washington and Du Bois and the other aforementioned factors, such as the emboldened agency of black troops and the great exodus, created a conducive environment for the birth of the Harlem Renaissance, an unprecedented cultural and literary explosion of African American artistry in the 1920s. Centered in Harlem, New York, the movement has been described as "the first creative awakening of Negro artists, as a group, in America. For the first time in American cultural history, African Americans became aware of their importance as creative persons and as spokesmen for their race" (Coleman 1988, 156). As literary scholar Karsten H. Piep points out, "influential studies ranging from Nathan Irvin Huggins's *Harlem Renaissance* (1973) to Ann Douglas's *Terrible Honesty: Mongrel Manhattan in the 1920s* (1996) have tended to describe the Harlem Renaissance as a local phenomenon, whose struggles with questions of cultural nationalism, civil rights, and race relations were confined to the US American scene" (2014, 110). This conceptualization of the Harlem Renaissance as a singularly American and regional phenomenon is thus the prevalent interpretative lens used in literary and cultural discourse to "read" the artistic intentions and productions of this era.

Piep calls regional readings of the Harlem Renaissance an "apparent critical oversight" (2014, 110) because seminal Harlem Renaissance novels like Nella Larsen's *Quicksand* and Claude McKay's *Home to Harlem* contain "transnational subtexts" (Piep 2014, 110) and are entangled in the geopolitics of imperialism and migration. I go a step further and argue that realizing the promise of the Harlem Renaissance often meant physically and philosophically leaving Harlem and the United States. The Harlem Renaissance, I must emphasize, was a uniquely American consciousness that, due to the afore-mentioned factors, could not have developed anywhere else in the world. However, at the turn of the twentieth century, the United States was still a fundamentally prejudiced society separated by the color line. Unlike other parts of the world like Europe, race dominated every aspect of American politics and society (Degler 1973, 757). Although European imperialism and ingrained Eurocentric ideologies about racial superiority fostered a comparable culture of racism in Europe, race was generally absent from the legal language of pre-Nazi Europe in the 1920s. In the United States, on the other hand, "racism . . . was translated into law-segregation and rested upon a genetic definition of the Negro" (Degler 1973, 757).

Herein lies what I have coined the Harlem Renaissance paradox. Although the United States was the only country in the world in the 1920s capable of producing a racially progressive movement like the Harlem Renaissance, the same United States had written racism into law and made it impossible for many Harlem Renaissance artists to cross the color line. Thus, striving to realize the promise of the Harlem Renaissance, the promise of unbridled creative freedom and black cultural expression, often meant seeking out alternative strategies and approaches in the transnational realm. Claude McKay's *Home to Harlem* (1928), for example, is set in Harlem. However, the existential tensions between individual and collective identities are thematized in negotiation with migration patterns and new imperialism, and the growing transnational consciousness of the character Ray, as a result, can no longer be contained within the restrictive racial milieu of the United States. For artists like singer and actress Josephine Baker and actor Paul Robeson, striving to achieve the Harlem Renaissance dream meant taking their creative agency across the Atlantic, to locations like Paris and London, in order to remap and reorient the parameters of black self-expression. These artists were engaging with a literary and cultural topography that existed and thrived beyond national borders. Their creative agency influenced and was influenced by transnational negotiations that sought to challenge and reconfigure racial hierarchies and political histories, transnational negotiations often in direct opposition with the rhetoric of American regionalism.

Some of the most famous writers and poets of the Harlem Renaissance include Claude McKay, Langston Hughes, Zora Neale Hurston, James Weldon Johnson, and Countee Cullen. By imbuing their work with novel and dynamic stylistic devices that spoke to the uniqueness and variedness of black self-expression, these writers showcased black art as a worthy subject of erudite analysis. According to African American history and culture scholar Leon Coleman, "the Harlem Renaissance created a new acceptance and a new recognition by the white public of the African American as a serious artist" (1998, 156). Before the 1920s, black artists were viewed as anomalies "who could not be judged by the ordinary criteria of excellence" (Coleman 1998, 156). Thanks to the Harlem Renaissance, and to the white patrons who supported the livelihood of black artists during this era (Stewart and Anderson, 302), this perception changed and "black artists were beginning to be measured by the same critical standards that were applied to white artists" (Coleman 1998, 156). This period also saw the explosion of trail blazing actors, actresses, and musicians who dabbled in experimental theater, innovative musical genres, and hybridized performance styles. Some of these artists include Josephine Baker, Paul Robeson, Bessie Smith, Duke Ellington, and Louis Armstrong, and the agency and authenticity these artists possessed was a stark contrast to "the Blackface and Minstrelsy shows that prevailed prior to the 1920s" (Stewart and Anderson 2007, 302). The origins of minstrel shows can be traced as far back as the 1820s and 1830s when white actors like Chris Matthews and Thomas "Daddy" Rice posed as African American characters by painting their faces black (aka "blackface") (Brooks 2019, 7). Blackface performances quickly garnered nationwide attention, and they amused crowds with stereotypical and exaggerated depictions of African American mannerisms, facial expressions, and speech (Brooks 2019, 7–10). Although black actors like Billy Kersands were later welcomed to the minstrel stage, minstrel shows continued to rely on offensive tropes about African American culture (Brooks 2019, 20). The Harlem Renaissance's emphasis on the integrity of black artistry was thus a momentous moment in American history and culture because after a century of the degradation of black art, African American artists were finally taking control of their narratives.

In 1922, Jamaican American writer Claude McKay published a poetry collection titled *Harlem Shadows*. White reviewers "were astonished to discover that none of it was written in Negro dialect" (Keller 1984, 156) and praised its "formal excellence and spirit of defiance" (Schwarz 2003, 88). *Harlem Shadows'* impeccable attention to classical form and structure positioned black authorship as high art and emerging poets like Langston Hughes, who would later become a prominent Harlem Renaissance figure, sought to achieve the same goal by emulating McKay's writing aesthetic (Schwarz 2003, 88). Although McKay was a crucial figure in the aesthetic and artistic development of the Harlem Renaissance, he was ironically absent from the United States for almost the entirety of the movement. In 1922, he left the United States for Soviet Russia to witness and support the Bolshevik revolution that disregarded the color line and emphasized a universal class struggle (Irmscher 2017). When American writer and political activist Max Eastman traveled to Soviet Russia, he was pleased to see McKay, his good friend, and he described the trailblazing Harlem Renaissance writer as "the prince of the revolution" who looked like a "'black pearl' among all the somber Bolsheviks" (Irmscher 2017). McKay's exalted status in Europe, at a time when black artists were facing widespread racial discrimination in the United States, influenced other Harlem Renaissance writers to look beyond regional borders and explore transnational opportunities (Wintz and Finkelman 2004, 301). McKay would remain abroad for twelve more years, visiting and living in multiple countries such as Morocco (Irmscher 2017); he did not return to America until 1934 (Barkan 2001, 232). This is important to point out because it illustrates that although the Harlem Renaissance was centered in Harlem, New York, its orientation was often transnational. McKay never stopped being a central figure in the Harlem Renaissance because he lived abroad. Rather, his transnational exposure remapped the depth of the literary discourse happening in Harlem and opened, I argue, a cosmopolitan portal that brought Harlem to the world and the world to Harlem. This cosmopolitan portal is evident in McKay's novel *Home to Harlem* (1928).

Two important themes *Home to Harlem* engages with are displacement and new imperialism. One of the central characters in the novel is Ray, a Haitian immigrant based in Harlem. He is educated, fluent in French (Haiti was a French colony), and utterly fascinated by Harlem's pulsating energy. In 1925, famed African American philosopher and writer Alain Locke proclaimed Harlem as a "race capital" (Locke 1995, 50). In Harlem, he argued, "Negro life is seizing upon its first chances for group expression and self-determination . . . That is why our comparison is taken with those nascent centers of folk-expression and self-determination which are playing a creative part in the world to-day" (Locke 1995, 50). Self-determination typically references the yearning of a community for the right to legitimate statehood, the right to fair political representation and governance. The statehood analogy is strengthened when Locke further states, "Harlem has the same role to play for the New Negro as Dublin has had for the New Ireland or Prague for the New Czechoslovakia" (Locke 1995, 50). Using nation-building terminology to describe what was happening in Harlem in the mid-1920s insinuates the growth of a unified national black identity demanding legitimate citizenship and cultural recognition from the dominant white society. Ray's Haitian background, however, complicates this national promise of Harlem as a race capital.

During the start of the twentieth century, the United States became an emergent superpower in the age of new imperialism (new imperialism generally refers to aggressive colonial expeditions and expansions in the nineteenth and early twentieth centuries, particularly by the British Empire in Africa and Asia and the Empire of Japan in Korea, China, and other neighboring Asian territories). The United States sought to compete with Europe and Japan by securing overseas territories and expanding its imperial sphere of influence. Haiti was one of the first casualties of this burgeoning colonial appetite. In 1915, the United States invaded the tiny Caribbean nation, and Haiti would remain under American military occupation for nineteen years (Renda 2004, 10).

As a black Haitian immigrant living in Harlem, the race capital, the occupation of Haiti leaves Ray profoundly shocked (the novel uses the word "quivering" to describe his reaction) (McKay 2000, 150). The novel ponders whether Ray can truly have a "claimed kinship" (McKay 2000, 153) with the African American community in Harlem fighting for representation and recognition in an imperial institution that has colonized his country of origin. This moment represents a form of existential and cultural displacement as the loss of Haiti's sovereignty represents the loss of Ray's sovereign identity. In countries like Haiti where an overwhelming majority of the population belongs to one racial group, national congruence/ethnic affiliations are naturally the primary identity markers and not race. Unlike African Americans, a racial minority group in the United States historically and primarily defined by racial categorization and marginalization, Ray is Haitian first and black second. Thus, his struggle to understand his sense of self after the colonization of Haiti by the United States inevitably creates a uniquely transnational political agenda not sufficiently reflected in the national priorities of black Harlem, a society still deeply divided and defined by the color line. For Ray and the diasporic black community of Harlem, the realization of statehood sentiments in Harlem cannot be achieved without reconciling, or at least confronting, the discrepancies between the national and the international. The argument here is not that the prioritization of national African American issues is misguided. Considering the traumatic history of American slavery and the equally traumatic failures of the reconstruction era, African Americans have every right to politically galvanize and prioritize their national interests. What McKay is deconstructing here, I argue, is the regional interpretation of the Harlem Renaissance as an almost utopic experience that creatively and existentially awakened and inspired a homogenized imaginary of black Harlem. For a transnational black being in Harlem like Ray, the Harlem Renaissance is ultimately not celebratory. The creative movement coincided with the loss of his sovereign identity, a multidimensional diasporic identity not properly represented by the restrictive black and white dichotomy of the color line in the United States. Although the revolutionary spirit of Harlem energizes Ray, the color line prevents him from realizing the promise of the movement, a full embrace and celebration of his Haitian/black/immigrant identity (McKay 2000, 196).

These transnational tensions in *Home to Harlem* evoke the concept of aesthetic imaginaries, as articulated by literary and cultural studies scholar Ranjan Ghosh. Ghosh describes the aesthetic as an imaginary, a rethinking, that is intertwined with the conflicts and incongruities of shared worlds (Ghosh 2017, 450). Although the aesthetic imaginary, Ghosh continues, is "built inside the borders of a nation, a culture, a society, a tradition, or an inheritance" (Ghosh 2017, 450), it allows for deconstructions and reconstructions "when exposed to the callings and constraints of cross-border epistemic and cultural circulations" (Ghosh 2017, 450). These reconstructions allow a process of micro and macro movements that bear out the promise of what Ghosh calls "shared realities" (Ghosh 2017, 450). In *Home to Harlem*, although there are shared realities between the African American experience and the Haitian American experience (racism, cultural influences from Africa, etc.), both identities are ultimately fundamentally different. The latter resists racial regionalism while the former adheres to it. Lucidly illustrated here is the Harlem Renaissance paradox: Ray admits that in Harlem, he had "known happiness . . . joy that glowed gloriousness upon him like the high-noon sunlight of his tropic island home" (McKay 2000, 187). In Harlem, he is inspired by the ingenuity of African American artistry and engages in passionate debates with the black educated elite about race, nationality, and class (McKay 2000, 169). Although the unparalleled vitality of these Harlem interactions encourages Ray to explore his transnational consciousness, he is also stifled, intellectually and emotionally, by the same Harlem interactions. As Piep points out, the segregationist policies enforced by the color line (McKay 2000, 109) ensure that race is Ray's "primary identity marker" in the United States (2014, 117). Thus, black diasporic identities significantly shaped by other characteristics such as social mobility, class, language, and so on lack adequate representation by the racial politics of black Harlem and white America. Most of Harlem, Ray states, is oblivious to the concept of a fluid transnational being; identity, they believe, is stable and regional (McKay 2000, 196). Ray ultimately feels like a "misfit" (McKay 2000, 109), and his story ends with his decision to migrate to Europe before he too becomes "one of the contented hogs in the pigpen of Harlem" (McKay 2000, 196). In summation, cultural circulations, despite their shared realities, often yield no satisfactory resolution.

Transcontinental migration to Europe is a recurrent theme in Harlem Renaissance narratives. Josephine Baker was arguably one of the most exciting performers in New York during the emergence of the Harlem Renaissance. As a chorus girl in the elite nightclub *The Plantation Club*, she showed great promise by imbuing her performances with an intoxicating vigor and sensual charisma (Schroeder and Wagner 2009, 26). She was later cast in the hit Broadway show *Shuffle Along*, "a play that was remarkable for being produced, written and performed entirely by African Americans" (Norman 2018). Racism and discrimination, however, remained rife and this meant the chances of mainstream success and leading lady status were slim to impossible (Schroeder and Wagner 2009, 26). Screen goddesses and stage stars like Lillian Gish, Fanny Brice, Gloria Swanson, and Joan Crawford dominated the 1920s; when African American actress Nina Mae McKinney was cast in the 1929 movie *Hallelujah*, she became "the first black woman to play a significant role in a Hollywood movie" (Wintz and Finkelman 2004, 783). *Hallelujah* was, however, a "black" film, a movie featuring all-black characters, with dehumanizing and stereotypical characters and despite its financial success at the box office, it remained relegated to the black aisle of the color line (Wintz and Finkelman 2004, 783). Due to the lack of opportunities available to African American actresses, McKinney was not able to replicate the success of *Hallelujah*, and she eventually left the United States to seek acting opportunities abroad (Wintz and Finkelman 2004, 783). African American singers fared slightly better. The 1920s saw the rise of blues entertainers like Ethel Waters, Bessie Smith, Ma Rainey, and Alberta Hunter, but despite their ability to sell records and emotionally move audiences, they still endured "challenges with racism, sexism, racial segregation, and exclusion" (Jackson 11 and Givens 2006, 53). The color line in the United States seemed inescapable, so when Josephine Baker was offered an opportunity to perform in Paris in 1925, she gladly took it. Years of discriminatory practices in the entertainment industry had taken its toll, and she was now ready to try her luck elsewhere. In Paris, her fortunes changed.

Her headlining performance in the show *La Revue Nègre* stunned Paris with its haunting melodies and vivacious primal sensuality, and she became an overnight sensation (Schroeder and Wagner 2009, 26). In the realm of Harlem Renaissance scholarship, Baker is often described as an example of a Harlem success story who was able to take her talents abroad and flourish. What is often not highlighted, however, are the skillful and strategic transnational elements Baker used to access agency and negotiate fame. Core musical aspects of her Paris performances, from the Charleston dance to the rhythm of the cymbals, relied on regional African American traditions that fascinated French people (Schroeder and Wagner 2009, 26). Her physical presentation, on the other hand, speaks to the colonial French imaginary of black femininity. Baker and her creative team shrewdly utilized gendered imagery of "savage" Africa to enthrall French audiences already intrigued by similar imagery coming out from their colonies in Africa and Asia. Baker's roaring cheetahs on stage, her barefoot dancing, scantily clad "banana outfits," and occasional leaps into the audience were met with waves of "frantic applause" (Schroeder and Wagner 2009, 33) and placed her "in the heat of the spotlight" (Schroeder and Wagner 2009, 33). Her artistic blend of colonial fantasy and African American rhythm was a winning formula that fed the European appetite for Indigenous savagery and the cultural explosion of black artistry in Harlem. There are of course problematic elements to appropriating the savage Indigenous imaginary. However, it is imperative to emphasize that "Josephine Baker," the Parisian celebrity persona and not the person, was an autonomous invention. Baker and her creative team were the architects of this image. They deliberately and shrewdly concocted a transnational femininity that allowed her to access a level of superstardom that was unprecedented for a black woman in the 1920s. As literary critic Cheryl A. Wall points out "Onstage she [Baker] usually appeared bare-breasted . . . girdled with her infamous bananas. Offstage she turned heads as she walked her pet leopard down the Champs Elysees. She traveled with a veritable menagerie. Wherever she went, Baker was always costumed to intensify the effect" (1995, 105).

Europe could not get enough of this strategically designed effect that spoke to their obsession with primitivist modernism. Picasso, for example, called Baker the Nefertiti of their times, her nude portrait by Jean-Gabriel Domergue was displayed in the Grand Palais and sculptor Alexander Calder drew her now infamous caricature and "captured 'Le Baker' in media as varied as the art they created. Yet the woman must rarely have recognized herself in the images they created . . . Baker was able to mock the role of exotic primitive even as she played it to the hilt" (Wall 1995, 105). She also became a European screen goddess, appearing as a leading lady in movies like *Siren of the Tropics* (1927), *Zouzou* (1934), and *Princess Tam Tam* (1935). *Siren of the Tropics* made Baker the "first woman of black African descent to star in a major motion picture" (Martone 2008, 52) and in 1927, the year the movie was released, she was "the highest paid entertainer in Europe and . . . had opened her own nightclub" (Martone 2008, 52).

Baker's self-awareness about her image reinforces her agency. She deliberately created a hybridized cross-border image that exploited transnational fantasies and prejudices and gave her access to the leading lady status she could never attain in the United States due to the rigidity of the color. Once again, the paradox resurfaces: the Harlem Renaissance awakened the talents of a young Baker and made her realize that she was just as talented as the screen goddesses and stage stars of the 1920s. However, the color line between black Harlem and white America meant she could never be the next Lillian Gish or Fanny Brice. Thus, in order to realize her Harlem Renaissance dream, she had to travel overseas and negotiate a new transnational persona. I am not insinuating here that Europeans at the turn of the twentieth century were more racially tolerant than Americans. Comparing and contrasting the magnitude of racial discrimination on both continents is not the focus of my research. I am instead pointing out that the absence of an American-style color line in Europe gave black artists like Baker the opportunity to infiltrate white spaces and negotiate greater agency. This argument is also corroborated by Baker's brief return to the United States in 1936. Already one of France's highest-paid entertainers (Otfinoski 2010, 15), Baker was lured back to New York in 1936 by producers Jake and Lee Shubert to star in the lavish Broadway production *Ziegfeld Follies* (Schroeder and Wagner 2009, 49).

When Baker arrived in New York, she was instructed to use the servants' entrance of the hotel because "many of the guests were from the South, the manager explained, and the sight of an African-American woman in the lobby might offend them" (Schroeder and Wagner 2009, 49). The humiliation did not end there. American critics harshly panned her performance in *Follicles*. They labeled her a "foreigner" due to her French accent and dismissed her voice as thin (Schroeder Wagner 2009, 49). *Time* magazine went a step further, calling her a "Negro wench . . . whose dancing and singing might be topped practically anywhere outside of Paris" (Schroeder and Wagner 2009, 49). Author and playwright Steven Otfinoski speculates that "Americans may have found her act too sophisticated and may also have resented a poor, black girl from St. Louis becoming a celebrity in Europe" (2010, 15). Despite being one of Europe's most glamorous and highest paid entertainers, there was no escaping the color line in the United States. A dejected Baker "returned to France and immediately became a French citizen" (Otfinoski 2010, 15). She would spend the rest of her life using her star power to champion for racial equality and democratic principles on both sides of the Atlantic (Schroeder and Wagner 2009, 93).

Another example of a performer who used the absence of the color line in Europe to negotiate greater agency is actor Paul Robeson. Like Baker, Robeson was one of the Harlem Renaissance's exciting new talents. He rose to prominence for his work as the titular character in *The Emperor Jones* (1924), a challenging expressionistic play by Eugene O'Neil. Robeson earned rave reviews for his performance; *The New York Times*, for example, called him "singularly fine," and he established himself as a star of the stage (Young 2012, 13). Months later, he would make his film debut in Oscar Micheaux's *Body and Soul*, a silent film about a deceptive preacher. Micheaux was categorically the most prolific black filmmaker of the Harlem Renaissance era, and unlike the stereotypical and offensive depictions of black life in Hollywood, he gave black actors the rare opportunity to play dignified and complex characters (Wintz and Finkelman 204, 377). As film history scholar Scott Allen Nollen points out, Robeson's decision in *Body and Soul* "to portray the bogus preacher . . . in a naturalistic style, rather than embracing the often exaggerated pantomime of the silent era, indicates that he instinctively understood the possibilities of cinematic acting" (2014, 19). In 1925, the same year Baker stunned Paris in *La Revue Nègre*, *The Emperor Jones* moved to the London stage and, once again, Robeson was a hit with the critics. Not only did they praise his acting, they were enthralled by his voice, and "Robeson believed that he had helped the London audiences 'see a modern Negro roll up the centuries and reveal primeval man'" (Ehrlich 1989, 75). The absence of the color line meant Robeson enjoyed greater mobility, physically and psychologically, and he was often stunned by the lack of overt racial hostility in London and other European locations he visited like the French Riviera and the Mediterranean (Ehrlich 1989, 78–80). Robeson would get the opportunity to return to London three years later. His performance in *Show Boat* (1928) on the London stage, once again, earned him ecstatic reviews and access to London high society (Ehrlich 1989, 84). The decision to make London his home was inevitable.

Like Baker, Robeson's career trajectory is an illustration of the Harlem Renaissance paradox. The creative opportunities in New York awakened a young Robeson's talents and solidified his potential as a leading man of the stage and screen. However, the ubiquitous presence of the color line meant that his talents were relegated to marginalized black spaces, and he would never attract the kind of top quality projects offered to his white counterparts. In London, not only was Robeson able to attract top-billed projects like Shakespeare's *Othello* (1930), where he starred alongside a white actress (such interracial pairings were a taboo in the United States at the time), but he also toured Europe extensively, exposing audiences to black folk music and jazz (Ehrlich 1989, 85). Moreover, London was central to the maturity of his political consciousness. Because the British Empire had colonized significant parts of the African continent, studies on African history and culture were easily accessible in London (Ehrlich 1989, 89–90). Robeson was thus able to learn about his African heritage and interact with black students from the African colonies (Ehrlich 1989, 89–90). He also strengthened his transnational identity by developing a global class consciousness among the oppressed working class (Ehrlich 1989, 90), and in movies like *Sanders of the River* (1935), *King Solomon's Mines* (1937), and *Proud Valley* (1940), he used "the British film industry to . . . reflect his investments in African culture and class struggle" (Perucci 2012, 9). Such opportunities to cultivate and reconcile his passion for acting and activism were rare to impossible in the United States due to the color line. Thus, like Baker, Robeson strategically found ways to realize the potential of the Harlem Renaissance dream by resettling in Europe and negotiating a transnational identity.

The Harlem Renaissance was a trailblazing creative movement that could have only happened in the United States. The amalgamation of the fighting African American spirit, from the trans-Atlantic slave trade to post-reconstruction, and the American democratic project and its philosophical orientation in ideologies such as liberty and exceptionalism laid the foundation for the creative explosion of black arts in 1920s Harlem. Ironically, the same United States, from its inception, enshrined racial segregation into its legal language and rigidly maintained a color line that deprived African Americans of their merited civil liberties as American citizens. Thus, realizing the promise of the Harlem Renaissance, for characters like Ray in *Home to Harlem* and for artists like Josephine Baker and Paul Robeson, often meant leaving the United

States and negotiating transnational identities that gave them access to white spaces and greater agency. Although these transnational black creatives were able to accrue impressive accomplishments abroad, resettlement in Europe, I must underscore, was not a utopic existence or even a long-term solution to the color line problem. Biographical details from McKay's life reveal that Europe is possibly not the Promised Land Ray is hoping to encounter when he decides to leave Harlem behind and sail across the Atlantic. Despite the warm welcome McKay received in Soviet Russia, financial difficulties persistently plagued his transnational explorations (Irmscher 2017). Making a living as a black creative, writing stories about the transnational negotiations of black characters, was an arduous challenge. Europe might have lacked an American-style color line but it did not offer McKay financial security. As a result, he "returned to the United States, hoping his earnings would improve" (Barkan 2001, 232). Unfortunately, they did not, and he was never able to replicate the critical and commercial success he enjoyed at the dawn of the Harlem Renaissance in the United States (Irmscher 2017).

In the case of Josephine Baker, she conquered the Parisian stage in the 1920s, but she had to do this by playing into racist tropes and colonial fantasies. Moreover, despite achieving screen goddess status in movies like *Siren of the Tropics* (1927) and *Princess Tam Tam* (1935), she always played the fetishized "exotic" and remained creatively constrained by colonial narratives in the realm of cinema. After World War II, when the world was grappling with the aftermath of fascism and colonial fantasies were losing their popularity, Baker, who had attained national hero status in France by assisting the French rebellion against Nazi occupation, rebranded herself as the dignified grand dame, focusing more on sophisticated performance modes and social causes (Phillips 2006). Baker sustained her groundbreaking career, well into the 1970s, by constantly reimagining herself, and while some might argue that perpetually reinventing and negotiating transnational identities echoes the absence of resolution, perhaps the aesthetic imaginary of cultural circulations in perpetuity was Baker's resolution. She was after all a woman who could not exist on either side of the color line.

For Robeson, although Great Britain gave him greater creative freedom than the United States, racist tropes and colonial propaganda were prevalent in the British film industry. Although he had hoped that his starring roles in movies like *Sanders of the River* (1935) and *King Solomon's Mines* (1937) would promote African culture and support the class struggle, these projects ended being "overt apologias for colonialism, including blatant primitivist representation of blacks" (Perucci 2012, 9). Furthermore, in movies like *Song of Freedom* (1936) and *The Proud Valley* (1940), he is relegated to racial tropes that reinforce stereotypes of black people as superstitious beings and helpmates "to whites" (Perucci 2012, 10). After World War II, both Great

Britain and the United States became increasingly hostile to communist sympathizers like Robeson (his advocacy for the working class had drawn him into communist circles), and for the rest of his professional career, he journeyed restlessly between both sides of the Atlantic, striving, usually unsuccessfully, to reconcile his transnational interests (Perucci 2012, 13–16). The last stop on Robeson's transnational expedition was, tragically, a private sanitarium in London in 1961; he later relocated to the United States and "lived the rest of his life out of the public eye with his sister in Pennsylvania" (Perucci 2012, 16).

Europe was unquestionably not a racial paradise for performers like Baker and for artists like Robeson; it ultimately could not accommodate their burgeoning transnational identities that now encompassed both race and class. However, the absence of an American version of the color line in European society gave Harlem Renaissance creatives like Baker and Robeson (and perhaps *Home to Harlem*'s Ray) the opportunity to find agency in unexpected spaces. And although these transnational negotiations were often marred with strife and heartbreak, narratives about McKay, Baker, and Robeson ascending to the pinnacle of European society, reorienting and disseminating black art and self-expression, must have inspired generations of African Americans still steeped in the racial politics of the color line. These transnational narratives must have inspired them to believe in a level of success that was previously thought to be impossible for people of their hue. As mentioned previously, McKay was at the forefront of the black literary exodus to Europe (Irmscher 2017), a trend that continued for most of the twentieth century and exposed Europe to writers like Richard Wright and James Baldwin. When we witness tributes like African American pop icon Beyoncé performing with a Baker-styled banana skirt in 2006 (Jerkins 2016), the generational influence of transnational Harlem Renaissance artists is evident. Although Robeson is not a comparably recognizable name in the American imaginary (possibly due to his communist leanings and overt support for Soviet Russia), his dignified interpretations of black masculinity on stage and on screen are the blueprint for acclaimed contemporary African American actors like James Earl Jones and Denzel Washington. In brief, the formidable presence of black representation in contemporary American media (music, movies, etc.), and its popularity abroad, has its roots in the trailblazing transnational negotiations of Harlem Renaissance artists.

WORKS CITED

Barkan, Elliot Robert. 2001. *Making It in America: A Sourcebook on Eminent Ethnic Americans*. Santa Barbara: ABC-CLIO.

Brooks, Tim. 2019. *The Blackface Minstrel Show in Mass Media: 20th Century Performances on Radio, Records, Film and Television.* Jefferson: McFarland.

Coleman, Leon. 1998. *Carl Van Vechten and the Harlem Renaissance: A Critical Assessment.* New York: Taylor and Francis.

Degler, Carl N. 1973. "The Problem of the Color-Line." *Journal of Interdisciplinary History* 3, no. 4 (Spring): 757–762.

Ehrlich, Scott. 1989. *Paul Robeson.* Los Angeles: Holloway House Publishing.

Ghosh, Ranjan. 2017. "Aesthetic Imaginary: Rethinking the 'Comparative.'" *Canadian Review of Comparative Literature/Revue Canadienne de Littérature Comparée* 44(3): 449–467.

Goodman, Jordan. 2013. *Paul Robeson: A Watched Man.* New York: Verso Books.

Greene, Kevin D. 2019. "We Never Get to Be Men." In *Black Veterans, Politics and Civil Rights in Twentieth-Century America*, edited By Robert F. Jefferson Jr., 1–20. Lanham: Rowman and Littlefield.

Healey, Joseph F. 2011. *Race, Ethnicity, Gender, and Class: The Sociology of Group Conflict and Change.* Thousand Oaks: Pine Forge Press.

Irmscher, Christoph. 2017. "Rejecting Claude McKay: An Author's Lost, and Last, Novel." *Library of America*, August 21, 2017. https://www.loa.org/news-and-v iews/1318-rejecting-claude-mckay-an-authors-lost-and-last-novel.

Jackson II, Ronald L., and Sonja M. Brown Givens. 2006. *Black Pioneers in Communication Research.* Thousand Oaks: SAGE Publications.

Jerkins, Morgan. 2016. "90 Years Later, the Radical Power of Josephine Baker's Banana Skirt." *Vogue*, June 3, 2016. https://www.vogue.com/article/josephine-baker-90th-anniversary-banana-skirt.

Keller, Bruce. 1984. *The Harlem Renaissance: A Historical Dictionary for the Era.* Westport: Greenwood Press.

Library of Congress. n.d. "NAACP: A Century in the Fight for Freedom." Accessed May 15, 2020. https://www.loc.gov/exhibits/naacp/the-new-negro-movement.html.

Locke, Alain. 1995. "The New Negro." In *Voices from the Harlem Renaissance*, edited by Nathan Irvin Huggins, 47–71. New York: Oxford University Press.

Martin, Lori Latrice. 2019. *Black Community Uplift and the Myth of the American Dream.* Lanham: Rowman and Littlefield.

Martone, Eric. 2008. "Baker, Josephine." In *Encyclopedia of Blacks in European History and Culture* [2 volumes], edited by Eric Martone, 50–53. Westport: Greenwood Publishing Group.

McKay, Claude. 2000. *Home to Harlem.* London: X Press.

Morrison, Michael A., and William G. Shade. 2010. *Encyclopedia of U.S. Political History.* Washington, D.C.: SAGE.

Nollen, Scott Allen. 2014. *Paul Robeson: Film Pioneer.* Jefferson: McFarland.

Norman, Dominique. 2018. "Black Excellence: The Ever Legendary Josephine Baker." *V Magazine*, February 23, 2018. https://vmagazine.com/article/black -excellence-josephine-baker/.Otfinoski, Steven. 2010. *African Americans in the Performing Arts.* Ann Arbor: Infobase Publishing.

Perucci, Tony. 2012. *Paul Robeson and the Cold War Performance Complex.* Michigan: University of Michigan Press.

Phillips, Suzanne. 2006. "Joséphine Baker: The 1st Black Superstar." Video, 39.33. https://www.youtube.com/watch?v=Ggb_wGTvZoU.

Piep, Karsten H. 2004. "Home to Harlem, Away from Harlem: Transnational Subtexts in Nells Larsen's *Quicksand* and Claude McKay's *Home to Harlem.*" *Brno Studies in English* 40(3): 109–121.Renda, Mary A. 2004. *Taking Haiti: Military Occupation and the Culture of U.S. Imperialism, 1915–1940.* North Carolina: University of North Carolina Press.

Schroeder, Alan, and Heather L. Wagner. 2009. *Josephine Baker: Entertainer.* New York: Infobase Publishing.

Schwarz, A. B. Christa. 2003. *Gay Voices of the Harlem Renaissance.* Bloomington and Indianapolis: Indiana University Press.

Stewart, James Benjamin, and Talmadge Anderson. 2007. *Introduction to African American Studies: Transdisciplinary Approaches and Implications.* Baltimore: Black Classic Press.

Wall, Cheryl A. 1995. *Women of the Harlem Renaissance.* Bloomington and Indiana: Indiana University Press.

Wintz, Cary D., and Paul Finkelman, eds. 2004. *Encyclopedia of the Harlem Renaissance: K-Y.* New York: Taylor and Francis.

Young, Jeff C. 2012. *Amazing African-American Actors.* Berkeley Heights: Enslow Publishing, LLC.

Index

Abbeville, S. C., 63–76; court square, 63, 65, 67–75; history, 63–66; memorial plaque, 64, 65; performance, 63

absence(s)/absent xiii, xiv, xv, xvii, xviii, 2, 3, 113, 148; Abbeville court square, 64, 75; Appiani family tomb, 9; history, 65; Indigenous, 79, 84–85, 91, 161–76; Joy Division, *Closer,* 8; medieval, 2; race, 191, 197, 198, 201; rape/Rape of Proserpina, 98, 99, 102, 105–7; *Sharp Objects,* 23–24; storytelling, 118, 121, 123; visual texts, 47, 49, 58–61. *See also* presence

aesthesis, 116, 143, 146, 154, 177, 183

aesthetic/aesthetics xviii, 4, 13, 146, 164, 70, 74, 101, 127–40; Bloom, Harold, 133; Derrida, Jacques, 135–36; of healing, 35; hegemonies, 131; heterotopic, 128, 131, 136, 140; Kant, Immanuel, 127–30; literature, 143–47; literary, 113, 118, 123; modern/modernist, 31, 36, 135; Nancy, Jean-Luc, 129–30, 134; of the nondescript, 49, 51–53, 59; post-Kantian, 131; Rancière, Jacques, 70, 74, 130–31, 133, 134, 164; regime, 4; suffering, xvi, 9, 108–9

aesthetic apprehension, xvi, xvii, 1, 6, 13, 17, 75, 98, 101, 164

aesthetic experience, 116, 118, 143, 145, 148, 152

aesthetic imaginary, xvi–xviii, 29, 78–80, 113, 115, 143–47, 153–54, 162, 163, 167, 194–95; cultural circulations, 78, 162, 195, 200; disruption of, 78, 91–93, 175; *Emerging Aesthetic Imaginaries,* xii; false familiarity, 79, 91–92; Ghosh, Ranjan, xvi, 78–79, 162, 194–95; National Park Service, xvi, 77–93; nostalgia, 80, 87

aesthetic understanding, 143–45, 148, 152; affect/affectivity, 92, 79; aesthetic, 130; "affect aliens," 85, 92; "affect imposter syndrome," 85; affective dissonance, 78; affect studies, 55; imaginary, 79; musical, 178; "wilderness affect," 92

Agawu, Kofi, 178

alien(s), 161–64, 175

allegory/allegorizing, 33, 97, 98, 101–3, 108, 109

anachronism, 3

analysis: aesthetic, 149–50; literary, 53, 146, 149–51

ancient/antiquity, 4, 8, 10, 35, 71, 117

Appiani family tomb, 8–10
apprehension/apprehending: as affective
    state, 67, 144; apprehensive(ness)
    xiii, 63–75; as understanding xi,
    xiii, xvi, xvii, 2, 5, 8, 10, 65, 69, 70,
    79, 85, 106, 144, 154, 178. *See also*
    aesthetic apprehension
archeological poetics, 164
Aristotle, 116–17, 119, 153
Atlanta, GA, 67–68

Baker, Josephine, 191–201
Barnes, Djuna, *Ryder*, xvi, 97–109
Barthes, Roland, 51
Bauhaus, 5, 12
beauty, 33–39, 104, 106, 137, 180–82,
    184–86. *See also* feminine, beauty
Bechdel, Alison, 50; *Fun Home: A*
    Family Tragicomic, 51
Berman, Marshall, 32, 36–37, 40
Bernstein, Charles, 154–55
Black femininity, 196–97
Blake, William, 108–9
Bloom, Harold, 132–34, 137
body, 19, 22, 27, 31–45, 64, 72, 78,
    90, 97, 101, 103–7, 163, 178,
    180, 185–86; aesthetics of, 33;
    cultures of, 33, 35, 39, 46. *See also*
    embodiment
border(s), xii, xix, 131, 136–37; cross-
    border, 78, 162, 195, 197; national,
    78, 93, 128, 162, 191, 195; regional,
    193; US-Canada, 79
Botticelli, *Birth of Venus*, 35, 42
Bragg, Melvyn, 132–34
Brooks, Cleanth and Robert Penn
    Warren, *Understanding Poetry*,
    147–48, 150–55
Burne Jones, Edward. *See* Pre-
    Raphaelites

Calhoun, John C., 72–73
Cather, Willa, "Coming, Aphrodite!",
    36–45
Charlottesville, VA, 66

chorography, 64, 70–71; choreography,
    73
Cimitero monumentale di Staglieno
    (Genoa). *See* Appiani family tomb
civil rights, 189, 190
class, 74, 121, 130, 136, 195, 199, 201;
    consciousness, 199; middle, 51;
    second-class citizens, 189; struggle,
    136, 192, 199, 200
classic/classical, xv, 7–8, 10, 13, 119,
    122, 134, 139, 192; classical studies,
    4, 37; classicist/classicism, 33–34;
    and modern, 2; music, xviii, 22;
    neo-, xiv, 2, 7; non-, 177; rock, 5;
    sculpture, 7, 37, 39, 44
close reading. *See* reading practices
Coast Salish, 79–80, 82–83
colonial fantasies, 3, 200
color line, 191–201
comic(s), 49–54, 162, 164–65, 170
comprehension/comprehending, xi–xiii,
    xvii, 1, 15, 24, 47, 51, 58, 60, 64, 72,
    122, 144, 146, 147, 149, 151, 153,
    154; in-, 154; un-, 42
Confederacy, 66, 68
confederate monuments. *See*
    monument(s)
critical immersion. *See* reading practices
Curtis, Ian, 10, 12

Dalí, Salvador, *Dream of Venus*, 35–36,
    43
Damned, the, 12
deaf/deafness, xviii, 162, 164–70, 174–
    75; superheroes, 162
Derrida, Jacques, xvii, 128, 131, 135–
    37, 139; hauntology, xvii, 135–36,
    139
desire, xi, 8, 25, 35, 40, 44, 48, 53,
    90, 99, 108–9, 116, 130, 178, 182;
    disruptive, 2; reader, readerly, 53,
    59, 117–18
Drnaso, Nick, *Sabrina*, xvi, 47–61

Eilish, Billie, 59

emblem, xvi, 97, 102, 108, 109
embodiment, xviii, 26, 107, 174, 178–
79, 182; disembodiment, 105, 179,
186; hyperembodiment, 186. *See
also* body
emotions, 54–55, 77–78, 85, 90, 108,
154. *See also* affect
Equal Justice Initiative, xvi, 64–65, 68,
73
eros, 182, 184
exceptionalism, 199

Falcoff, Marc, 137–38
false familiarity(ies), xii–xiii, xvi, xvii,
xviii, 1–3, 51, 74–75, 77–95, 103,
114, 119, 127–42, 155, 164, 174, 175
family, xv, 17–21, 23–24, 28, 98,
105, 121, 174; Crawford family,
64; Ryder family, 98–99. *See also*
Appiani family tomb
female/feminine/femininity, 18, 25, 28,
38, 43, 48, 50, 120–21, 123, 180,
196; beauty, 34, 38; body, 33, 41,
100, 102–4, 105, 108; experience,
xv, 104; grotesque, 104; identity,
25, 28, 29; suffering, xvi, 106, 108,
109; virtues, 106. *See also* Black
femininity; mother-daughter; Venus
feminism/feminist, 18, 21, 132
focalization, 99, 123
frontier, 80, 82

Ghosh, Ranjan, 78, 79, 92, 162, 194–95
Giotto di Bondone, 10–11
goth/gothic, 1, 5, 11–13; Southern
Gothic, 25. *See also* post-punk gothic
graphic narrative, novel/novella, xv, 47–
50, 60, 162, 165. *See also* comic(s);
illustrated novel
Greco-Roman mythology: Aphrodite/
Venus, xv, 7, 33–39, 42, 44; Artemis,
39; Demeter and Persephone,
19–20; Ovid's *Metamorphosis*, 106;
Proserpina, xvi, 98–108. *See also*
Cather, Willa, "Coming, Aphrodite!"

Greenham, David, 151, 153, 154
grotesque, 102, 104, 108. *See also*
female, grotesque
Guantánamo Bay, xvii, 128, 137–39

Harlem renaissance, 189–203; artists,
191, 201; paradox, 191, 195, 199;
writers, 191–93, 201
hauntology. *See* Derrida, Jacques
Heaney, Seamus, 134, 137, 139, 140
heterotopia/heterotopic, xvii, 74, 75, 93,
127–28, 131–37, 140

icon/iconic, xvi, 6, 34, 35, 42, 77, 149,
201
iconographic/iconography, 102, 104,
106; religious, 10, 13
identity, 10, 51, 167, 178, 194;
American, 84; black, 193, 194;
diasporic, 194; female, 25, 28;
immigrant, 194; national, xviii, 77;
racial, 167; transnational, 199
illustrated novel, 98. *See also* graphic
narrative
imagination, 12, 103, 122, 129
immigrant(s), 86, 193–94; identity, 194
imperialism xviii, 135, 190–91, 193
Indian/Indigenous/Native American,
xvi, xvii–xviii, 77–87, 89, 90–93,
161–75, 196; art, 165; *Cowboys and
Aliens*, 163–64; *The End of the Trail*,
164, 174; *The Last of the Mohicans*,
164. *See also* Coast Salish; Kanaka
Maoli
Indigenous. *See* Indian
indisciplinary, 131, 134–37, 139–40
inferencing. *See* reading practices
intimacy, xv, 18–28, 120, 121
invisibilization, 97, 109
invisual/invisuality, xvii, 161–76
Irigaray, Luce, 182

jazz, xviii, 178–80, 184–85, 186, 199;
jazz novel, 177
Jim Crow, 189–90

Joy Division, 5, 12; *Closer*, 1–15
justice, xvii, 69, 128, 133–40. *See also*
    Equal Justice Initiative
just literature, 127–42

Kanaka Maoli, 79, 86, 88
Kant, Immanuel, 128–30, 134–36
Kramer, Lawrence, 178

Landrieu, Mitch, 66
landscape, 80, 82, 86–88, 90–91, 163
listen/listening, xi, xii, xiv, xviii, 47, 49,
    60–61, 120, 122, 177, 179, 181, 183,
    185; close listening, 154; Nancy,
    Jean-Luc, 47, 60–61, 177
literacy, 98; cultural, 91; visual, 47, 48.
    See also reading practices
literary aesthetic. *See* aesthetic
literature, xi, xvii, 128–40, 143–59,
    165; American, 162; canonical, 26;
    reader, 47, 53, 145–59; Western, 87;
    women, 109. *See also* just literature
logos, 177, 131, 183

Mack, David, 162, 165–75
McCloud, Scott, 170
McKay, Claude, 191–95, 200–201
medieval/Middle Ages/medievalism,
    xiv–xvi, 1–6, 9–13
medium/mediality, xviii, 35, 128, 134,
    136, 146, 153, 165
memorial(s), 63, 66, 71, 74, 77–79, 84–
    88, 93; Confederate, 67; Crawford,
    Anthony, 63–65, 68–71, 73–74;
    Guards, 12; Lynching Memorial, 64;
    National Memorial for Peace and
    Justice, 64; USS *Arizona*, 79, 84–85,
    87–88. *See also* monument(s); Sand
    Creek Massacre National Historic
    Site; San Juan Island National
    Historic Park
metaphor, 98, 102, 108, 113, 117–18
metonymy/metonymic, xvi–xvii, 103,
    108, 113–26; displacement, 97, 98
migration, xviii, 133, 190–91, 195

minstrel show, 192
modern, xv, 1–5, 8, 13, 22, 118, 129;
    architecture, 78; body, 31–46; early,
    10, 134; music, 8; Negro, 198; non-
    modern, 4; unmodern, 3. *See also*
    aesthetics
modernism, 31–33, 36; primitivist, 197
modernity, 2, 20, 31–34, 36–37, 39–42,
    164, 169, 170
monument(s), 65, 66, 71, 73–75;
    absence, 65, 75; Confederate xv,
    63–68, 71; dialogue, 65, 67–71;
    figure, 67, 69–71, 75; silence, 64,
    70, 72, 79; site-specificity, xv–xvi,
    63–64, 66, 69, 72, 74–75; World
    War II Valor in the Pacific National
    Monument, 79, 84–88. *See also* Sand
    Creek Massacre National Historic
    Site; San Juan Island National
    Historic Park
mother-daughter, 18–21, 26, 28
multimodal(ity), xvii, 154–55, 164;
    music, 5, 7–8, 13, 22–23, 38, 137,
    149, 163, 177–87. *See also* jazz;
    myth, xvi, 43, 99, 104–6. *See also*
    Greco-Roman mythology

Nancy, Jean-Luc, xii, xiii–xiv, 47, 60,
    127–34, 177, 183, 185, 186
narrative, xv, xvi–xvii, 10, 17–27, 38,
    48, 52, 56, 69, 70, 72, 79, 81, 83,
    88, 91, 98, 99, 103, 107–8, 113–23,
    139, 164, 172, 177, 186, 192;
    colonial, 200; discourse, 114, 116;
    epic, 117; frame, 122; frontier, 82;
    grand, 70; graphic, 60, 165; Harlem
    Renaissance, xviii, 195; indigenous,
    165; master, 27; metonymic/
    metonymy, xvi–xvii, 113, 115,
    117, 119, 122–23; micro, xvii, 113,
    118; mother-daughter, 18–20; and
    music, xviii, 177; national, 74; and
    nostalgia, 86–87; progress, 84;
    and rape, 97, 100, 105, 106, 109;
    romance, 99, 107; transnational, 201;

visual, 49, 57, 58, 98; voice, 54,
    122–23
narratology, xviii, 114, 117
narrator, xviii, 28, 40, 42, 43, 115, 116,
    120–23, 164
National Parks Service, 77–96
Native American. *See* Indian
new critics/new criticism. *See* reading
    practices
Northern Ireland, xvii, 128, 137–38
nostalgia/nostalgic, xvi, 19, 22, 78–80,
    86–87, 91, 132

Ovid, 123; *The Metamorphoses,* 106

parataxis, 57
parkitecture, 78
parody, 98–99, 101, 109
pastoral, 80
patriot(s)/patriotism, 78–80, 84, 85, 92;
    nostalgic, 79, 91; techno-patriotism,
    88
peace/peaceful, 55, 79–81, 84–85, 88,
    131; National Memorial for Peace
    and Justice, 64; Nobel, 134, 137
Pearl Harbor, 85–89. *See also*
    monument(s), World War II Valor in
    the Pacific National Monument
Pig War, 80, 83–84
plot, emplotment, 18, 26–28, 114–21,
    148, 150, 153, 161–63, 175
post-punk gothic, xiv, 1–15
practical criticism. *See* reading practices
Pre-Raphaelites, 107; Burne Jones,
    Edward, 107; *Proserpine,* 107;
    Rossetti, Dante Gabriel, 107
presence/presencing, xii, xv, 23, 48,
    61, 64–66, 72, 73, 75, 155, 169,
    177, 185; absence, absent, 113, 123;
    Indigenous, 79, 85; military, 87; self,
    155, 178, 185; silence, silent, 1, 9,
    123, 171
primitivist modernism. *See* modernism
Prosperina. *See* myth

quest, 18, 21, 134–35, 174, 180–81,
    183; *Echo: Vision Quest* (David
    Mack), 161–76; race, 190–91, 193–
    95, 201. *See also* color line

Rancière, Jacques, xvi, 24, 74–75,
    127–40; aesthetic apprehension, 164;
    aesthetic heterotopia, 74, 93, 127,
    135; aesthetics, 70, 74, 78, 90–91,
    130–31; figures of the thinkable, 69;
    sensible experience, 70; topography
    of the thinkable, xi–xii, xvii, xviii,
    69, 92, 131, 164, 170, 172
rape, 27; allegorization, xvi, 97–112;
    Proserpina. *See* myth
reading practices, 113–26, 143–59;
    close reading, 53, 59, 143–59;
    critical immersion, xvii, 143–59;
    inferencing, 50; misreading, 47, 55,
    60; new critics/new criticism, 132,
    145, 148–51; practical criticism,
    145, 148–51; slow reading xvi, 59,
    113–23
Robeson, Paul, xix, 191–92, 198–201
Rossetti, Dante Gabriel. *See* Pre-
    Raphaelites

Sand Creek Massacre National Historic
    Site, 88–91
San Juan Island National Historic Park,
    79–83
Satrapi, Marjane, *Embroideries,* 47–48
Saville, Peter, xiv, 6–8, 10, 13, 14
Sedgwick, Eve Kosofsky, "paranoid
    reading," 55
Self, xviii, 20, 61, 178, 179–86, 194;
    expression, 182, 191, 201; sameness,
    182, 185; sonic self, 182, 183, 185
settler colonialism, xviii, 85, 90, 93,
    162, 163, 165, 171
Shakespeare, 26, 134–36, 139, 199
sign language(s), 167–70
silence(s), xiii, xvi, xvii, xviii, 18, 22,
    26, 52, 79, 92, 97, 105, 109, 113,

118, 123, 161–76; and absence(s), xviii, 2, 164, 58–61, 113, 163

silencing, 18, 92, 106, 109, 116, 123, 136–39, 155, 163, 168–69, 174

Siouxsie and the Banshees, 5, 12

site, xv, xvi, 7, 17, 31, 65, 66, 69, 72, 74, 75, 77–80, 85, 86, 88–91; aesthetics, 74; body, 31, 33–34; false familiarity, 2; historic, 79, 88; performativity, 72; place, 17, 27, 64, 69, 71, 74, 80; remembering, 80, 94; site-specific installation, xvi, 69, 72–74; site-specific performance, 63–76; as text, 63, 69, 71, 72; of trauma or harm, 17, 74

Slahi, Mohamedou Ould, 138–40

slow reading. *See* reading practices

soft fascination, 81

space/spatiality, xi, xv, 4, 20, 24, 26, 65, 69, 70, 72, 73, 75, 85, 93, 146, 183, 184; of intimacy, 19, 20, 23, 28; militarized, 86; of the page, 164; and place, 64, 70, 71, 93; rhetorical, 86; and time, xi, 9, 32–33, 85, 114, 144, 152; of understanding, 65

Stabat mater, 9

subject/subjectivity, 28, 32; modernity, 34

superhero/superheroes, xvii, 162

survivance, 171, 174

synecdoche/synecdochic, 69, 113, 114, 117

time, temporality, 3, 8–9, 12, 23, 70–71, 73, 116–18, 168, 185; disjunction, 3, 4, 26, 121, 136; localizing, 7; political, 4; teleological, 149. *See also* chorography

topography of the thinkable. *See* Rancière, Jacques

tradition, 32, 70–71; affect, 85, 92; national identity, 77; the National Parks Service mission, 78, 82

Trail of Tears, 171–72

transnational, 191, 193–94; and identity, 195, 197, 199–201

trauma, 19, 22–23, 72

uncanny, 19, 23

Venus, 33, 35; Botticelli's *Birth of Venus*, 35; Dalí's *Dream of Venus,* 35, 43; ideal of feminine beauty, 34; Venus de Milo, 34. *See also* Greco-Roman mythology

victor-victim reversal, 162

visual/vision/visuality/visualization, 13, 47–61, 98, 100, 106–7, 109, 153, 164, 169; indeterminacy, 49, 56; literacy, 47–48; parataxis, 57; semiotics, 50; text, 49, 53, 60, 165

Williams, Raymond, 5

Wimsatt, W. K., 149

About the Editors

Jena Habegger-Conti, associate professor of English at the Western Norway University of Applied Sciences in Bergen, Norway, teaches and researches in English literature and culture with a particular focus on reading practices related to visual and transcultural forms. Her recent publications include "Reading the Invisible in Marjane Satrapi's *Embroideries*" (2019) and "Transcultural Literacy: Reading the 'Other,' Shifting Aesthetic Imaginaries" (2018).

Lene M. Johannessen is professor of American literature, University of Bergen. Her research interests are in American Studies, including Chicano and Postcolonial studies. More generally, Johannessen's interests circle the ideological, cultural, social and aesthetic manifestations and negotiations of the en-route/migration, and aesthetics in spatial practices. Among the most recent publications are *Emerging Aesthetic Imaginaries* (2018, edited with M. Ledbetter) and "Regional Singularity and Decolonial Chicana/o Studies" (*Routledge Handbook of Chicana/o Studies*, 2018).

About the Contributors

Aidan Conti is professor of medieval Latin at the University of Bergen where his present research investigates affective interactions with the medieval in late twentieth-century cultural productions. Recent publications include "Creating Absence" on the rhetoric of writing in early Scandinavian histories (2019) and a chapter on medieval Latin for the *Handbook of Pre-Modern Nordic Memory Studies* (2018).

Janne Stigen Drangsholt is associate professor of English in the Department of Culture and Language Studies at the University of Stavanger. She has published four novels in Norwegian, among other critical and creative works. Her main fields of expertise are contemporary poetry and myth studies. Her most recent publication is a book essay in the anthology *Ted Hughes in Context*.

Ingrid Galtung teaches in the Department of Language and Culture Studies, University of Stavanger. She is currently completing her doctoral dissertation at the University of Agder, focusing on the impact of early twentieth-century body culture on the aesthetics of modernist narrative.

Jennifer Ladino, associate professor of American literature at the University of Idaho, teaches and researches representations of nature, understood as landscape, symbol, everyday environment, or simply "space." She is the author of *Memorials Matter: Affect and Environment at American Memory Sites* (2019) and *Reclaiming Nostalgia: Longing for Nature in American Literature* (2012).

Helle H. Lapeniene is a doctoral candidate in American literature at the University of Bergen. Her project examines text–image relations in Djuna

Barnes's composite works. Research interests include literature and aesthetics, American literature, visual culture, and modernism.

Genevieve Liveley holds the position of reader in Classics at the University of Bristol. Liveley's research and teaching center upon narratologically inflected studies of the ancient world. Her most recent book, *Narratology* (2019) exposes the dynamic (mis)appropriation of ancient scripts that gives modern narratology its shape. Her new research, on the ancient and future (hi) stories of AI and robots, builds on this work, and seeks a better understanding of the frames, schemata, and scripts that program cultural narratives about human interaction with artificial humans, automata, and AI.

Ruben Moi is associate professor of English literature at UiT, The Arctic University of Norway. His research focuses on Irish literature and culture and Border Aesthetics but also includes modernism and visual arts. Other fields of interest are the Renaissance, Romanticism, and didactics. Moi's most recent book is *Paul Muldoon and the Language of Poetry* (2020).

Timothy Saunders, associate professor of English literature at Volda University College researches the reception of classical antiquity in English and European literature, the interaction between literature and the natural environment, literary form, and reading history and reading strategies, as witnessed in the recent "Peripheral Figures: British and Irish Receptions of Nordic Literature and Culture" (special edition, *Scandinavica* 56.1)

Sara L. Spurgeon, professor of American literature at Texas Tech University, works in literatures of the American West and Southwest as well as nature/environmental writing, gender studies, and postcolonial theory. She is the author of *Exploding the Western: Myths of Empire on the Postmodern Frontier*, coauthor of *Writing the Southwest*, and editor of the critical anthology *Cormac McCarthy*.

Zoltan Varga is associate professor of English Literature at the Western Norway University of Applied Sciences. His academic background includes English literature, ancient Greek, gender studies, and musical semiotics. His recent research focuses on modernist fiction, aesthetic critical literacy, and intercultural dialogue. His most recent publication is a collaborative article, "We Are Invited to Imagine: Using a Literary Text to Encourage Cross-Cultural Dialogue about Citizenship," published in the *Cambridge Journal of Education* (2020).

Nahum Welang is a research fellow in American Literature and Culture at the University of Bergen's Department of Foreign Languages (Norway). His work has appeared in journals like *Open Cultural Studies* and *Cineforum*, and his research interests include American popular culture, African American literature, film noir, transnational narratives, and intermediality.